# THE TRANSFORMATIONAL POWER OF BIBLICAL FASTING

## WITH QUESTIONS & ANSWERS

GOD'S GATEWAY TO SPIRITUAL BREAKTHROUGH

## VICTOR I. IRUOBE

Copyright © 2021 Victor I. Iruobe

All rights reserved. No part of this publication may be produced, distributed, or transmitted in any form or by any means, including photocopying, recording, or other electronic or mechanical methods, without the prior written permision of the publisher, except in the case of brief quotations embodied in critical reviews and certain other noncommercial uses permitted by copyright law.

For permission requests, write to the publisher, addressed "Attention: Permissions Coordinator" at the email address below:

**Life and Success Media Ltd**

e-mail: info@abookinsideyou.com

www.abookinsideyou.com

Unless otherwise stated, all scripture quotations are taken from the Holy Bible, New King James Version. Quotations marked NKJV are taken from the HOLY BIBLE, NEW KING JAMES VERSION. Copyright © 1973, 1978, 1984 by International Bible Society. Used by permission of Hodder and Stoughton Ltd, a member of the Hodder Headline Plc Group. All rights reserved. "NKJV" is a registered trademark of International Bible Society. UK trademark number 1448790.

Quotations marked KJV are from the Holy Bible,

King James Version.

ISBN Number: 978-1-7398859-6-0

Cover Design: **MIA**Design.com

# CONTENT

| | |
|---|---|
| DEDICATION | 9 |
| ACKNOWLEDGEMENTS | 10 |
| THE FATHER'S CLARION CALL TO FASTING | 12 |
| INTRODUCTION | 15 |

**PART ONE**
**UNDERSTANDING BIBLICAL FASTING** — 23

**CHAPTER 1**
FASTING DEFINED — 25
What Is Fasting? — 27
What Fasting Is Not? — 32

**CHAPTER 2**
FASTING FUNDAMENTALS — 37
Beyond The Sacrifice — 37

**CHAPTER 3**
GOD'S ESTIMATION OF THE FAST:
THE WRONG AND RIGHT FASTS — 43
When The Wrong Person Fasts — 43
Prophet Isaiah's Condemnation Of Wrong Attitude To Fasting. — 45
Seventy Years of Fasting: All But In Vain! — 50
Man Looks At His Fast; God Looks At The Heart. — 52

**CHAPTER 4**
THE RIGHT FAST — 57
The God-Honoured Fast — 57
Eight Characteristics Of A God's Chosen Fast — 58
Loose The Bands Of Wickedness — 61
Let The Oppressed Go Free — 63
Fasting Breaks Every Yoke — 64

**CHAPTER 5**
FASTING AND GOOD DEEDS — 67
"Bring the poor that are cast out into thy house" — 69
"When thou seest the naked, that thou cover him" — 70

## PART TWO
## GOD'S PURPOSE FOR FASTING — 75
### CHAPTER 6
### USUAL REASONS TO FAST — 77

| | |
|---|---|
| Fasting As A Means Of Self-Humbling | 80 |
| Fasting As An Effective Tool of Repentance | 84 |
| Fasting For Self-Examination | 87 |
| Fasting As A Tool For Averting Crises | 93 |
| Fasting To Strengthen Your Faith | 97 |
| Fasting To Gain victory In Battle | 101 |
| Fasting To Prepare For Ministry | 104 |
| Fasting For Revelation: | |
| Interceding Against The Powers Of Darkness | 107 |
| Fasting To Overcome The Flesh –The Daniel Fast | 112 |
| Fasting As An Instrument of Worship To God | 116 |
| Fasting As A Refilling Process | 119 |

## PART THREE
## UNDERSTANDING THE DIFFERENT TYPES OF FASTS — 125
### CHAPTER 7
### THE DIFFERENT TYPES OF FASTS — 127

| | |
|---|---|
| PROCLAIMED OR PUBLIC AND PERSONAL FAST | 128 |
| THE PROCLAIMED FAST | |
| – CALLING THE CHURCH OR NATION TO FASTING | 128 |
| PROCLAIMED AND REGULAR FAST | 129 |

### CHAPTER 8
### PERSONAL FAST — 139

| | |
|---|---|
| Key Points to Note About Personal Fast | 141 |

### CHAPTER 9
### NORMAL, PARTIAL AND ABSOLUTE FAST — 145

| | |
|---|---|
| The Normal Fast | 146 |
| Fasting and Sleep | 147 |
| The Partial Fast | 148 |
| The Absolute Fast | 151 |
| Queen Esther | 152 |
| Prophet Ezra | 153 |

| | |
|---|---|
| Saul of Tarsus (Paul) | 154 |
| King David | 154 |
| Fasting Beyond Three Days Absolute | 155 |
| Moses | 156 |
| Elijah | 156 |

**PART FOUR**
| | |
|---|---|
| UNDERSTANDING JESUS' TEACHING ON FASTING | 159 |
| CHAPTER 10 | |
| WHAT JESUS TAUGHT ABOUT FASTING | 161 |
| The Appearance Of The Fasting Saint | 163 |
| CHAPTER 11 | |
| WHO SHOULD SEE AND REWARD THE FAST? | 171 |
| Who Sees The Fast? | 171 |
| Who Rewards The Fast? | 173 |
| The Believers Fasting Account In Heaven | 175 |
| CHAPTER 12 | |
| EXCEPT BY PRAYER AND FASTING | 181 |
| CHAPTER 13 | |
| THEY SHALL FAST | 185 |
| The Early Church Fulfilled The Prophecy | 189 |
| A Grave Misinterpretation of the Statement in context | 193 |
| CHAPTER 14 | |
| JESUS EMPOWERED THROUGH FASTING | 195 |
| Moving Beyond The "In-Filling" Process | 197 |
| Jesus' Disciples And The Divine Process | 198 |

**PART FIVE**
| | |
|---|---|
| THE FASTING MINISTRY OF JESUS | 201 |
| Chapter 15 | |
| JESUS IN THE MINISTRY OF FASTING | 203 |
| Why Did Jesus Fast? | 205 |
| Jesus Fasted To Establish A Closer Walk With The Father | 206 |
| Jesus Fasted To Launch His Public Ministry | 207 |
| Jesus Fasted To Demonstrate His Humanity | 211 |
| Jesus Fasted To Leave An Eternal Legacy For The Would-Be Disciples | 212 |

# THE TRANSFORMATIONAL POWER OF FASTING

PART SIX
UNDERSTANDING THE GUIDELINES FOR
PERSONAL AND COLLECTIVE FASTS    215
CHAPTER 16
GUIDELINES FOR PERSONAL AND COPORATE FASTINGS    217
Deciding The Parameters Of Your Fast    219
Guidelines For Collective Fasting    231

PART SEVEN
UNDERSTANDING THE RELATIONSHIP
BETWEEN PRAYER AND FASTING    235
CHAPTER 17
THE RELATIONSHIP BETWEEN PRAYER AND FASTING    237
Divergence Of Opinion    241

PART EIGHT
UNDERSTANDING THE BENEFITS OF BIBLICAL FASTING    245
CHAPTER 18
REWARDS AND BENEFITS OF BIBLICAL FASTING    247
Answered Prayer    249
Fasting Strengthens Intimacy With God    255
Fasting Brings Victories In Difficult Situations    259
Fasting Helps Us Discover God's Will    263
Fasting Intensifies The Power Of Prayer    264
Fasting Nourishes Our Faith    267
An Aid To Mortification    268
Fasting Helps Sustain The Anointing    271
Fasting Deepens Our Understanding Of The Word Of God    273
Fasting Defines And Equips The Vessel Of God    277
Fasting Is A Catalyst For Spiritual Growth    283
Fasting Turns Defeat To Triumph    284
Fasting Averts God's Impending Judgment    287
Fasting Helps To Stir The Gifts Of God In The Believer    292
Fasting Brings Deliverance    294
Fasting Quickens Your Spirit    296
Fasting Precipitates The Latter Rain And Serves As A Gateway To Restoration    298

| | |
|---|---|
| Fasting As A Means Of Ministering TO the Lord | 301 |
| Fasting Helps To Turn the Battle Against The Enemy | 303 |

**CHAPTER 19**

| | |
|---|---|
| THE HEALING VALUE OF FASTING | 313 |

**CHAPTER 20**

| | |
|---|---|
| THE OPEN REWARD OF THE SECRET FAST OF THE BELIEVER | 319 |
| Personal Reward For Fasting According To Prophet Isaiah | 321 |

**CHAPTER 21**

| | |
|---|---|
| SPECIAL FASTING BLESSINGS | 325 |
| Other Promised Blessings Associated With Fasting | 333 |
| Joy, Gladness And Cheerfulness | 333 |
| God's Open Reward | 334 |
| Spiritual Powers Over Demons | 334 |
| Divine Empowerment And Supernatural Publicity | 334 |

**PART NINE**

| | |
|---|---|
| QUESTIONS AND ANSWERS ON BIBLICAL FASTING | 335 |

**CHAPTER 22**

| | |
|---|---|
| FASTING: QUESTIONS AND ANSWERS | 337 |
| What Is Fasting? | 338 |
| Why Should A Believer Fast? | 338 |
| How Should I Prepare For A Fast? | 339 |
| How Do I Begin My Fast? | 341 |
| Will Fasting For More Than One Prayer Request Diminish My Reward? | 342 |
| Should I Always Withdraw To A Solitary Place During My Fast? | 344 |
| Should I Carry On With My Usual Business Of Life While I Am Fasting? | 347 |
| What Are The Usual Indicators That You Need To Fast? | 351 |
| Can The Practice Of Fasting Be Abused? | 353 |
| I Want To Fast But Cannot Because Of An Illness | 355 |
| Should I Take Multi-Vitamins During A Fast? | 356 |
| Will My Fasting Be Rewarded? | 357 |
| Why Is Fasting Important? | 358 |
| Does Jesus Expect The Christians To Fast? | 358 |
| How Often Can I Fast? | 359 |
| How Should I Go About Fasting? | 360 |

| | |
|---|---|
| How Do I Know What Type Of Fast To Observe? | 361 |
| Why Should I Consider Fasting? | 362 |
| Is Fasting Always Voluntary? | 365 |
| Should I Always Fast In Secret? | 368 |
| Can I Fast And Not Let My Wife Or Husband Know? | 369 |
| Are There Circumstances That Make Giving Knowledge Of Our Fasting To Others Legitimate Or Unavoidable?? | 370 |
| Does Fasting Require Abstention From Water? | 372 |
| Are There People That Should Not Fast? | 375 |
| Is The Discipline Of Fasting Taught Through Out Scripture? | 377 |
| What Scriptures Do You Recommend For Study During Fast? | 378 |
| How Often Should A Christian Fast? | 378 |
| How Do I Know When To Quit Fasting? | 381 |
| How Do I Overcome Satan's Temptation To Violate My Fast? | 382 |
| Was Fasting Practised By The Early Church? | 383 |
| Fasting As Practiced And Taught In The Epistles. | 387 |
| How Should I Break A Fast Successfully? | 389 |
| | |
| FASTING FROM THE LEGENDS' PERSPECTIVES | 391 |
| | |
| EPILOGUE | 403 |
| Various Fastings In The Bible And Their Durations | 407 |
| Part Of The Day Fast | 407 |
| One Day Fast | 407 |
| Three Days | 409 |
| Further Records Of Three Day Fasts | 411 |
| Seven Days | 412 |
| Fourteen Days | 413 |
| Twenty One Day Fasts | 413 |
| Forty Day Fasts | 414 |

# Warning

The fasts suggested in this book are not for everyone. It's not meant to diagnose any disease or in any way serve as a remedy for any ailment. Consult your Medical Practitioner before embarking on any fasts, no matter how short. Although fasting is healthful to many, God would not command a physical exercise that would harm people physically or emotionally.

# Dedication

To all God's generals, past and present, who have used fasting to bring down the fullness of God's presence to the earth, through obeying the Master's prophetic mandate upon our generation.

*"But the days will come, when the bridegroom shall be taken away from them, and then shall they fast in those days," says Jesus (Luke 5:35).*

May the fruit of their labour ever remain with us!

# Acknowledgements

This book is a product of dogged and unwavering determination, grim persistence, unflinching courage, endless hours of research and writing. I am eternally grateful to the Holy Spirit, Who has been my indwelling Inspiration, Teacher, Counsellor, Comforter, and Helper over the period it took to write this book.

Nothing in life is ever successful without the corporate effort of many gifted people God has brought along one's way in the journey of life. People are assets; special gift from God. I am always reminded that we are an embodiment of all the people we have known, met, and learnt from. This work is therefore the product of the countless individuals whom I have met and learnt from at the various stages of my life.

I would like to express my enormous gratitude to my wife -Pastor Omowunmi Ann Iruobe - who has been my faithful companion, lover, a personal source of encouragement and inspiration, and prayer partner in the glorious institution of marriage and ministry together. Without her compelling enthusiasm, humour, imagination and new idea each time we got stuck in the course of editing this book, which she did single-handedly, this work might never have been finished.

I wish to thank my children - Gloria, Sarah, Joshua and David – Vincent, for their enormous passion and contributions to the building of God's kingdom; you are each a special treasure! Thank you for the great joy you have all brought to our lives. We love you all deeply. You are individually the best!

Finally, I am indebted to the leadership, staff and members of Hope of Glory International Christian Centre, especially my very able administrators – Minister Andrew and Evelyn Ettienne - thank you for your great work in God's kingdom over the years. May heaven reward you abundantly in Jesus name.

# The Father's Clarion Call to Fasting

*Blow the trumpet in Zion, sanctify a fast, call a solemn assembly: Gather the people, sanctify the congregation, assemble the elders, gather the children, and those that suck the breasts: let the bridegroom go forth of his chamber, and the bride out of her closet. Let the priests, the ministers of the LORD, weep between the porch and the altar, and let them say, Spare thy people, O LORD, and give not thine heritage to reproach, that the heathen should rule over them: wherefore should they say among the people, Where is their God? Then will the LORD be jealous for his land, and pity his people. Yea, the LORD will answer and say unto his people, Behold, I will send you corn, and wine, and oil, and ye shall be satisfied therewith: and I will no more make you a reproach among the heathen:*

*But I will remove far off from you the northern army, and will drive him into a land barren and desolate, with his face toward the east sea, and his hinder part toward the utmost sea, and his stink shall come up, and his ill savour shall come up, because he hath done great things. Fear not, O land: be glad and rejoice: for the LORD will do great things. Be not afraid, ye beasts of the field: for the pastures of the wilderness do spring, for the tree beareth her fruit, the fig tree and the vine do yield their strength. Be glad then, ye children of Zion, and rejoice in the LORD your God: for he hath given you the former rain moderately, and he will cause to come down for you the rain, the former rain, and the latter rain in the first month.*

*And the floors shall be full of wheat, and the vats shall overflow with wine and oil. And I will restore to you the years that the locust hath eaten, the cankerworm, and the caterpiller, and the palmerworm, my great army which I sent among you. And ye shall eat in plenty, and be satisfied, and praise the name of the LORD your God, that hath dealt wondrously with you: and my people shall never be ashamed. And ye shall know that I am in the midst of Israel, and that I am the LORD your God, and none else: and my people shall never be ashamed. And it shall come to pass afterward, that I will pour out my spirit upon all flesh; and your sons and your daughters shall prophesy, your old men shall dream dreams, your young men shall see visions:*

*And also upon the servants and upon the handmaids in those days will I pour out my spirit. And I will shew wonders in the Heavens and in the earth, blood, and fire, and pillars of smoke. The sun shall be turned into darkness, and the moon into blood, before the great and terrible day of the LORD come. And it shall come to pass, that whosoever shall call on the name of the LORD shall be delivered: for in mount Zion and in Jerusalem shall be deliverance, as the LORD hath said, and in the remnant whom the LORD shall call (Joel 2:15-32).*

*Almost everywhere at all times fasting has held a place of great importance since it is closely linked with the intimate sense of religion. Perhaps this is the explanation for the demise of fasting in our day. When the sense of God diminishes, fasting disappears* – **Edward Farrell.**

# Introduction

We are unarguably, living in tempestuous days! It should be no surprise to anyone familiar with end-time prophecies that the latter days are stormy days. Fear and hatred stalk the world today. In addition to the latest man-made deadly devices – nuclear, atomic and biological weapons nations of the world have been stockpiling for decades, ready to be deployed at the slightest opportunity, nature has come to give us something even more devastating to grapple with – a pervasive pandemic! Yes, it's been a time of great loss and of great pain and great frustration.

Many dreams have been shattered. People have seen so many things we rely and depend on – fail! This might well not be the greatest crisis the world will know yet! No one knows to what use world governments will put their newly discovered nuclear- war-heads (North Korea for instance, with her Ballistic Missiles), atomic and biological energy.

With the global pandemic, no one can doubt that we are living in uncertain times; only a fool would shrug his shoulders in denial and remain unmoved by recent events on the planet. With the said pandemic that has claimed tens of millions lives worldwide, with bereaved families left in excruciating pain, the planet earth in biblical terms, reminisce *"a land that eats up its inhabitants"* (Num. 13:32).

Yet, climate change poses no less concern for humanity. Volumes of studies lend scientific credibility to the fact that we are on the cusp of an existential crises, as climate change constitutes the single greatest danger to humanity.

Developments in this area may well 'mark the beginning of the end', as they usher in signs preceding the second coming of Christ as foretold in Luke 21:26-27:

> *"Men's hearts failing them for fear, and for looking after those things which are coming on the earth: for the powers of heaven shall be shaken. And then shall they see the Son of man coming in a cloud with power and great glory"* (emphasis added).

Far more concerning is the fact that we live in a world that is so resistant to God and His Spirit, that I believe today's generation needs the weapon of fasting and prayer to survive the challenges and demands of our time. Individuals need it, the Church (God's end-time army) needs it, and the nations of the world need it, as exemplified in the Bible by God calling nations to fasting:

> *Gird yourselves, and lament, ye priests: howl, ye ministers of the altar: come, lie all night in sackcloth, ye ministers of my God: for the meat offering and the drink offering is withholden from the house of your God. Sanctify ye a fast, call a solemn assembly, gather the elders and all the inhabitants of the land into the house of the LORD your God, and cry unto the LORD. (Joel 1:13-14).*

While we welcome the great awareness and renewal in this regard, we whole-heartedly believe a lot more needs to be done to sustain the great move of God a return to a life of fasting has orchestrated in the Church.

I strongly believe Bill Bright profoundly alluded to this fact when he famously wrote:

**I believe the power of fasting as it relates to prayer is the spiritual atomic bomb that our Lord has given us to destroy the strongholds of evil and usher in a great revival and spiritual harvest around the world.**

We live in a very dangerous world that threatens those things that are most spiritual. All over the world morals are on a downward trend, the wind of spiritual apathy and apostasy is blowing within the church of Jesus Christ in an unprecedented and unimaginable proportion. Sins and spiritual diseases have invaded the church, with evil spirits constantly attacking it in a way that has not been seen for centuries.

King Solomon wrote,

> *"So I returned, and considered all the oppressions that are done under the sun: and behold the tears of such as were oppressed, and they had no comforter; and on the side of their oppressors there was power; but they had no comforter" (Eccl. 4:1).*

We, too – probably much more than Solomon – live in an age of oppression and incredible pain. If we had access to the naked truth, our times would probably be recognised as having unprecedented anguish. More people are being martyred for their faith in Christ Jesus in our days than in all the previous centuries combined. Besides these persecuted believers, multitude more can be added to the rolls of suffering souls – each precious one a victim of those who have no fear of God and who in their consuming, unbridled lust brutally inflict and wound others in the rage of their passion. Think of the children, women and men who have suffered unspeakable emotional, physical, and sexual abuse. Perhaps you too have experienced such pain – enough to be awakened, sympathetic, and sensitive to the hurt of others. You might at times feel lonely in your pain. Or maybe your pain is actually born of loneliness, which is one of the most common hurts people deal with today. This shouldn't be true of those in the body of Christ, but unfortunately it is.

Pain is everywhere. Its victims may camouflage their inward suffering by external decorum, but *"Even in laughter the heart is sorrowful; and the end of that mirth is heaviness"* (Prov. 14:13). Life is fraught not only with stress and tense relationships and everyday disappointments but also with acute, piecing pain.

At such a time as this we must use the emergency powers at our disposal – fasting and prayer. It was with this solution in mind, and at a time reminiscent to our present dispensation that Prophet Joel proclaimed:

> *"Blow the trumpet in Zion, sanctify a fast, call a solemn assembly" (Joel 2:15).*

We need a solution no doubt; we need God now more than ever before! The insightful words of Frederick Douglas must reverberate with far greater meaning now than ever before: "It is not light that we need, but fire; it is not the gentle shower, but thunder. We need the storm, the whirlwind, and the earthquake" It is, therefore, time to heed God's call to usher in some sense of order and sanctity, and rise in the power of the Holy Spirit and fight! "Therefore also now," saith the Lord,

> *"turn ye even to Me with all your heart, and with fasting, and with weeping, and with mourning" (Joel 2:12).*

It is no doubt, our "time of Jacob's trouble." Thank God the message does not end there.

> *"Alas! for that day is great, so that none is like it: it is even the time of Jacob's trouble; but he shall be saved out of it" (Jer. 30:7).*

Verse 5 describes a time of great fear and trembling. Verse 6 delineates this time in a way that pictures men going through the pains of childbirth, again indicating a time of agony. But there is hope for Judah and Israel (the Church) for though this is called "the time of Jacob's distress" (NASB), the Lord promises He will save Jacob, referring to Judah and Israel (the Church) out of this time of great trouble (verse 7).

This material has been developed in response to the apparent need of our time, to help the end-time believer understand and face some key issues that relate to fasting that many struggle with today. The author has worked hard to bring a comprehensive work on the subject, offering clear insight, teaching and illustrations on a broad range of areas of the subject and other issues related thereto. God's eternal and essential principles must be firmly grasped and communicated if we hope to survive. Within these pages are ancient yet, profoundly relevant and valuable truths, presented in today's terms for today's believer, facing today's challenges as we explore the undisputable transformational power that fasting and prayer offer.

Each chapter is carefully crafted to deal with different realities that will, if applied, increase your confidence and ability to navigate through life's challenges, because they rest on the bedrock of the time-tested wisdom of the Scriptures, as it applies to the greatest needs of today's believer. Here and only here, will we find counsel that is inspired of God, workable, realistic and full of promise. Best of all, the Bible is ever relevant, never limited or anchored to the lifestyle of a particular era. Things we are about to discover are for us today just as much as they were for the people to whom they were originally written. Indeed, the word of God transcends generational boundaries.

Specifically, the purpose of this book is to provide the believer with the much-needed understanding that would help him know what fasting is, how to properly engage in the act, but most significantly, have an in-depth knowledge of not just the call of God on the Church to fast, but of the purpose and power of God's chosen fast. This, we believe, will ultimately help to dispel many of the myths and deadly misconceptions associated with biblical fasts, by exploring the subject from different perspectives.

Included in this book is a vast section of 'Questions and Answers'. Answers are offered drawing on the wealth of breath-taking teachings on the subject of fasting by various characters in the Bible, not least our Lord Jesus Christ who not only taught why and how we should fast but also wholeheartedly authenticated same by engaging in the act Himself. It is to the examination of these questions that this book is mainly devoted. In the grandstands are all the faithful disciples (past and present) who have run before us, encouraging us to run strong. Before us is the track, one prepared beforehand by God (Heb. 12:1). At the end is the finish line, where Jesus is standing, waiting to congratulate all who cross it. May you be found a worthy winner!

It is a privilege to write again on this very sensitive, but highly significant subject as inspired and directed by the Holy Spirit, and from personal experience. My desire is that this book leaves you fired up to take this time-honoured instrument of worship and proven weapon of warfare that is instrumental to bringing down demonic strongholds, and apply it in your life.

No book on any one subject is exhaustive, but a great deal of effort has been geared towards incorporating in this volume as much materials as deemed necessary.

As you read this book, we encourage you to put the principles and teachings it brings to you into practice and let same inspire you to include fasting in your walk with God.

# PART ONE

# UNDERSTANDING BIBLICAL FASTING

# 1
# FASTING DEFINED

This section is devoted to helping the believer understand some critical aspects of biblical fasting that have been greatly misunderstood, which has rendered the practice of it almost unthinkable for many.

Most of the problems often associated with fasting stem from the legalistic, rigid and ritualistic view of what biblical fasting is and is not. According to R. A. Torrey, "There are those who think that fasting belongs to the old dispensation; but when we look at the [Bible] we find that it was practiced by the earnest men of the apostolic day." Most people erroneously believe that unless they engage in very lengthy fasts, they would not be able to gain God's attention; while some others think that they have to observe a certain kind of fast in order to get God to do what perhaps, He would not do otherwise. It must

> **Fasting, at its best, changes man and positions him spiritually, to better receive from God.**

be made abundantly clear that in no way does the fasting of man change God. Fasting, at its best, changes man and positions him spiritually, to better receive from God. Second, no one can access the throne of grace successfully, even with the most lengthy and gruesome fast, while living in sin. The Bible admonishes, "the **sacrifice of the wicked** is an abomination [detestable, ISV] to the LORD: but the prayer of the upright is his delight" (Pro. 15:5, emphasis added). Jesus taught, "Ye shall seek me, and shall not find me" (John 7:34). However, Jesus had admonished His disciples in the Sermon on the Mount, "Ask, and it shall be given you; seek, and ye shall find; knock, and it shall be opened unto you…" (Matt. 7:7); apparent contradiction? Of course not!

The underlying factor or issue at stake is the condition of the heart that is set on seeking God. The point is driven home in Jeremiah 29:13,

> *"And you shall seek me, and find me,* **when you shall search for me with all your heart**" *(emphasis added).*

The key factor to be considered always is the condition and motive of the heart that seeks the Lord. If the heart is right and the motive is genuine, the fast will invariably, be acceptable to God. The Bible says by the mouth of Paul the Apostle:

> **"Nevertheless the foundation of God standeth sure,** having this seal, **The Lord knoweth them that are his..."** (2 Tim. 2:19 emphases added).

Also Habakkuk 1:13 describes God as, "… of purer eyes than to behold evil, and canst not look on iniquity:" This remains God's criteria in His dealings with man.

## WHAT IS FASTING?

*The Fasting is often associated with a sense of spiritual desperation. Joel 2:12 says, 'Turn to me now, while there is time!' Notice the sense of urgency and desperation. Fasting is not so much about food as it is about focus. Fasting is not so much about saying "no" to the body as it is about saying "yes" to the Spirit. Fasting is not about doing without, it is about looking within. Fasting is an outward response to an inward attitude and cry of the soul…Fasting is not about the externals. In Joel 2:13, God says, "Don't tear your clothing in grief, instead tear your hearts." It is entirely possible to go without food and not have a true fast. Fasting is the response of a broken heart…Fasting is the humble response to immense responsibility. Joel calls a solemn assembly* – **Lance Witt.**

Fasting is a practice found throughout the Bible. According to Unger's Bible Dictionary, the word "fast" in the Bible is from

> *If the heart is right and the motive is genuine, the fast will invariably, be acceptable to God.*

the Hebrew word meaning "to cover" the mouth, or from the Greek word nesteuo meaning "to abstain."

The noun translated "fast" or "a fasting" is *tsom* in the Hebrew, and nesteia in the Greek language. It means the voluntary abstinence from food. The literal Hebrew translation would be "not to eat." The literal Greek means "no food."

A fast in the Bible is usually an intentional, voluntary and total abstinence from food, for a set time, for the purpose of devoting oneself to seeking God. Fasting denies the flesh what it wants so that we can focus more clearly on strengthening our spirits. Fasting shifts our attention from the things of the flesh to the things of the Spirit, and it is an act of full and total surrender to the Lord.

Through fasting, we confirm the words uttered by Jesus in the face of temptation during His forty-day fast,

> *"Man does not live by bread alone, but by every Word that proceeds from the mouth of God" (Matthew 4:4).*

However, William Thrasher's caution must be heeded,

# FASTING DEFINED

"The abstinence is not to be an end in itself but rather for the purpose of being separated to the Lord and to concentrate on godliness. This kind of fasting reduces the influence of our self-will and invites the Holy Spirit to do a more intense work in us."

Fasting is a designated time the believer consciously and voluntarily neglects the most natural necessities of life the body desires, for the purpose of pursuing God with greater intensity and alertness to do something supernatural in his life, home, business, church, even the nation, as in the cases of Israel in the book of Joel, when God's unequivocal demand was,

> "Gird yourselves, and lament, ye priests: howl, ye ministers of the altar: come, lie all night in sackcloth, ye ministers of my God: for the meat offering and the drink offering is withholden from the house of your God. Sanctify ye a fast, call a solemn assembly, gather the elders and all the inhabitants of the land into the house of the LORD your God, and cry unto the LORD" (Joel 1:13-14).

> "Therefore also now, saith the LORD, turn ye even to me with all your heart, and with fasting, and with weeping, and with mourning: Gather the people, sanctify the congregation, assemble the elders, gather the children, and those that suck the breasts: let the bridegroom go forth of his chamber, and the bride out of her closet. Let the priests, the ministers of the LORD, weep between the porch and the altar, and let them say, Spare thy people, O LORD, and give not thine heritage to reproach,

> *that the heathen should rule over them: wherefore should they say among the people, Where is their God?"* (Joel 2:12, 16-17).

the heathen and wicked nation of Assyria, as recorded in the book of Jonah,

"Now the word of the LORD came unto Jonah the son of Amittai, saying, Arise, go to Nineveh, that great city, and cry against it; for their wickedness is come up before me" (vv 1-2),

the Jews in Shushan,

> *"Then Esther bade them return Mordecai this answer, Go, gather together all the Jews that are present in Shushan, and fast ye for me, and neither eat nor drink three days, night or day: I also and my maidens will fast likewise; and so will I go in unto the king, which is not according to the law: and if I perish, I perish"* (Est. 4:15-16).

Finally, Judah under the reign of Jehoshaphat,

> *"Then there came some that told Jehoshaphat, saying, There cometh a great multitude against thee from beyond the sea on this side Syria; and, behold, they be in Hazazontamar, which is Engedi. And Jehoshaphat feared, and set himself to seek the Lord, and proclaimed a fast throughout all Judah"* (2 Chr. 20:2-3),

to mention but a few.

During the time of a fast, the individual would devote himself to seeking the Lord and His will. Fasting typically fosters a heart and attitude of dependence as one relies upon God for His strength and sustenance.

> **The desired outcome of fasting is a stronger spirit and a deeper focus on God**

The desired outcome of fasting is a stronger spirit and a deeper focus on God, instead of earthly matters.

In Kenneth Copeland's view,

"fasting is a willingness to separate yourself from the things of this world and put your focus solely on the Lord. It has been a powerful spiritual tool used by Christians and ministry leaders the world over and was modelled in biblical contexts throughout Scripture in times of trial, in seeking divine direction, and for deliverance from sin and evil."

Fasting is a crucial part of our walk with the Lord, and although it is not commanded, we can clearly see in Scripture that Jesus expects His followers to fast. However, biblical fasting is not to be considered a method for achieving any other purpose than for growing into deeper communion with God, being more in tune with His Spirit, seeking His power, knowing His direction on critical issues, engaging in warfare and desiring breakthroughs in life.

In the words of Andrew Murray,

> "Prayer is reaching out after the unseen; fasting is letting go of all that is seen and temporal. Fasting helps express, deepen, confirm the resolution that we are ready to sacrifice anything, even ourselves to attain what we seek for the kingdom of God."

Fasting, therefore, helps us deny oneself and one's needs to grow one's dependence and reliance on God. It is a part of our sacrificial living for the purpose of bringing our spirits in alignment with His. In James 4:8, the Apostle calls on the believer to draw near—to move closer—to God. This comes with an additional promise: God will respond by moving closer to us. That is an incredible act of mercy on God's part. The God of the universe owes us nothing, including His closeness. Fasting aids us in accomplishing this end. Fasting is ultimately a call to return to God (Joel 2:13). Israel's first need, like that of the prodigal son, was to return to the Father (Luke 15:11-32). God does not talk about the people's need for better plans, programs, or strategies. He is simply saying to us: You have been unfaithful to me; come home. May we heed the call!

## WHAT FASTING IS NOT

It must be made clear from the outset, that fasting is not a magical rite that invokes blessings on the fasting believer.

We are not trying to bribe God or secure His divine favour through His appreciation of our performance of a fast or some duties we deem qualify us for any special consideration by God. Elmer Towns agrees,

"Even if we wanted to, we could not manipulate God. We fast and pray for results, but the results are in God's hands. One of the greatest spiritual benefits of fasting is becoming more attentive to God—becoming more aware of our own inadequacies and His adequacy, our own contingencies and His self-sufficiency—and listening to what He wants us to be and do."

Further, biblical fasting is not dieting. Whereas dieting has a physical end in mind, biblical fasting always works towards a spiritual end. Fasting is a sacrificial, voluntary abstinence from food, and sometimes from drink (Est.4:16), pre-planned for a definite period of time, for the singular purpose of engaging in the act of intense seeking of God's face. As said, the Greek word for fast, *nesteuo*, literally means, to not eat. But this should not imply that biblical fasting is simply not eating. Biblical fasting is a physical self-denial of food (and sometimes of drink) for a spiritual purpose. The purpose for any fast is critical; and should be given due attention. The reason must be well defined, and the motive must be right.

Prophet Jeremiah writes,

> "Thus saith the Lord unto this people, Thus have they loved to wander, they have not refrained their feet, therefore the

*Lord doth not accept them; he will now remember their iniquity, and visit their sins. Then said the Lord unto me, Pray not for this people for their good. When they fast, I will not hear their cry; and when they offer burnt offering and an oblation, I will not accept them: but I will consume them by the sword, and by the famine, and by the pestilence" (Jer. 14:10-12).*

Finally, fasting is not a legalistic exercise. Simply engaging in fasting as a habitual practice is not what the Bible teaches either. God is never interested in our rote performance. God wants obedience, but He wants it to come from a heart that loves Him and that longs to be in fervent communion with Him. Biblical fasting must flow from a heart that first, loves God, and submits fully to His Lordship. Isaiah 58.1 recounts God's condemnation of Israel's legalistic practice of fasting, while ignoring the divine commands to be holy, to oppose oppression, and to feed and care for the needy:

*"Cry aloud, spare not, lift up thy voice like a trumpet, and shew my people their transgression, and the house of Jacob their sins. Yet they seek me daily, and delight to know my ways, as a nation that did righteousness, and forsook not the ordinance of their God: they ask of me the ordinances of justice; they take delight in approaching to God. Wherefore have we fasted, say they, and thou seest not? Wherefore have we afflicted our soul, and thou takest no knowledge?*

## FASTING DEFINED

*Behold, in the day of your fast ye find pleasure, and exact all your labours. Behold, ye fast for strife and debate, and to smite with the fist of wickedness: ye shall not fast as ye do this day, to make your voice to be heard on high. Is it such a fast that I have chosen? A day for a man to afflict his soul? Is it to bow down his head as a bulrush, and to spread sackcloth and ashes under him? wilt thou call this a fast, and an acceptable day to the Lord? Is not this the fast that I have chosen? to loose the bands of wickedness, to undo the heavy burdens, and to let the oppressed go free, and that ye break every yoke?" (Isaiah 58: 1-6).*

So, you see that what matters here is not man's perception of His sacrifice to God, but God's assessment of the motive behind the sacrifice; a very valuable lesson Prophet Samuel learnt in the very early days of his ministry, when God etched the following words in his heart,

*"Look not on his countenance, or on the height of his stature; because I have refused him: for the LORD seeth not as man seeth: for man looketh on the outward appearance, but the LORD looketh on the heart" (I Sam. 16:7).*

# 2

# FASTING FUNDAMENTALS

## BEYOND THE SACRIFICE

*Cry aloud, spare not, lift up thy voice like a trumpet, and shew my people their transgression, and the house of Jacob their sins. Yet they seek me daily, and delight to know my ways, as a nation that did righteousness, and forsook not the ordinance of their God: they ask of me the ordinances of justice; they take delight in approaching to God. Wherefore have we fasted, say they, and thou seest not? Wherefore have we afflicted our soul, and thou takest no knowledge?* **Behold, in the day of your fast ye find pleasure, and exact all your labours. Behold, ye fast for strife and debate, and to smite with the fist of wickedness:** *ye shall not fast as ye do this day, to make your voice to be heard on high. Is it such a fast that I have chosen? A day for a man to afflict his soul? is it to bow down his head as a bulrush, and to spread sackcloth and ashes under him? wilt thou call this a fast,*

> **Acceptability hinges on one supreme factor - the condition of the heart!**

*and an acceptable day to the LORD? (Isaiah 58:1-5, emphasis added).*

Francis Dixon had the answer when he said, *"No gift is acceptable to God until we have given Him our hearts; even if we pray, or give our money, He will not accept these unless we have first given ourselves to Him (Prov. 15:8; 28:9). God wants our hearts, He wants us, [all of our hearts; not part of it]."*

This is the dividing line between the fast that is acceptable to God and the one that is not. The spiritual condition of our hearts remains critical, as the determining and decisive factor of the fasting that is acceptable to God. As far as God is concerned, the length of the fast carries little or no significance, in this regard! Acceptability hinges on one supreme factor - the condition of the heart! All the precautions and principles of biblical fasting earlier examined flow from this overriding factor. If the heart is right, motive will invariably be right! Further, if the heart is right, the fasting believer will not seek men's approval at the expense of honouring God with his fasting and attracting His reward. Finally, if the heart is right, the fasting will be based purely on and conducted in the spirit of the word of God entirely!

No doubt, the huge lesson of Proverbs 4: 23 reverberates with significant caution: *"**Keep thy heart** with all diligence; for out of it are the issues of life" (emphasis added)*. Truly, everything about life depends on the spiritual state of the heart, as the wellspring of life.

Accordingly, if the fast is to be accepted by God, the heart must of necessity, be judged right by God. This divine order cannot be circumvented; because this foundation too, stands 'sure' (2 Tim. 2:19).

On a broader perspective, what we have discussed in this section so far revolves round the fundamental pillar that defines and shapes man's dealings with God - the core of his tie and relationship with God. It must be seen beyond the quality of the sacrifices, for example, prayer, fasting, offerings or any other services, that man renders to the Lord. None of these, as argued, is as close to the heart of God as the spiritual condition of the heart that renders them. In Scripture, we see God in constant demand for the heart of man.

*"My son, give me thine heart, and let thine eyes observe my ways"* (Prov. 23:26); in essence asking for the totality of man's will and submission to Him.

The heart in scripture signifies the seat of affections, also of wisdom and understanding; it is the centre of a man's being. This is the greatest demand of God from man, and it is the centre-piece of what binds both together in a healthy relationship. The yielding of a man's heart to God is a precondition for a healthy and fruitful relationship with Him (Heb. 11:6). Consequently, God will not allow man access to Him, unless he (man) first, allows God access to his heart and makes it His habitation, and there continues to be a friendly, harmonious, and indeed, an unbroken affinity with the God, thereafter. Jesus' relationship with His father exemplifies this; and He puts the position succinctly: *"I and My Father are one."* (John 10:30).

In consequence, we must never think of fasting as a measure designed to force God's hand, and get our own way! Fasting cannot be used to try to push God into a corner. Fasting does not change God; it changes man! God's requirements for dealing with man cannot be altered.

The position is made explicit in 2 Kings 17:16-17:

> *"And they left all the commandments of the Lord their God, and made them molten images, even two calves, and made a grove, and worshipped all the host of Heaven, and served Baal. And they caused their sons and their daughters to pass through the fire, and used divination and enchantments, and sold themselves to do evil in the sight of the Lord, to provoke him to anger."*

How did God react to Israel's state of apostasy? God's judgment was swift and harshly delivered! In verse 20, the Bible records:

*And the LORD rejected all the descendants of Israel, and afflicted them, and delivered them into the hand of plunderers, until he had cast them out of his sight.*

God's reaction to sin is consistent through-out the Bible. For instance, in Judges 2:14, we read:

*In his anger against Israel the LORD gave them into the hands of raiders who plundered them. He sold them into the hands of their enemies all around, whom they were no longer able to resist.*

God would always judge sin because, in His sight and His Holiness, He cannot endure to "look toward iniquity":

*You are of purer eyes than to behold evil, and cannot look on iniquity… (Habakkuk. 1:13).*

Sin separates us from God. Prophet Isaiah lays the blame squarely on the sins of the sinner:

*Behold, the LORD's hand is not shortened, that it cannot save; neither his ear heavy that it cannot hear: But your iniquities have separated between you and your God, and your sins have hid his face from you, that he will not hear (Isaiah 59:1-2).*

While man focuses on his sacrifice, its nature, its size etc., God focuses on the heart, the motive, and man's relationship with Him. The fast that satisfies God therefore, puts the heart before the sacrifice.

# 3

# GOD'S ESTIMATION OF THE FAST: THE WRONG AND RIGHT FASTS

## WHEN THE WRONG PERSON FASTS

At the end of the whole process, a believer's fast is either accepted or rejected. God is the sole judge, not man (Psalm 75:6). He is the assessor; He weighs the believer's sacrifice against His pre-laid down standard, and decides whether the man's sacrifice bears any divine relevance before Him

> **When a man out of tune with God fasts, the fast is wrong ...**

or he has merely served his self-centred ego (Isaiah 58:1-6).

Consequently, when a man out of tune with God fasts, the fast is wrong, and it bears no significance with God. As a matter of fact, before a man fasts or prays, he must qualify to engage in the act. In other words, he must have recognition before God, for his sacrifices to be accepted. The sacrifice of the wicked (the unsaved and the backslidden), is an exercise in futility. The Bible says, "The sacrifice of the wicked is an abomination to the LORD: but the prayer of the upright is his delight" (Prov. 15:8). The prayer, fasting, giving or other sacrifices that proceed from a wrong heart is a futile effort at taking God for granted. They bear no spiritual fruits whatsoever!

Martin Luther argues:

*...genuine Christian fasting is a fruit of repentance... it helps keep the flesh in check and is a fine outward training in preparing to better receive God's grace.*

He was not alone in the condemnation of wrong attitude to fasting. John Calvin – exposing the abominable fasting habits of the Ancient Roman Catholic Church - taught that fasting is of no value to God, unless the heart is right and fasting is accompanied by genuine repentance, humiliation, and sorrow in the presence of an awesome God.

# PROPHET ISAIAH'S CONDEMNATION OF WRONG ATTITUDE TO FASTING

The 58th chapter of Isaiah presents us with a clear picture of what God regards as wrong attitude in fasting, and, of course, the wrong fast.

Isaiah took to task those who went through the motions of religious observance while at the same time, not having the right standing with God; and engaging in corrupt practices. The kind of fasting that God is pleased with includes a desire to live an upright life, help the poor and the oppressed.

The Lord instructed Isaiah to proclaim loudly the sins of the nation. This includes the outward righteousness of the people as they went to the temple, obeyed God's laws, fasted, and appeared eager to serve the Holy One of Israel. However, the Lord who sees the heart (1 Sam. 16:7), was not impressed with the external religious rituals.

> **The kind of fasting that God is pleased with includes a desire to live an upright life, and help the poor and the oppressed.**

God says:

*What are all your sacrifices to Me? ... I have had enough of burnt offerings and rams and the fat of well-fed cattle; I have no desire for the blood of bulls, lambs, or male goats.... Stop bringing useless offerings. I despise [your] incense.... I hate your New Moons and prescribed festivals. They have become a burden to Me; I am tired of putting up with [them]. When you lift up your hands [in prayer], I will refuse to look at you; even if you offer countless prayers, I will not listen (Isaiah. 1:11-15).*

Quoting Isaiah 29:13, Jesus offered a similar rebuke to the religious leaders of His day:

*These people honour Me with their lips, but their heart is far from Me. They worship Me in vain, teaching as doctrines the commands of men (Matt. 15:8-9).*

The important lessons embedded in these scriptures, no doubt, speak audibly to Christians today. The question should be constantly asked, is our worship a humble response to God's grace, or a self-centred effort to draw attention to ourselves or to curry God's favour? This position finds consensus with the view expressed by Warren Wiersbe, when he said:

## GOD'S ESTIMATION OF THE FAST: THE WRONG AND RIGHT FASTS

*When we worship because it is the popular thing to do, not because it is the right thing to do, then our worship becomes hypocritical.*

The Jews were commanded to observe only one fast per year, on the Day of Atonement (Lev. 16:29-31). However, they were permitted to fast personally at other times. Somehow, the permission to fast devolved into a contest among God's people to gain His attention. Quite expected, they complained that the Lord's attention was not drawn to their fasting.

Hear the outcry of the people:

> *Wherefore have we fasted, say they, and thou seest not? wherefore have we afflicted our soul, and thou takest no knowledge? Behold, in the day of your fast ye find pleasure, and exact all your labours (Isaiah 58:3).*

These people only wanted to gain God's attention at all costs, while buried in their evil traditions and unbiblical practices.

God's response was swift:

> *Behold, you fast for strife and debate, and to strike with the fist of wickedness: you shall not fast as you do this day, to make your voice to be heard on high. Is it such a fast that I have chosen? a day for a man to afflict his soul? is it to bow down his head as a bulrush, and to spread sackcloth and*

> *ashes under him? will you call this a fast, and an acceptable day to the LORD? (Isaiah 58:4-5).*

**Abstaining from food alone, therefore, is not what makes and defines the fast.**

The people in Isaiah's day were fasting for all the wrong reasons! They fasted to draw attention to themselves, while at the same time, hypocritically appeared righteous.

The problem with the fasting in this regard, of course, is that it was an empty religious ritual, observed to satisfy religious requirements. It was fasting characterised with injustice to others, and as you would expect, ended in strife and contention; there was no self-humbling or repentance from sins whatsoever!

Fasting is meant to encourage believers to respond positively to God's commands. As we deprive ourselves of certain physical needs – food, sleep, sexual relations, for example, we are better able to see the weakness of our flesh. This creates spiritual alertness, and ability to hear God's voice clearly.

Although the people of Israel were fasting, they had clearly neglected the instructions from the Lord to care for the less fortunate among them and treat them as members of their own family who, at one time, had been slaves in Egypt. In others words, they were overlooking the very essential elements of a true fast. Fasting should result in self-denial, not self-indulgence. When believers share with others, it serves as a reminder that all they own ultimately belongs to God.

The message here to us is unequivocal! There is no degree of cry by man or any group of persons that would move God to alter His standard. God rejected their fasting because God is looking for fasting that merits His attention and reflects His nature, that is, fasting that exemplifies His love for humanity. If the fasting fails to meet God's criteria, He is not interested.

Abstaining from food alone, therefore, is not what makes and defines the fast. There are other equally weighty matters that have to always be considered, such as the condition of the heart, as earlier discussed, and the alignment of our fast with the dictates of Scripture. Failure at this level means an outright failure! Once the heart is wrong, and the conduct of the fast is in contravention to the word of God, the fasting becomes ineffective. The heart is the bed-rock of everything we do for, and with God. The Bible asks, *"If the foundation be destroyed, what can the righteous do" (Prov. 11:3).*

# SEVENTY YEARS OF FASTING: ALL BUT IN VAIN!

*Speak unto all the people of the land, and to the Priests, saying, When ye fasted and mourned in fifth and seventh month, even those seventy years, did ye at all fast unto me, even to me? (Zech. 7:5).*

There is a pathetic account in the book of Zechariah 7: 1-3, that further highlights the great premium God places on His pre-ordained criteria for accepting the fasts of the believer:

*And it came to pass in the fourth year of King Darius, that the word of the Lord came unto Zachariah in the fourth day of the ninth month, even in Chisleu, when they had sent unto the house of God Sherezer and Regemelech, and their men, to pray before the LORD of hosts, and to the prophets; saying Should I weep in the fifth month, separating myself, as I have done these so many years?*

The people of Zechariah's day had fasted, albeit ritualistically, for a staggering period of seventy years - every fifth and seventh month of the year! The people would have carried on with this wistful liturgical practice, had God not intervened! In verse 5, after a practice that had spanned through seven decades, as indicated, God

## GOD'S ESTIMATION OF THE FAST: THE WRONG AND RIGHT FASTS

finally expressed His disgust at what the people regarded as "a fast unto the lord."

Says God:

> *Speak unto all the people of the land, and to the Priests, saying. When ye fasted and mourned in fifth and seventh month, even those seventy years, did ye at all fast unto me, even to me? (Zech. 7:5).*

Fasting for seventy years without approval from God? How awful! No doubt, the people were fully persuaded that they were fasting unto the Lord those seventy years. The length of time the people had engaged in this wrongful fast did not move God to condone their practices or sidestep His divine standard!

God would always distance Himself from whatever is at odds with His purpose and requirements. What is the implication of this, you may ask? A man could choose to fast for as long as he wishes, but if the fast is conducted in defiance to God's criteria, the fasting is wrong, and bears no consequence with God. Further, as earlier indicated, if a man in his sinful nature fasts, his fasting is an abomination to God; he receives no reward but condemnation in return. How tragic!

> *The sacrifice of the wicked is abomination: how much more, when he bringeth it with a wicked mind? (Prov. 21:27, KJV).*

*The sacrifice of the wicked is detestable-- how much more so when brought with evil intent! (Prov. 12:27 NIV).*

# MAN LOOKS AT HIS FAST; GOD LOOKS AT THE HEART

Here exists a fundamental principle: while man focuses on 'his fast', God looks at the heart of the 'fasting believer! If the heart is right with Him, then God looks at the fast.

*For the LORD sees not as man sees: man looks on the outward appearance, but the LORD looks on the heart (I Sam.16:7).*

The same goes for prayers, giving, and indeed, all our services in God's kingdom. If our heart is right then God considers our services. But if the heart is wrong or is in opposition to His will, then God takes His eyes away from us.

It never ceases to amaze me how very often, Spirit-filled believers take these fundamental principles of faith for granted; walk in defiance to God's laid down principles, while at the same time, expect God to be moved by their much fasting. Dear Saint, God is not mocked! David says *"If I regard iniquity in my heart, the Lord will not hear me" (Psalm 66:18)*. The Master is looking for His life reflected in the believer that fasts; a life fully yielded to Him.

## GOD'S ESTIMATION OF THE FAST: THE WRONG AND RIGHT FASTS

Obedience to the word of God cannot be substituted with sacrifice. Hear the conclusion of the matter:

> *"... Hath the Lord as great delight in burnt offerings and sacrifices, as in obeying the voice of the Lord? Behold, to obey is better than sacrifice, and to hearken than the fat of rams." (I Sam. 15:22).*

This was recorded concerning a beloved saint – Gaius.

> *The elder unto the wellbeloved Gaius, whom I love in the truth. For I rejoiced greatly, when the brethren came and testified of the truth that is in thee,* **even as thou walkest** *in the truth (3 John 1:3, emphasis added).*

And of Demetrius the testimony runs:

> **Demetrius hath good report of all men, and of the truth itself:** *yea, and we also bear him record; and ye know that our record is true (3 John 12, emphasis added).*

We are called to be a reflection of the message of the Bible. Apostle Paul calls the believer a written epistle "known and read of all men" (2 Cor. 3:2). And in 2 Corinthians 2:14-15, he writes;

> *"Now thanks be unto God, which always causeth us to triumph in Christ,* **and maketh manifest the savour of his knowledge by us in every place. For we are unto God a sweet savour of Christ**, *in them that are saved, and in them that perish" (emphasis added).*

These exemplify the hearts that the Master is seeking. "Those that will worship [serve] the father in spirit and in truth" (John 4:23).

Still on the subject of wrong fast, Jesus says:

> *Moreover, when you fast, be not as the hypocrites, of a sad countenance, for they disfigure their faces, that they may appear unto men to fast. Verily I say unto you. They have their reward. But thou when thou fastest anoint thine head, and wash thy face. That thou appear not unto men to fast but unto God thy father which is in secret, shall reward thee openly (Matt. 6:16-18).*

In this passage, Jesus tells the believer how to engage in fasting that honours God and attracts His blessings: they are to anoint their heads and wash their faces. In Jewish custom anointing one's head and washing one's face was not done for daily hygiene or cosmetic reasons. Rather, they were reserved for joyous occasions. So, unusual religious sorrow within should be compensated for by outward signs of an opposite sort. Reality in the sight of God rather than appearance in the sight of man must be the believer's priority.

The phrase, *"your Father,"* used twice in verse 18, points to the personal relationship between the individual and God. This is elsewhere expressed powerfully by the use of the Aramaic term *"Abba"*, which can be translated, *"Daddy"* (Mark 14:36; Rom. 8:15). Acts of piety such as fasting

## GOD'S ESTIMATION OF THE FAST: THE WRONG AND RIGHT FASTS

must be performed solely and exclusively for the believer's *"Father"* with no concern for one's reputation before others. God "is in secret," and He "sees in secret." The double use of the word "secret" in Matthew 6:18 emphasises the hiddenness of the virtuous act of fasting, in order to be performed for God alone. These secret acts are noticed by God and will be rewarded by Him.

The passage closes with the assuring words "thy Father … will reward you…"

As with almsgiving and prayer, the believer should practice fasting as an act of private piety. His main concern was their inner spirit with which fasting was performed. They were to be pure in motive as they fasted and not to fast as a means of gaining approval from others.

# 4

# THE RIGHT FAST

## THE GOD-HONOURED FAST

*God is attracted to weakness. He cannot resist when we humbly and honestly admit how desperately we need Him. When we are empty vessels, He longs to fill us with His grace, love and goodness. This is God's law of attraction* —**Jentezen Franklin.**

Having examined the negative fast, we must now turn our attention to consider the positive fast – the kind of fast that honours the Master, which consequently, attracts His reward! Let us examine this first, in the life of Jesus Himself.

> *And ... being full of the Holy returned from Jordan. and was led by the Spirit in the Wilderness. Being forty days tempted of the devil. And in those days he did eat nothing. and when they were ended. he was afterward hungered (Luke 4:1-2).*

After the Lord fasted, the Bible says, *"And Jesus returned in the power of the Spirit..." (v.14).* What are the implications

> **Notice that Jesus was already full of the Holy Ghost when he entered the fast, but he was overflowing with the Holy Spirit when he finished.**

of the verse in context? First, being full of the Holy Spirit does not necessarily cause one to walk in the power of the Spirit. One of the ways to walking in power as a believer is fasting and prayer. Second, Jesus was full of the Holy Spirit when He entered into forty days fast. But how did He come out of it? The Bible says, He *"returned in the power of the Spirit into Galilee, and there went out the fame of him through all the region around about"* *(LK 4:14).*

# EIGHT CHARACTERISTICS OF A GOD'S CHOSEN FAST

*Is not this the fast that I have chosen? to loose the bands of wickedness, to undo the heavy burdens, and to let the oppressed go free, and that ye break every yoke? Is it not to deal thy bread to the hungry, and that thou bring the poor that are cast out to thy house? when thou seest the naked, that thou cover him; and that thou hide not thyself from thine own flesh? (Isaiah 58:6-7)*

The above scripture lists eight key characteristics of the kind of fast that is pleasing to God. In other words, every God-centred and God-focused fast must seek to accomplish the following tasks, to honour and attract His rewards. They add weight to our sacrifices unto the Lord.

> **Our faith must have practical works in our relationship with others, to be genuine.**

1. Loose the bands of wickedness
2. Undo the heavy burden
3. Let the oppressed go free
4. Break every yoke
5. Deal thy bread to the hungry
6. Bring the poor that are cast out into thy house
7. Cover the naked
8. Not hide thyself from thine own flesh.

The issues raised in these verses of Scripture are fundamental and significant. They further buttress the need to combine faith with works. It is not enough to have faith. Our faith must have practical works in our relationship with others, to be genuine. From the expository teaching of Apostle James on the subject, we can conclude that emphasis on faith at the expense of works renders faith ineffective, as our fasting.

Apostle James writes:

> *What does it profit, my brethren, if someone says he has faith but does not have works? Can faith save him? If a brother or sister is naked and destitute of daily food, and one of you says to them, "Depart in peace, be warmed and filled," but you do not give them the things which are needed for the body, what does it profit? Thus also faith by itself, if it does not have works, is dead. But someone will say, "You have faith, and I have works." Show me your faith without your works, and I will show you my faith by my works. You believe that there is one God. You do well. Even the demons believe—and tremble! But do you want to know, O foolish man, that faith without works is dead?*
>
> *Was not Abraham our father justified by works when he offered Isaac his son on the altar? Do you see that faith was working together with his works, and by works faith was made perfect? And the Scripture was fulfilled which says, "Abraham believed God, and it was accounted to him for righteousness." And he was called the friend of God. You see then that a man is justified by works, and not by faith only. Likewise, was not Rahab the harlot also justified by works when she received the messengers and sent them out another way? For as the body without the spirit is dead, so faith without works is dead also (James 2:14-26 NKJV).*

The church, to be effective in its mission, cannot afford to be in isolation and out of touch with the needs of the people it is called to serve.

We see a great deal of consensus from the writings of various Bible personalities on the subject.

Says Apostle Paul,

> *As we have therefore opportunity, let us do good unto all men, especially unto them who are of the household of faith (Galatians 6:10).*

And Apostle John was emphatic in his view:

> *But whoever has this world's good, and sees his brother have need, and shuts up his bowels of compassion from him, how dwells the love of God in him? My little children, let us not love in word, neither in tongue; but indeed and in truth (1 John 3:17).*

## LOOSE THE BANDS OF WICKEDNESS

According to Webster's New Explorer Encyclopaedic Dictionary, a band is "something that confines or constricts while allowing a degree of movements; something that binds or restrains legally, morally, or spiritually…"

When the enemy wants to have his way, alter the course of an individual, family, or, even, a church's life and take full control of the affairs of their destiny, he uses bands – the bands of wickedness.

> **The church can no longer ignore the command to loosen the bands of wickedness and undo the heavy burdens.**

Too many of God's people are in one form of bondage or another. Some are experiencing fiery trials that have defiled prayers, many are drowning in depression. Some believers are under the bands that bound them long before they met Christ and are still being haunted. These individuals, families, even churches find themselves under the weight of bands of afflictions, yokes of set-backs and frustration in life. Jesus says this kind only comes out by prayer and fasting. I believe He is referring to the type of prayer and fasting described in the book of Isaiah, as discussed, to lose the bands of wickedness and destroy the yokes of depression.

Today, churches are full of well-meaning people and families who satan has limited, confined and restrained to a life of misery and reproach. How sad! These people have prayed all kinds of prayers and attended all kinds of special meetings: conventions, conferences, seminars, all-night prayer meetings, to mention but a few, seeking solutions, but to no avail!

The church can no longer ignore the command to loosen the bands of wickedness and undo the heavy burdens. To do so is to shy away from God's mandate for the church. Our fasting destroys the yoke the enemy has placed on people both in the church, our cities and nations. God's prescription for losing the bands of wickedness is His *"chosen fast."* Men and women must rise in the power of the Holy Ghost to bring deliverance and freedom from the bands of wickedness.

## LET THE OPPRESSED GO FREE

One of the greatest objects of fasting is to set the oppressed free. To be oppressed means the following:

1. Burden with cruel or unjust impositions or restraints; subject to a burdensome or harsh exercise of authority or power: a people oppressed by totalitarianism.

2. To lie heavily upon (the mind, a person).

3. To weigh down, as sleep or weariness does.

4. To put down; subdue or suppress.

5. To press upon or against; crush.

According to Strong's Exhaustive Concordance of the Bible, the Greek word for oppression – *katadunasteuo* – means "to exercise dominion against." The Hebrew word for oppression or to be oppressed *"ratsats"* means "to crack in pieces, to break, bruise, crush, discourage, oppress, struggle together."

Thank God! The Bible says:

*How God anointed Jesus of Nazareth with the Holy Spirit and with power, who went about doing good and healing all who were **oppressed** by the devil, for God was with Him (Acts 10:38, emphasis added).*

There is healing for the oppressed! God has mandated His church to set the oppressed, hurting people free. Jesus says:

*The Spirit of the Lord is upon me, because he hath anointed me to preach the gospel to the poor; he hath sent me to heal the brokenhearted, to preach deliverance to the captives, and recovering of sight to the blind, to set at liberty them that are bruised (Luke 4:18).*

*"... the Lord is that Spirit: and where the Spirit of the Lord is, there is liberty" (2 Cor. 3:17).*

There is freedom for you if you are in any form of oppression in Jesus' name. Engage God's infallible weapon (fasting), and secure your freedom from the evil of oppression!

## FASTING BREAKS EVERY YOKE

Literally, a "yoke" is a device laid across the necks of animals to harness them together so they can work as a team, and their load is attached to it. It was also widely used by slave traders in the transportation of slaves. A yoke was a sign of absolute slavery and captivity. In a sense, they played the role of modern day "hand-cuffs", often used by the police on suspects. Yokes are designed to restrain movement. They were also used as vindictive instruments to humiliate, despise, and enslave prisoners.

If a yoke was not properly attached to the animals, or if the load was too heavy for them to pull, the yoke would chafe the animals painfully and hinder their productivity.

However, its use gave rise to a couple of figurative meanings in the New Testament.

Jesus employed its use when He taught His audience: "My yoke is easy and My burden is light" (Matt. 11:30), wherein He was contrasting the "difficulties" of following Him with the difficulties of keeping the Law of Moses.

Apostle Peter described the harsh requirements of the Law the young converts in Antioch were asked to satisfy to be accepted into the Christian faith, as a yoke.

He said:

> Now therefore, why do you test God by putting a **yoke** on the neck of the disciples which neither our fathers nor we were able to bear? (Acts 15:10, emphasis added).

The other major figurative meaning refers to the way a yoke places animals side-by-side. This is to compel them to move together in order to accomplish anything. This aspect is the basis of the teaching, *"Do not be unequally yoked together with unbelievers." (2 Cor. 6:14)*. This teaching is not exclusive to marriage; in fact, Paul was not even talking about marriage in this passage. It more broadly applies to any relationship that would compel two people to *"work together as one."*

The only weapon, according to the Bible, that destroys yokes is the anointing of the Holy Spirit working through a human vessel.

> *"And it shall come to pass in that day, that his burden shall be taken away from off your shoulder, and his yoke from off your neck, and the yoke shall be destroyed because of the anointing" (Isaiah 10:27).*

Nothing fuels the anointing as much as biblical fasting. The vessels of God are empowered to the degree that they submit themselves to God. It is God that fills His vessels with the divine ability that is needed to accomplish kingdom assignments. The Word says, *"… we have this treasure in earthen vessels, that the excellency of the power may be of God, and not of us." (2 Cor. 4:7)*.

Sadly, despite the authority Christ has given the church, countless numbers of people live in perpetual darkness under the yoke of satanic bondage. The same applies to millions of Christian homes. Child of God, you do not have to bear that burden any more. The Bible says, *"his [Satan's] burden shall be taken away from off your shoulder" (Isaiah 10:27)*. Every yoke, no matter its intensity.

# 5
# FASTING AND GOOD DEEDS

*Is it not to deal thy bread to the hungry, and that thou bring the poor that are cast out to thy house? when thou seest the naked, that thou cover him; and that thou hide not thyself from thine own flesh? (Isaiah 58: 7).*

The seventh verse of Isaiah 58 is extremely vital to our study, as it takes our discussion to an altogether new dimension. It must be stressed that God greatly blesses generosity to the needy.

To have adequate understanding of what this verse conveys, it is important to examine its various segments or requirements distinctly.

Most translations of the Bible take an interpretative approach, taking "flesh" to mean, significantly, 'one's own family.' For examples:

*"...and do not hide from relatives who need your help" (NLT)*

*"...and not to turn away from your own flesh and blood" (NIV)*

*"...and to not ignore your own flesh and blood?" (HCSB)*

Let us now examine the various components of the said verse:

*"Is it not to deal thy bread to the hungry?"*

Christlikeness is more to do with how we treat the poor. It sounds like what our modern societies have labelled charitable work. Yes, God teaches that if our fasting must meet His criteria, it must have something to do with taking care of the poor. The greatest 'charity worker' that ever lived was Jesus; He healed the sick, raised the dead and fed the poor, all for nothing in return. The Bible says:

> *He that has pity upon the poor lends unto the LORD; and that which he has given will he pay him again (Prov. 19:17)*

> *He that giveth unto the poor shall not lack: but he that hideth his eyes shall have many a curse (Prov. 28:27).*

As John Kilpatrick puts it:

*The Church has grown accustomed to letting soup kitchens and relief agencies feed the hungry...There is something about hand-on ministry and sharing that transforms the heart and the soul. There is something about rubbing shoulders with the hungry, the lost, and the wounded that keeps our eyes on Jesus Christ and our egos on the ground, where they belong. God planned it this way because He knows that when we personally share our bread with another person, we also share love, encouragement, and reassurance that the person we serve is valuable and precious in the sight of both God and man.... our religion becomes a lifestyle of Christlike sharing, loving, and redeeming. After all, if Jesus were to walk among us today, where would we find Him-with the satisfied or the hungry?*

### "Bring the poor that are cast out into thy house"

It must be noted that concerning these requirements, God is not looking for something we do just when we are fasting, but an act that is habitual – a lifestyle!

Knowing or recognising the poor does not require prayer and fasting, Saints! You do not need a special word of knowledge to know who is poor and who is not. The poor are easy to identify. Jesus says, *"For you have the poor **always** with you…"* (Matt. 26: 11, emphasis added).

I know it could be very risky sharing your shelter with people you do not know so well, but you know what? Be led by the Spirit of God. The dividends of sharing our bounty and shelter with others are immeasurable. We are enjoined by Scriptures *"not to forget to entertain strangers: for thereby some have entertained angels unawares" (Heb. 13:2)*.

There is great joy and fulfilment in the lives of people that have made it a practice to open their homes to the needy. They are tremendously rewarded. The Bible says,

> **For God is not unrighteous to forget your work and labour of love**, *which ye have shewed toward his name, in that ye have ministered to the saints, and do minister (Heb. 6:10, emphasis added).*

Fasting, to be effective, must go hand-in- hand with good works. We cannot engage in one without the other!

> *"When thou seeth the naked, that thou cover him"*
> *(Isaiah 58:7, ASV).*

In our world today, too many people are naked. With the global pandemic, and all its resultant effects, millions of people, families, and even churches are faced with gruesome challenges. Many live with the excruciating pains of lack and abject poverty daily. Notice what this scripture says "when thou seest the naked;" and not *'if'* thou seest the naked'. Dear saint, the global pandemic has claimed its victims, beyond the dead! The ripple effects still reverberate worldwide. Hundreds of thousands of people have either lost their jobs or businesses – their only source of livelihood. The rate of unemployment has skyrocketed all over the world, at an unprecedented level. As a result, the destitute are all around us; they are not hard to find. People are hungry! It is our responsibility – the church and not that of any formal institutionalised system to feed the poor and needy, both within and outside our churches. Multitudes of people are naked – exposed to the elements and eyes of the world. The church must step in and show these people that someone cares.

The naked, according to John Kilpatrick, also include those who are damaged by the words and criticisms of the accusers and the self-righteous – fellow believers. We need to learn to stand together in times of trouble and crisis. The sad reality is that believers who are going through painful situations find more assistance and sympathy out in the world than in the Body of Christ, in an attitude Mahesh Chavda regarded as acting like sharks.

He said:

*We have trained ourselves to act more like sharks than believers when we see someone who is wounded, bleeding and floundering in the waters of adversity or failure. The members of the Body of Christ seem more determined to attack and cut up their wounded members than to rush to their side with support, healing, and gentle correction if needed. We are to support each order in grace and mercy because we are yoked together and united in Christ. If one falters, we all falter. That is why the fasting family of God wants to see every individual family in its body blessed. If one is affected, we are all affected, so it behoves us to stick together.*

The Bible says,

*"Hatred stirs up strife: but love covers all sins" (Prov. 10:12).*

*"And that thou hide not thyself from thine own flesh?"*

The saying: *"you can choose your friends, but cannot choose your family members"* holds true in all ramifications – in relation to our earthly family and the family of believers. We cannot pick and choose our family members.

Majority of Christians have not come to terms with the huge significance God has placed on the family structure. As a result, many have accepted the wander and roam plan of the world system, casting off all obligations to family members, as well as the local church. This is quite dangerous! Family life and church life are paramount in God's plan. This is true because the character of God is best formed in the heat and pressure of long-term, mandatory fellowship with other people who may or may not agree with you on every detail. Family is important to God! Well-structured learning and long-term character formation and growth take place in the crucible of family life than in any other area of human institutions.

In the words of John Kilpatrick:

*The family is God's safety net for a lifetime. Modern society, in its wisdom, has tried to dismantle the family. However, the family structure has worked for thousands of years in every culture on earth. Long before there were welfare agencies, government assistance programs, and Social Security, there was family. The family not only provided for the physical necessities of its members but also policed those among them who were not diligent about seeking work or meeting their responsibilities... Even the Church has fallen into the "let the government do it" mentality.*

*Personal responsibility and duty were once at the heart of all family relationships. Children knew that they had an inherent responsibility to care for the parents in old age, just as their parents had cared for them in infancy. The sick, the disabled, and failing were never abandoned...after all they were family. Where personal responsibility and duty are discarded, the family safety net fails. It is time for the Church to restore God's standard of responsibility to every Christian home and congregation.*

Paul was explicit in his declaration on the subject:

> But if anyone does not provide for his own, and especially for those of his household, he has denied the faith and is worse than an unbeliever (1Tim. 5:8).

Let us consider the verse in summary (Isaiah 58:7):

I believe the verse in context is using "flesh" in the normal, literal sense, not in the figurative sense. The figurative sense "relatives" is used in scripture, but not nearly as much as the literal sense. Giving to the needy is not only to be engaged in when we are enjoying prosperity; we are to give even if it seems like such giving will place us in need, ourselves. As a matter of fact, it is such sacrificial giving that breaks the yokes of poverty off the life of the giver and releases abundance (Luke 6:38).

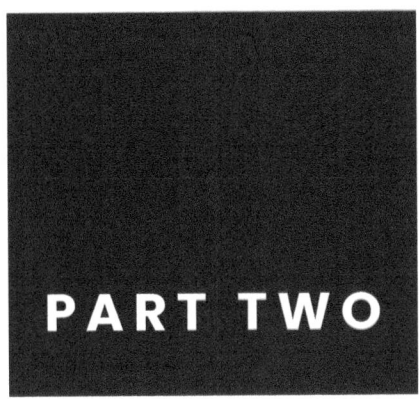

# GOD'S PURPOSE FOR FASTING

# 6

# USUAL REASONS TO FAST

*Without a purpose and plan, it's not Christian fasting. It's going hungry"* – **David Mattis**.

The question for our consideration under this heading is: why fast? Why should a believer set apart a specific period of time to deny himself the basic necessities of life, for the purpose of seeking God?

There are several reasons why a believer would make a firm decision to fast. Fasting should, therefore, always have specific objectives in view. As David Livingstone puts it, "Fastings … without a special object in view are time run to waste. They are made to minister to a sort of self-gratification, instead of being turned to good account." You fast for specific purpose(s); a fact alluded to by Arthur Blessitt when he said, *"In my personal life, fasting has been for specific purpose,"* you do not fast for the sake of fasting. Whatever aims at nothing achieves nothing! Napoleon Hills concurs; and as part of his laws of success, he enjoins the believer, "Plan your work, and work your plan." The same principle applies to fasting. Those who would make success of their fasting endeavour must aim to 'plan their fast and work their fasts.'

> **Fasting should, therefore, always have specific objectives in view.**

Fasting is not to be some religious ritual we go through. Every true fast should be purpose-driven. Our objectives need to be well defined before we take up a fast; we should have a specific reason for it, something we want to accomplish as a result of our fast. It can be for something very simple, as well as something complex and desperate.

You need to ask yourself the question: Why am I fasting? Is it for spiritual renewal, for guidance, for healing, for the resolution of problems, for special grace to handle a difficult situation? Ask the Holy Spirit to clarify His leading and objectives for your fast. This will enable you to pray more specifically and strategically, and be fully focused throughout the journey.

There are several reasons, as said, that could make a Christian decide to fast. Usually, you fast as a means of seeking God. God said, *"When you seek me with all your heart, I will be found by you" (Jer. 29:13, 14)*. When a man or woman is willing to set aside the legitimate appetites of the body to concentrate on the work of praying, they are demonstrating that they mean business; that they are seeking God with all their heart. To Zachariah Fomum, this is what fasting entails "...*the deliberate abstention from food **for the purpose of concentrating on deeper fellowship with the Lord and the renewal of spiritual power**" (emphasis added)*. Every Bible – based fast must be for a well-defined reason, an aim, and an objective to be achieved and must, therefore, answer the question, why should I fast?

Since fasts in the Old Testament were in response to calamities and were to demonstrate humility and repentance, it would seem that the same purpose and attitude would hold true for New Testament believers. Jesus hinted that this should be the purpose for fasting among His disciples.

His disciples would fast after the bridegroom was taken away (Matt. 9:14-15; Mark 2:18-20; Luke 5:33-35), Jesus says. The departure of the Bridegroom from His Bride would normally be considered as a tragedy that would evoke a felt need. In times of tragedies and headaches of life, therefore, Jesus' true disciples should fast.

Fasting, therefore, is a legitimate response to dangers, trial or sorrows. In times of physical or spiritual needs, the believer realises his inadequacy, and in humility and repentance looks up to the Lord, sentiment well expressed by Jehoshaphat, King of Judah in 2 Chr. 20:12:

*"O our God, wilt thou not judge them? for we have no*

*might against this great company that cometh against us;* **neither know we what to do: but our eyes are upon thee"** (emphasis added).

Let us now examine some specific purposes of fasting; reasons why the believer could and should set time aside to fast:

# FASTING AS A MEANS OF SELF-HUMBLING

As human, we are prone towards pride, unless we deal with our hearts. Pride is the default mode of the human heart. It is a besetting sin, and the root of all sin that we must continually seek to be conscious and repentant of. Pride is dealt with throughout the Bible in the sternest of terms. God's emotion towards pride is "hate" (Prov. 8:13). His action toward the proud is punishment (Prov. 16:5), that includes "destruction" and a "fall" (Prov. 16:18). Humility enables us to gain access to God. God's grace is only available to the humble; and fasting is God-ordained means of self-humbling.

This was particularly so in the life of David. He says *"I humble myself soul with fasting" (Psalm 35:13)*. Humility is not a transcendent experience, or a vague emotional experience. Humility is a way of life that becomes part of our 'being' as we make conscious, determined effort to incorporate it as part of the qualities that define us.

According to Saint Augustine, *"Fasting cleanses the soul, raises the mind, subjects one's flesh to the spirit, renders the heart contrite and humble, scatters the clouds of concupiscence, quenches the fire of lust, and kindles the true light of chastity. Enter again into yourself."*

We must bear in mind that God will not humble us, because He has given us the responsibility to work out humility for ourselves. David, in the scripture just referenced, showed us how to incorporate humility as an integral part of our lives. The Bible is inundated with teachings on the value of humility. It is an established principle of God, that whoever goes the way of humility receives the Master's lifting.

> "Humble yourselves, therefore, under God's mighty hand, that he may lift you up in due time" (I Peter. 5:6).

Further, in Matthew 23: 12, the Bible says,

> "And whoever shall exalt himself shall be abased; and he that shall humble himself shall be exalted."

From these two scriptural references, it is very appropriate to conclude that in life, the 'way up' is 'down'. The choice therefore, is whether to be exalted or abased.

It was the choice of John the Baptist to humble himself before the Master.

*"He must increase, but I must decrease" (John 3:30)*, was his resolve!

John was saying in essence, 'This is the assigned moment for the Master to take the centre stage, while I slip off to the side-line'.

Since John's mission was to go before Jesus and prepare the way for Him (Mark 1:2-3), the time came when John needed to fade into the background of the Jesus' era and allow Jesus His place. It is with considerable grace and humility that John says, *"He must increase, but I must decrease" (John 3:30)*. What can we learn from this statement, and indeed, attitude? The answer is to be found in a similar bold statement made by John,

> "I indeed baptise you with water unto repentance, but He who is coming after me is mightier than I, whose sandals I am not worthy to carry. He will baptize you with the Holy Spirit and fire" (Matt 3:11).

John had no pretensions about the superiority of Jesus' mission to his. The Pharisees sent a list of questions to John—whether he was the prophet, or the Christ, or Elijah resurrected. John never rashly agreed to any inaccurate designation (John 1:19-26). John knew who He was, and that he was inferior to Jesus—and that did not bother him. Instead his declaration, "He must increase, but I must decrease" reflects a mind-set of complete humility in the face of one greater.

John shows us that passing the torch is natural, yet still requires humility. *"He must increase, but I must decrease"* is the thought of each passing generation of God's leaders who are looking to the future of Christ's cause. It was the thought of Moses preparing Joshua, David preparing Solomon, and Paul preparing Timothy and Titus. Yet we should never think that the need for a new generation to take the reins of leadership in God's work means that relinquishing those reins is easy for a generation accustomed to them! We desperately need the humility to say that we are not as important as the fate of a local church, or the development of leaders in worship and preaching, or the confidence of young believers. Let us promote and encourage them; acknowledging that they must increase, and we must decrease, or at best, admit the reality that one day, we must vacate the stage for a younger, more vibrant generation of leaders, preachers, administrators, songwriters in the Church. This is the reality of life! And it must be welcomed with open arms.

John reminds us that God's word is more important than any one person. Surely his followers warned him to be quiet about Herod's adulterous marriage (Matt 14:4), so that he could stay out of trouble and keep preaching—yet the word of God was more important than what happened to John. Further, consider what might have happened had John not stepped aside for Jesus—a power struggle, competing teachers and disciples, and a prevention of many disciples from coming to Jesus. Yet

John conceding to Him enabled Jesus to say, *"Assuredly, I say to you, among those born of women there has not risen one greater than John the Baptist..." (Matt. 11:11).* Why? Because God gives us more grace when we humble ourselves before Him. The Scripture says: *"God opposes the proud but gives grace to the humble" (James 4:6).* We may advance the gospel, or detract from its advancement yet, it remains far bigger than we are, individually! We must guard against an inflated sense of self in spiritual matters! *"He must increase, but I must decrease"* is a distillation of a humble heart. Are we pursuing this humility? Having examined the inestimable worth or benefit of humility in our lives, whatever facilitates it must be appreciated greatly.

# FASTING AS AN EFFECTIVE TOOL OF REPENTANCE

Repentance holds great value before God. He places high premium on it. Fasting softens the heart of the believer, and creates sin consciousness. The Bible is deluged with instances where the people of God employed fasting as a means of registering first, remorse or contrition for wrongful deeds, followed by ultimate acts of repentance. Let us examine some of such cases:

> *Now in the twenty and fourth day of this month the children of Israel were assembled with fasting. and with sackclothes, and earth upon them. And the seed of Israel*

*separated themselves from all strangers, and stood and confessed their sins, and the iniquities of their fathers. And they stood up in their place, and read in the book of the law of the Lord their God one fourth part of the day; and another fourth part they confessed, and worshipped the Lord their God (Neh. 9:1-3).*

*"Gird yourselves, and lament, ye priests: howl, ye ministers of the altar: come, lie all night in sackcloth, ye ministers of my God: for the meat offering and the drink offering is withholden from the house of your God. Sanctify ye a fast, call a solemn assembly, gather the elders and all the inhabitants of the land into the house of the Lord your God, and cry unto the Lord" (Joel 1:13-14).*

*"Therefore also now, saith the Lord, turn ye even to me with all your heart, and with fasting, and with weeping, and with mourning: And rend your heart, and not your garments, and turn unto the Lord your God: for he is gracious and merciful, slow to anger, and of great kindness, and repenteth him of the evil. Who knoweth if he will return and repent, and leave a blessing behind him; even a meat offering and a drink offering unto the Lord your God? Blow the trumpet in Zion, sanctify a fast, call a solemn assembly: Gather the people, sanctify the congregation, assemble the elders, gather the children, and those that suck the breasts: let the bridegroom go forth of his chamber, and the bride out of her closet. Let the priests, the ministers of the Lord, weep between the porch and the altar, and let them say, Spare thy people, O Lord, and give not thine heritage to reproach, that*

*the heathen should rule over them: wherefore should they say among the people, Where is their God?" (Joel 2:12-17).*

The value of repentance is immeasurable! Its outcome, to say the least, is astonishing. Repentance is the renewal of life. It is man freeing himself from his past negative self and turning towards the best he can possibly be. *"No sin,"* says Elder Thaddeus, *"is unforgivable except the sin of unrepentance."* George Eliot concurs, *"Who with repentance is not satisfied, is not of Heaven, nor earth."* And that is what repentance is in its entire ramifications. Thomas Merton could not be more precise when he said, *"… the man who is not afraid to admit everything that he sees to be wrong with himself, and yet recognizes that he may be the object of God's love precisely because of his shortcomings, can begin to be sincere. His sincerity is based on confidence, not in his own illusions about himself, but in the endless, unfailing mercy of God."* And he finds consensus in the view expressed by Jim Anderson:

*The world is full of men who want to be right, when actually the secret of a man's strength and his pathway to true honor is his ability to admit fault when he has failed. God wants to fill the church with men who can say they are wrong when THEY ARE WRONG…*

Fasting helps to accomplish this objective in the life of the believer. Fasting, as an act of contrition or penitence, says to God, "behold my repentance, forgive me."

Further examples of this are found in Deuteronomy 9:18; 1 Samuel 7:6; 1 Kings 21:27; Ezra 10:6; Jonah 3:5; and Acts 9:3-9. In the Old Testament, when people wished to demonstrate that they were serious about repenting from their sin, they fasted. The case of the people of Nineveh stands out amongst many. After Jonah pronounced judgment against the city of Nineveh, the king covered himself with sackcloth and sat in the dust. He ordered the people to fast and pray. Jonah 3:10 says,

> *"When God saw what they did and how they turned from their evil ways, He relented and did not bring on them the destruction He had threatened."*

Our willingness to sacrifice shows the depth of our commitment and in this case, fasting is a pictorial way of saying to the Lord, *"I am sorry for my sins and failures, I care more about getting right with You, God, than I do about even my own life, behold my repentance."* Fasting as self-chastisement will prevent many chastisements of the Lord from coming upon us.

# FASTING FOR SELF-EXAMINATION

*Search me, O God, and know my heart: try me, and know my thoughts: And see if there be any wicked way in me, and lead me in the way everlasting (Psalm 139:23-24).*

> **Self-examination helps us to avoid many pitfalls in life…**

"The unexamined life is not worth living" (Socrates).

The significance of self-examination in our relationship with God is profound, and cannot be overemphasised. Self –examination helps to restore a believer to a glowing relationship and fellowship with Christ. This doctrine presumes that as human; we are vulnerable and prone to failure; in consequence, often wander away from the ways and precepts of God. As a loving Father, God keeps the way back to a right standing with Him in such circumstances, ever open. However, it is expected, as responsible children of God, to keep our eyes focused on Jesus and constantly weigh matters regarding the health of our relationship with Him.

Paul enjoins the saints:

> *Wherefore seeing we also are compassed about with so great a cloud of witnesses, let us lay aside every weight, and the sin which doth so easily beset us, and let us run with patience the race that is set before us,* **Looking unto Jesus [fixing our eyes on Jesus,** *NIV]* *the author and finisher of our faith: who for the joy that was set before him endured the cross, despising the shame, and is set down at the right hand of the throne of God (Heb. 12:1-2, emphasis added).*

Such matters must, therefore, be constantly kept under review; this is what self-examination calls for. *"Let us search and try our ways, and turn again to the LORD" (Lam.3:40)*, Jeremiah admonished.

In one of the land-mark parables of Jesus – the parable of the Prodigal Son - we see this lesson clearly illustrated:

According to Jesus,

> *"A certain man had two sons. And the younger of them said to his father, 'Father, give me the portion of goods that falls to me.' So he divided to them his livelihood. And not many days after, the younger son gathered all together, journeyed to a far country, and there wasted his possessions with prodigal living. But when he had spent all, there arose a severe famine in that land, and he began to be in want. Then he went and joined himself to a citizen of that country, and he sent him into his fields to feed swine. And he would gladly have filled his stomach with the pods that the swine ate, and no one gave him anything. "But when he came to himself, he said, 'How many of my father's hired servants have bread enough and to spare, and I perish with hunger!* **I will arise and go to my father...**" *(Luke 15: 11-17, NKJV, emphasis added).*

Note the dramatic turn of events in the life and destiny of this young man, whose account vividly depicts the life of a believer, momentarily out of tune with God. The phrase, *"... when he came to himself..."* is significant. This is what self-examination is; it is 'a coming back to oneself' after we have pre-judged ourselves. Pauls tells us that such self-imposed judgement helps us avoid the harsher judgement of the Lord, and the punishment that follows.

*"For if we would judge ourselves"*, Paul affirms, *"we should not be judged. But when we are judged, we are chastened of the Lord, that we should not be condemned with the world" (1 Cor. 11:31-32).*

It is observed that one of the primary reasons many believers struggle to draw near to God in an earnest, deeper way, in the spirit of self-examination, is because they know that such a pursuit may initially involve a painful, even excruciating encounter. Many of us avoid prescribed medical examinations and precautionary procedures not only because of the dread of discomfort or humiliation, but also for fear of what the good doctor may find? That should really not be the case with our relationship with God, it must be stressed. The merits of engaging in self-examination far out-weigh the fleeting and transitory discomfort it often occasions. The process of cutting out a cancerous cell is no doubt painful, but when it's gotten rid of, the life of the patient is preserved.

No doubt, to properly seek God and enjoy the fullness of the blessings it brings, requires an honest and consistent examination of our true position in Christ. The Latin word *'inquistion'* means the examining or discerning of conscience, conveying the idea of our on-going need for an accurate assessment of the true condition of our hearts.

Self-examination helps us to avoid many pitfalls in life generally. Full, total self-knowledge is the bread by which we are sustained. Socrates (an Ancient Greek Philosopher) was famous for saying, *"The unexamined life is not worth living."*

No Christian discipline enables the believer to engage in self-examination as much as fasting. In the Old Testament, the need for re-examination was established by God as a duty to be observed once a year. The Day of Atonement was instituted by God for Israel to reflect on their spiritual state:

> *Also on the tenth day of this seventh month there shall be a day of atonement: it shall be an holy convocation unto you; and ye shall afflict your souls, and offer an offering made by fire unto the LORD (Lev. 23:27).*

In Jeremiah 36:6, the Prophet Jeremiah wrote,

> *"Therefore go thou, and read in the roll, which thou hast written from my mouth, the words of the LORD in the ears of the people in the LORD'S house upon the fasting day: and also thou shalt read them in the ears of all Judah that come out of their cities."*

In the process of self-denial, God wanted His people to examine their spiritual state.

The New Testament believer is expected to do likewise, albeit, not as a duty, imposed by the harsh demands of the law, but as a means of drawing closer to God. Apostle Paul invites the believer to constantly and relentlessly engage in the discipline of self-examination in his walk with the Lord.

He admonishes:

> *"Examine yourselves, to see whether you are in the faith. Test yourselves. Or do you not realize this about yourselves, that Jesus Christ is in you?—unless indeed you fail to meet the test!"(2 Cor. 13:5),*

which draws consensus with Apostle Peter's notion,

> *"Therefore, brothers, be all the more diligent to confirm your calling and election, for if you practice these qualities you will never fall. For in this way there will be richly provided for you an entrance into the eternal kingdom of our Lord and Savior Jesus Christ" (2 Peter 1:10-11).*

# FASTING AS A TOOL FOR AVERTING CRISES

There are occasions when death or danger threatens us; we can see from the Scripture that it is certainly appropriate to employ fasting as a means of receiving God's protection during these times. When Ezra was carrying a large consignment of gold and silver to the temple in Jerusalem along a route infested with bandits, he records: *"I proclaimed a fast…that we might humble ourselves before our God, to seek from him a straight way for ourselves, our children, and all our goods" (Ezra 8:21,23,31).*

Other examples of fasting for protection are found in the following scriptures:

> *"And it came to pass in the fifth year of Jehoiakim the son of Josiah king of Judah, in the ninth month, that they proclaimed a fast before the LORD to all the people in Jerusalem, and to all the people that came from the cities of Judah unto Jerusalem" (Jer. 36:9).*

> *When Mordecai perceived all that was done, Mordecai rent his clothes, and put on sackcloth with ashes, and went out into the midst of the city, and cried with a loud and a bitter cry; And came even before the king's gate: for none might enter into the king's gate clothed with sackcloth. And in every province, whithersoever the king's commandment*

> A period of spiritual crisis should be met with God's supernatural weapon of mass – destruction (fasting)

*and his decree came, there was great mourning among the Jews, and fasting, and weeping, and wailing; and many lay in sackcloth and ashes (Est. 4:1-3).*

A period of spiritual crisis should be met with God's supernatural weapon of mass – destruction (fasting). This is the weapon that would break the most fiendish satanic oppression, opposition and affliction. Satan cannot stand against the power of a praying believer or church that resorts to fasting as its response to all forms of satanic attacks. We find a similar experience in 2 Chronicles 20. In verse 1-2, the Bible says:

> *"It came to pass after this also, that the children of Moab, and the children of Ammon, and with them other beside the Ammonites, came against Jehoshaphat to battle. Then there came some that told Jehoshaphat, saying, There cometh a great multitude against thee from beyond the sea on this side Syria; and, behold, they be in Hazazontamar, which is Engedi" (2 Chr. 20:1-2).*

In verse 3, Jehoshaphat included fasting in his measures to combat this imminent threat from foreign invaders: *"And Jehoshaphat feared, and set himself to seek the Lord, and proclaimed a fast throughout all Judah."* What was the outcome?

*"Then upon Jahaziel the son of Zechariah, the son of Benaiah, the son of Jeiel, the son of Mattaniah, a Levite of the sons of Asaph, came the Spirit of the Lord in the midst of the congregation; And he said, Hearken ye, all Judah, and ye inhabitants of Jerusalem, and thou king Jehoshaphat, Thus saith the Lord unto you, Be not afraid nor dismayed by reason of this great multitude; for the battle is not yours, but God's. Tomorrow go ye down against them: behold, they come up by the cliff of Ziz; and ye shall find them at the end of the brook, before the wilderness of Jeruel. Ye shall not need to fight in this battle: set yourselves, stand ye still, and see the salvation of the Lord with you.*

*O Judah and Jerusalem: fear not, nor be dismayed; tomorrow go out against them: for the Lord will be with you. And Jehoshaphat bowed his head with his face to the ground: and all Judah and the inhabitants of Jerusalem fell before the Lord, worshipping the Lord. And the Levites, of the children of the Kohathites, and of the children of the Korhites, stood up to praise the Lord God of Israel with a loud voice on high. And they rose early in the morning, and went forth into the wilderness of Tekoa: and as they went forth, Jehoshaphat stood and said, Hear me, O Judah, and ye inhabitants of Jerusalem; Believe in the Lord your God, so shall ye be established; believe his prophets, so shall ye prosper. And when he had consulted with the people, he appointed singers unto the Lord, and that should praise the beauty of holiness, as they went out before the army, and to say,*

*Praise the Lord; for his mercy endureth for ever. And when they began to sing and to praise, the Lord set ambushments against the children of Ammon, Moab, and mount Seir, which were come against Judah: and they were smitten. For the children of Ammon and Moab stood up against the inhabitants of mount Seir, utterly to slay and destroy them: and when they had made an end of the inhabitants of Seir, every one helped to destroy another (2 Chr. 20:14-23).*

First, God spoke in the assembly of His fasting people and gave them firm assurance of victory in the impending battle (verse 14), Most significantly, God said to Jehoshaphat and Judah,

*"... Hearken ye, all Judah, and ye inhabitants of Jerusalem, and thou king Jehoshaphat, Thus saith the Lord unto you,* **Be not afraid nor dismayed by reason of this great multitude; for the battle is not yours, but God's** *(verse 15, emphasis added).*

Finally, because the people of Judah prayed and fasted; after the people of God had engaged the weapon of fasting in their hour of crisis…

*"the Lord set ambushments against the children of Ammon, Moab, and mount Seir, which were come against Judah: and they were smitten. For the children of Ammon and Moab stood up against the inhabitants of mount Seir, utterly to slay and destroy them: and when they had made*

an end of the inhabitants of Seir, every one helped to destroy another" (verses 22-23).

# FASTING TO STRENGTHEN YOUR FAITH

*Fasting gives birth to prophets and strengthens the powerful; fasting makes lawgivers wise. Fasting is a good safeguard for the soul, a steadfast companion for the body, a weapon for the valiant, and a gymnasium for athletes. Fasting repels temptations, anoints unto piety; it is the comrade of watchfulness and the artificer of chastity. In war it fights bravely, in peace it teaches stillness.* **– St. Basil the Great.**

There are answers to prayer, such as healing, restoration, financial blessings and breakthroughs in life generally; that you will never experience without the combo power of prayer and fasting. There are heights in life a believer can never scale without it. In Matthew 17, we read about a man who took his epileptic son to Jesus' disciples for healing, but they could not heal him. When Jesus heard about it, He said,

> "O faithless and perverse generation, how long shall I be with you? How long shall I bear with you? Bring him here to Me." Jesus rebuked the demon, and it came out of him; and the child was healed from that very hour" (Matt. 17:17-18).

Later, when the disciples asked Jesus why they were unable to cast the demon out of the boy, and thereby heal him, Jesus put it down to a grave situation that defiles the life of faith we are called to live in Christ Jesus. He said,

> *"Because of your unbelief; for assuredly, I say to you, if you have faith as a mustard seed, you will say to this mountain, 'Move from here to there,' and it will move; and nothing will be impossible for you. However, this kind does not go out except by prayer and fasting" (Matt. 17:20-21).*

According to Jesus, the reason the disciples failed in this regard was due to their unbelief, given the "faithless and perverse generation" they lived in. It is important to realise that Jesus may have blamed them for their unbelief, but this by no means indicate outright failure in their ministry. Jesus was only showing them a situation that needed to change.

Being faithless has to do with a disconnection from God, and being perverse has to do with a connection to the world. The admonition of Paul to the Roman Christians was to be transformed and not to be "conformed to this world" (Romans 12:1). The remedy Jesus gave for this was prayer and fasting. Prayer connects you with God, and fasting disconnects you from the world. Together, they help you "become blameless and harmless, children of God without fault in the midst of a crooked and perverse generation, among whom you shine as lights in the world, holding fast the word of life…" (Phil. 2:15-16).

If we neglect fasting, our spiritual lives will always be far less than God intends it. We will be weak in the combat against our passions, and the forces of evil. Worst off, we will easily succumb to temptations, and never truly overcome our inherent selfishness and self-indulgence. Our failure in this regard, often keeps us from realising our full potential as Christians. The Bible says, *"For whatsoever is born of God overcometh the world: and this is the victory that **overcometh the world, even our faith**" (1 John 5:4, emphasis added).*

As believers in Christ Jesus, our desire should be to strengthen ourselves and be the best we can be. We should rely on the Holy Spirit to train us to be strong and valiant in battle.

The Psalmist shares his intriguing experience, "Blessed be the LORD my strength, which teacheth my hands to war, and my fingers to fight" (Psalm 144:1). In Psalm 18: 34-39, he states further, He [God] teacheth my hands to war, so that a bow of steel is broken by mine arms. Thou hast also given me the shield of thy salvation: and thy right hand hath holden me up, and thy gentleness hath made me great. Thou hast enlarged my steps under me, that my feet did not slip. I have pursued mine enemies, and overtaken them: neither did I turn again till they were consumed. I have wounded them that they were not able to rise: they are fallen under my feet. For thou hast girded me with strength unto the battle: thou hast subdued under me those that rose up against me."

There is no better way to begin this spiritual training than through the practise of fasting. Fasting is God's weapon of warfare, highly potent and dynamic in its operation.

In the words of Paul:

> "... though we walk in the flesh, we do not war according to the flesh. **For the weapons of our warfare are not carnal but mighty in God for pulling down strongholds,** casting down arguments and every high thing that exalts itself against the knowledge of God, bringing every thought into captivity to the obedience of Christ" (2 Cor. 10:3-5, emphasis added).

Furthermore, the Scripture presents us with a gallery of heroes and heroines of faith who:

> "...**through faith subdued kingdoms,** wrought righteousness, obtained promises, stopped the mouths of lions. Quenched the violence of fire, escaped the edge of the sword, out of weakness were made strong, waxed valiant in fight, turned to flight the armies of the aliens. Women received their dead raised to life again: and others were tortured, not accepting deliverance; that they might obtain a better resurrection" (Heb. 11:33-35, emphasis added).

Interestingly, the Bible says, *"And these all...**obtained a good report through faith...**" (v 39, emphasis added)*. May same be said of us!

In Christianity we are called into a profession of faith. It can only function by faith, otherwise it is not Christianity. In Hebrews 11:6, we are admonished, *"But without faith it is impossible to please him: for he that cometh to God must believe that he is, and that he is a rewarder of them that diligently seek him."* Also in Romans 14:23, Paul was emphatic when he said, *"...for whatsoever is not of faith is sin."* Fasting helps us tremendously to booster our faith.

# FASTING TO GAIN VICTORY IN BATTLE

In 2 Chronicles 20, Jehoshaphat and the people of Judah came under the invasion of foreign army which they could not overcome militarily, given the size and the advancement of the weapons of the invading enemy.

> "It came to pass after this also, that the children of Moab, and the children of Ammon, and with them other beside the Ammonites, came against Jehoshaphat to battle. Then there came some that told Jehoshaphat, saying, There cometh a great multitude against thee from beyond the sea on this side Syria; and, behold, they be in Hazazontamar, which is Engedi" (2 Chr. 20:1-2).

However, Jehoshaphat and the nation of Judah humbled themselves before God in fasting and prayer.

God intervened and totally defeated the enemies of Judah. There is no doubt, He is just as willing to intervene on our behalf when we seek Him in the same manner.

Further, the nation of Judah, after losing forty thousand men in battle in just two days, cried out to God for help. The people assembled in Bethel and fasted all day before the Lord.

The next day, the Lord gave them victory over the Benjamites.

> *"Then all the children of Israel, and all the people, went up, and came unto the house of God, and wept, and sat there before the Lord, and fasted that day until even, and offered burnt offerings and peace offerings before the Lord" (Judges 20:26).*

What the nation of Israel did after they had suffered catastrophic defeats on two different occasions changed the dynamics of this strange battle. Israel finally prevailed over their adversary, after the people of God had spent time in fasting before the Lord. There is hope, no matter the level of challenges or obstacles you face in your life, home, business or ministry, today. In the words of another, *"There is not one time in the Bible that God tells us: "Stress about it," "Worry about it," "Figure it out," He clearly says many times… "Trust Me."* Winston Churchill famously said, *"success is not final, failure is not fatal: it is the courage to continue that counts."* While in his view, Napoleon Hill asserts *"most worries are not half as serious as their owners think they are."*

The great Psalmist teaches that the,

> *"The righteous cry, and the Lord heareth, and **delivereth them out of all their troubles. The Lord is nigh unto them that are of a broken heart**; and saveth such as be of a contrite spirit. Many are the afflictions of the righteous: but the Lord delivereth him out of them all. He keepeth all his bones: not one of them is broken" (Psalm 34:17-20, emphasis added).*

Paul had a very personal experience in this regard,

> *"But thou hast fully known my doctrine, manner of life, purpose, faith, longsuffering, charity, patience, Persecutions, afflictions, which came unto me at Antioch, at Iconium, at Lystra; what persecutions I endured: but out of them all the Lord delivered me" (2 Tim. 3:10-11).*

There is a sure victory ordained for you in your situation. *"Even the darkest night will end and the sun will rise,"* says Zig Ziglar.

# FASTING TO PREPARE FOR MINISTRY

*When we fast and pray we put more spiritual "octane" on our service and ministry to the Lord. Fasting and prayer boosts the intensity of everything we do for Jesus. In addition, fasting and prayer helps us recognize the open doors God places before us. Why wouldn't we want all of this?* – **Kiev Bowman.**

Jesus spent forty days and nights in the wilderness, fasting and praying before He began His earthly ministry. He needed time alone to prepare for what His Father had called Him to do (Matt. 4:1-17; Mark 1:12-13; Luke 4:1-14). He appears to be setting a precedent for the would-be ministry worker.

After He fasted, the Bible says, *"**And Jesus returned in the power of the Spirit** into Galilee: and there went out a fame of him through all the region round about" (Luke 4:14, emphasis added).* Jesus was infused with tremendous power after His fasting encounter. That was undoubtedly, Jesus' gateway into His earthly ministry.

Every follower of Christ who seeks God with fasting can experience incredible spiritual opportunities, even if those opportunities were never apparent before.

## USUAL REASONS TO FAST

In Acts 13, a prayer forum involving a handful of key leaders of the church in Antioch, opened unexpected doors of ministry as they were worshipping, fasting and praying. Paul, Barnabas and three other gifted and significant leaders had been in

> *....As the devoted team fasted and prayed a long awaited door suddenly flung opened!*

the midst of a genuine city-wide spiritual awakening in Antioch for well over a year. Hungry to know the steps they were to take next, they pulled away from the day to day routine of ministry to hear from God.

The Holy Spirit spoke to them clearly and gave them a vision and a direction they had apparently never considered before. A period nearing two decades had passed since the resurrection and ascension of Jesus and since the Great Commission had been given, but no one had made any substantial efforts to reach the Gentile world with the gospel. As the devoted team fasted and prayed, a long awaited door suddenly flung opened! The Holy Spirit clearly and specifically directed them to spread the gospel to the Gentiles. That unexpected door led to what would later be known as Paul's first missionary journey:

> *"Now there were in the church that was at Antioch certain prophets and teachers; as Barnabas, and Simeon that was called Niger, and Lucius of Cyrene, and Manaen, which*

> *It orchestrated a worldwide revival that was unprecedented and definitely, unimaginable…*

had been brought up with Herod the tetrarch, and Saul. As they ministered to the Lord, and fasted, the Holy Ghost said, Separate me Barnabas and Saul for the work whereunto I have called them. And when they had fasted and prayed, and laid their hands on them, they sent them away" (Acts 13:1-4).

The impact this simple act of obedience has had on not only these fasting saints, but the universal Church and the entire world, especially on world evangelism, has been phenomenal. It orchestrated a worldwide revival that was unprecedented and definitely, unimaginable. A tidal wave of the Spirit of God swept through the whole earth, from coast to coast, continent to continent, with exceptionally widespread manifestation of the Spirit.

Having learnt the lesson first-hand, Paul and Barnabas would go on to pray and fast for the elders of the churches they had established through their missionary work, before committing them to the Lord's service.

> "And when they had ordained them elders in every church, and had prayed with fasting, they commended them to the Lord, on whom they believed" (Acts 14:23).

# FASTING FOR REVELATION: INTERCEDING AGAINST THE POWERS OF DARKNESS

*I believe the power of fasting as it relates to prayer is the spiritual atomic bomb that our Lord has given us to destroy the strongholds of evil...* –Bill Bright.

The second account of Daniel's fast was to receive special revelation. Unusual levels of insight from God were sometimes, given to the prophets and others during periods of fasting, as in the case just examined. In the book of Daniel we find an account in relation to the prayer (intercession) and fasting for revelation about the future. This would, undoubtedly, challenge our prayer life if we can fully grasp it. Daniel sought God with fasting to ask Him to fulfil His promise to restore Jerusalem (Daniel 9:9, 18 and compare with Jer. 29:10-13).

He received, through the angel Gabriel, a wonderful unfolding of God's plan for Israel that would not have been unveiled otherwise. If we have sought God fervently for a period of time without any apparent physical manifestation or result for the fulfilment of key promises in our lives, our Churches, our communities, and even our nations, perhaps this is an indication that it is time to incorporate fasting to our seeking, as Daniel did.

> *"And I set my face unto the Lord God, to seek by prayer and supplications, with fasting, and sackcloth, and ashes.... whiles I was speaking in prayer, even the man Gabriel ... talked with me, and said O Daniel... at the beginning of thy supplications the commandment came forth..." (Dan. 9:3-21).*

The Daniel fasting experience is replete with thrilling insights for today's believer. In the first place, this portion of scripture makes it abundantly clear that there are different ways to engage in fasting, and that fasting does not always have to involve total abstinence from food, as we see in Daniel 10:2,3.

Daniel says,

> *"In those days I Daniel was mourning three full weeks. I ate no pleasant bread, neither came flesh nor wine in my mouth, neither did I anoint myself at all, till three whole weeks were fulfilled."*

In the tenth to the thirteenth verse, he said:

> *"And, behold, a hand touched me, which set me upon my knees and upon the palms of my hands. And he said unto me, O Daniel, a man greatly beloved, understand the words that I speak unto thee, and stand upright: for unto thee am I now sent. And when he had spoken this word unto me, I stood trembling. Then said he unto me, Fear not, Daniel: for from the first day that thou didst set thine*

*heart to understand, and to chasten thyself before thy God, thy words were heard, and I am come for thy words. But the prince of the kingdom of Persia withstood me one and twenty days: but, lo, Michael, one of the chief princes, came to help me: and I remained there with the kings of Persia."*

> **Perhaps, more time in the presence of God, ... with fasting, will explain the mystery.**

It is worth noting that the angel was not sent from Heaven to Daniel with the message of restoration, until he had prayed and fasted! It should be noted too, that there was an extended period of time between Daniel's fasting and the time he had the answer through. God heard his request, from the beginning of his supplication. Indeed, God sent the answer the very first day, but the answer was delayed for twenty-one days. Here lies a valuable lesson we should ponder over: sometimes when we pray and we do not have answers to our prayers instantly, this should not be seen as a refusal or reluctance on the part of God to answer our requests. Perhaps, an extended time in the presence of God, as in this case, with fasting, will not only explain the mystery but will, without a shadow of doubt, deliver your long-awaited miracle to you. Daniel's choice to persist in prayers and supplications, in the face of all odds paid off after-all! I agree wholeheartedly with Tom Ziglar when he said, "The right direction in life is determined by choice, not by chance."

In the words of Roger Lee, "...*All the struggles and hardships that you've conquered so far has shaped you into the person you are today. Life is a battle and you were born with the strength to survive it.*"

Arthur Wallis observes that, in spite, of the resistance Daniel experienced in the spirit realm, his "earnest, desperate cry would not stop until the answer came." "Thus", continues Wallis, "*we see that fasting was sometimes involved in earnest and prolonged supplication. When the Heavens remained as brass despite earnest and persistent prayer, men were sometimes driven in their desperation to fasting as the only solution.*"

This biblical account confirms, explicitly, the reality and intensity of spiritual warfare. There existed a spiritual kingdom of darkness over the earthly kingdom of Persia with a Satanic Prince heading it. It was this Satanic Prince that held up the answer that God had dispatched to Daniel. He did not want the angel to get through with the answer because of its significance to the Persian kingdom and, indeed the world. The message that God dispatched had to do with the dissolution of the Medo-Persian kingdom, and the institution, in its stead, of the Grecian Kingdom that would, ultimately be replaced by the Roman Kingdom that would rule over Jerusalem. So, we can see that the spiritual impact and significance of the revelation Daniel needed from God went beyond the immediate region of the Persian Kingdom.

With the reinforcement from another angel (Archangel Michael), the message finally got through on the twenty-first day of Daniel's fast. The fact that Daniel did not give up praying and fasting the whole period this saga lasted, leaves with us with a very startling lesson.

Upon arrival, the reinforcing angel said, "… now will I return to fight with the prince of Persia: and when I am gone forth, lo, the prince of Grecia (Greece) shall come" (verse 20).

We are given a clear picture of the continual spiritual battles we (believers) very often have to contend with, in Ephesians 6:12:

"For we wrestle not against flesh and blood, but against principalities, against powers, against the rulers of the darkness of this world, against spiritual wickedness in high places."

With fasting victory is guaranteed!

# FASTING TO OVERCOME THE FLESH – THE DANIEL FAST

*In the third year of the reign of Jehoiakim king of Judah came Nebuchadnezzar king of Babylon unto Jerusalem, and besieged it. And the Lord gave Jehoiakim king of Judah into his hand, with part of the vessels of the house of God: which he carried into the land of Shinar to the house of his god; and he brought the vessels into the treasure house of his god. And the king spake unto Ashpenaz the master of his eunuchs, that he should bring certain of the children of Israel, and of the king's seed, and of the princes; Children in whom was no blemish, but well favoured, and skilful in all wisdom, and cunning in knowledge, and understanding science, and such as had ability in them to stand in the king's palace, and whom they might teach the learning and the tongue of the Chaldeans. And the king appointed them a daily provision of the king's meat, and of the wine which he drank: so nourishing them three years, that at the end thereof they might stand before the king. Now among these were of the children of Judah, Daniel, Hananiah, Mishael, and Azariah: Unto whom the prince of the eunuchs gave names: for he gave unto Daniel the name of Belteshazzar; and to Hananiah, of Shadrach; and to Mishael, of Meshach; and to Azariah, of Abednego (Daniel 1:1-5).*

Daniel and the other Hebrew youths; Shadrach, Meshach and Abednego were Jews captivity in Babylon. These men were highly respected for their purity and absolute devotion to God. It was required that as people in captivity, and serving in the king's palace, that they be educated in the way of the Chaldeans.

Part of the process of training these young Jews for the Babylonian civil service was to rob them of their identities. They were given Babylonian names. They were taught the Babylonian language. They were to eat Babylonian food. And the Enemy of our souls uses the same tactics today. This was, particularly a testing time for these Hebrew men - their devotion to God was put to test.

It is not particularly known why Daniel accepted a Babylonian name and way of life, but not the food. Daniel 1:5 records that the king's servants assigned them a daily amount of food and wine from the king's table (NIV). It was the intention of the King to keep them on this special rich diet of meats, fats, and sugary pastries and wine (the sort of unhealthy food gladly consumed in our society today) for three years, at the end of which they were to be presented to the king.

Just as we do not know how Daniel and his friends were feeling, we do not know why Daniel was so concerned about food. Some people think it was because the food would not conform to the Law of Moses - for example, it might contain pork. But, if that was the problem, why would Daniel refuse wine? Some think it is because the food would have been offered to idols. But would not the vegetables he was prepared to eat (see verse 12) also have been offered to idols? Some think that to accept food from the King's table would have been an expression of friendship that would not have been appropriate. But Daniel was prepared to accept other food, as well as clothing, accommodation, education and, I expect, money from the king. To repeat, we do not know.

In verse 8, we see the nature of the attitude that is generally needed to go through a fast. Daniel made up his mind that he would not defile himself with the king's rich and delicious meats or with the wine which he drank; so he sought permission from the commander of the officials that he might not defile himself.

> *"But Daniel purposed in his heart that he would not defile himself with the portion of the king's meat. nor with the wine which he drank: therefore he requested of the prince of the eunuchs that he might not defile himself."*

It is highly significant for us to know that Daniel believed that it would have defiled him to eat food from the king's table. Daniel did what he believed was right - he acted with integrity. It has been suggested that Daniel could have rejected the king's food and wine because they did not meet the requirements of Jewish dietary laws or because these could have, first been offered to idols.

This is in keeping with Apostle Paul's caution in Romans 12:1-2:

> *"Therefore, I urge you, brothers, in view of God's mercy, to offer your bodies as living sacrifices, holy and pleasing to God — this is your spiritual act of worship. Do not conform any longer to the pattern of this world, but be transformed by the renewing of your mind. Then you will be able to test and approve what God's will is—his good, pleasing and perfect will."*

So Daniel made a request of the prince of the eunuchs:

> *"Test your servants for ten days: Give us nothing but vegetables to eat and water to drink. Then compare our appearance with that of the young men who eat the royal food, and treat your servants in accordance with what you see. So he agreed to this and tested them for ten days"* (verses 12-14, NIV).

Accordingly, Daniel and the other three Hebrew youths lived a fasted life for three years on vegetarian diets instead of the king's food and water instead of the king's wine while learning and studying in the king's court. Heaven moved on their behalf to honour their partial fast.

At the end of the ten days fast, Daniel and his friends not only "looked healthier and better nourished than any of the young men who ate the royal food" (verse 15 NIV), but God granted them favour, wisdom and insight that could not be matched by their contemporaries who fed on the king's food.

We read in verses 18-20:

> *"At the end of the time set by the king to bring them into his service, the chief official presented them to Nebuchadnezzar. The king talked with them, and he found none equal to Daniel, Hananiah, Mishael and Azariah; so they entered the king's service. In every matter of wisdom and understanding about which the king questioned them, he found them ten times better than all the magicians and enchanters in his whole kingdom."*

This biblical account teaches us that God honours those who honour Him with fasting. The Daniel fast eliminates rich and tempting food we easily want to reach for. Though not an absolute fast, God was greatly honoured nonetheless; Daniel and his Hebrew associates were greatly rewarded, as a result.

# FASTING AS AN INSTRUMENT OF WORSHIP TO GOD

*There was also a prophet, Anna, the daughter of Penuel, of the tribe of Asher. She was very old; she had lived with her husband seven years after her marriage, and then was a widow until she was eighty-four. She never left the*

## USUAL REASONS TO FAST

*temple but worshiped night and day, fasting and praying. Coming up to them at that very moment. she gave thanks to God and spoke about the child to all who were looking forward to the redemption of Jerusalem (Luke 2:36-38. NIV. emphasis added).*

> **One purpose of prayer and fasting is to bring our hearts to a place of being filled with a sacrificial love...**

Jesus by His example and teaching demonstrates that prayer and fasting are important, and an integral ingredients in the lives of His followers. One purpose of prayer and fasting is to bring our hearts to a place of being filled with a sacrificial love that results in godly attitude in our lives. True fasting will draw us closer to God and His purposes.

Often, we think of fasting as an individual discipline, but Scripture clearly has a place for corporate fasts as well. In Joel 2:12, for example, we see God calling the old covenant community to repent and fast so as to avoid impending judgment. Ezra called for fasting to gain the Lord's protection, when he led the exiled Israelites back to the Promised Land (Ezra 8:21–23). In the New Testament, we read of the church at Antioch worshiping and fasting just before setting apart Barnabas and Saul for their missionary work (Acts 13:1–3).

Under the new covenant, corporate worship takes place primarily on the Lord's Day, as that was when the

> As seen in Acts 13:2, as the elders of the church "ministered to the Lord, and fasted ..."

Apostles gathered with the early Christians to remember the great salvation purchased by Christ (Acts 20:7). That did not mean however, that corporate worship should never take place at other times. Significant streams of Church tradition have long recognised that the church does call for corporate worship on other days, as long as these special occasions of worship are not made mandatory.

We see then, that fasting can be a part of public worship no less than it can be observed in private worship (Matt. 6:16–18). But why should we fast? It cannot be to primarily merit an answer to prayer, for we do not earn God's favour by depriving ourselves of His good gifts. Instead, fasting can serve, first, as an instrument of worship to God, and as opportunity to pray more intently with greater focus. As we feel hunger pangs, we are reminded of our commitment to set aside time we would normally be eating in order to pray for the situation that inspired the fast. Fasting also reminds us of our vulnerability and dependence. We are ever tempted to believe that we are self-sufficient, but the hunger we experience in fasting should help us recall that we are needy creatures.

In Luke 2:37 we have the inspiring account of an eighty-four-year-old prophetess named Anna. The Bible says, *"She never left the temple but worshiped night and day, fasting and praying."* Anna was devoted to God, and fasting was one expression of her love for Him. As seen in Acts 13:2, as the elders of the church *"**ministered to the Lord, and fasted**, the Holy Ghost said, separate me Barnabas and Saul for the work whereunto I have called them"* (emphasis added).

# FASTING AS A REFILLING PROCESS

*Whatever you do in the kingdom, at whatever time you no longer sense that 'cutting edge unction', be it in preaching, singing, praying, or you sense that the more you pray, the less results you actually have, or you face a situation of outright 'power-seizure', what is required is simply, to suspend all the 'labouring' and seek the 'unction to function' – go for "a-refill"*
**– Jentezen Franklin.**

Fasting is a spiritual tool devised by God to offer the believer the opportunity to reconnect to the power source for fresh supply of the anointing. God is the anointer, and He gladly gives it to whoever He wishes. Jesus, His begotten was anointed by Him. The Bible says, *"How God anointed Jesus of Nazareth with the Holy Ghost and with power: who went about doing good, and healing all that were oppressed of*

> **Fasting is a spiritual tool devised by God to offer the believer the opportunity to reconnect to the power source, for fresh supply of the anointing.**

*the devil; for God was with him" (Acts 10:38).* Later, Jesus would go on to admonish the believer, *"Verily, verily, I say unto you, He that believeth on me, the works that I do shall he do also; and greater works than these shall he do; because I go unto my Father" (John 14:12)*; because, says Jesus, *"... the anointing which ye have received of him abideth in you..." (1 John 2:27).*

A common problem I have seen in the body of Christ for so long, is that too many of God's people that are committed to ministry assignments, often get to the place where they judge themselves too 'busy' with ministry responsibilities, to find time to get in their closet to undergo this 'refilling' process; the very process, it must be said, they cherished in their early days in ministry. Here is the principle: the immature are preoccupied with doing things for God, while the mature prioritise His presence.

The Bible – the source of all our inspirations – leaves us in no doubt as to the legitimate source of the anointing. The anointing of God on our lives makes the difference! It is what qualifies us for the great and enduring work of the kingdom; not personality, not names, and definitely, not academic qualifications. The Bible is very clear, "...

*for by strength shall no man prevail" (1 Sam. 2:9)*, a lesson God had to further amplify to the Church through one of His great generals of the kingdom, *"Then he answered and spake unto me, saying, This is the word of the LORD unto Zerubbabel, saying, Not by might, nor by power,* **but by my spirit, saith the LORD of hosts***" (Zech. 4:6, emphasis added).*

Jesus could not discharge His kingdom mandate without the anointing of the Holy Ghost, and you should not either. In addition, it takes the anointing of the Holy Ghost do exploits in God's kingdom.

> "...but the people that do know their God shall be strong, and do exploits" (Dan. 11:32).

In Acts 10:38, earlier referenced, the Bible says, *"for God was with Him" (Acts 10:38)*. This statement adds tremendous weight to our line of thought; however, its significance is sadly, often overlooked. While Jesus was engrossed with the work of the ministry, "doing good, healing all that were oppressed of the devil' - He maintained an unwavering and unbroken intimacy with His Father – the source of His enabling power. The busy nature of His ministerial itinerary did not affect, in the least, the grip Jesus had on His source; this ensured an incessant flow of power from the Father to the Son, to discharge His earthly mandate. And He would go on to declare His well-grounded commitment, devotion and absolute loyalty to His divine assignment, when He said, *"My meat is to do the will of him that sent me,* **and to finish his work***" (John 4:34, emphasis* *added)*. The same sentiment shared by Apostle Paul, when he said, *"I have fought a good fight,* ***I have finished my course,*** *I have kept the faith:* **Henceforth there is laid up for me a crown of righteousness***, which the Lord, the righteous judge, shall give me at that day: and not to me only,* ***but unto all them also that love his appearing"*** *(2 Tim. 4:7-8, emphasis added)*.

The busier Jesus was, the greater His grip on His power-source for the requisite anointing to fulfil the task at hand. Here is a glowing example the Master has left for all kingdom workers. We should therefore, eschew the habit of allowing kingdom responsibilities get on the way of our time with God, in order to constantly engage in this refilling process.

Martin Luther was once quoted as saying, *"I have so much to do that I shall have to spend the first three hours in prayer."* He understood the secret!

Martin Luther believes that the divine power to carry out Kingdom responsibilities is derivable from the presence of God.

For today believers, and a good number of kingdom labourers, we tend to disassociate or disconnect from the source of the anointing, the moment we sense a degree of success in the ministry. This is the sad reality!

While we may not consciously sever our relationship with the power-source, we very often discover that, unless we keep a constant watch in this regard, through unceasing fellowship with God, that there exists a great tendency to substitute kingdom duties, achievements, accomplishments, even accolades, for what truly matters - the all-important need of constantly tarrying in His presence, until we are endued with power for the present and future levels of our ministerial calling. Undoubtedly, this can have far-reaching consequences. We could be left operating not with the optimum level of the power God intends for us, but a latent residue of such power. This can be tragic!

# UNDERSTANDING THE DIFFERENT TYPES OF FASTS

# 7

# THE DIFFERENT TYPES OF FASTS

*There is a fast which is total abstention from food. That has value. There is also fasting that is both total abstention from food and withdrawal from human company. That has added value. There is fasting that is total abstention from food, total abstention from human company and total investment on waiting on God in prayer. This is the best and this what the Lord Jesus carried out. In there any wonder that it had such far-reaching consequences*
– Zachariah Tanee Fomum.

Just as there are different kinds of prayer, such as prayer of petition, intercession, prayer of thanksgiving, binding and loosing, prayer of biblical praise, payer of consecration and dedication, in the same way, there are various kinds of fasting, such as proclaimed or public fast, personal fast, the normal fast, the absolute fast and the partial fast.

## PROCLAIMED OR PUBLIC AND PERSONAL FAST

There are, broadly speaking, two categories of fasting – proclaimed or public fast (Joel 1:14) and personal fast, as Jesus described in Matthew 6: 1-18. These fasts can take the form of a normal, absolute or partial fast, as will be examined in due course.

## THE PROCLAIMED FAST – CALLING THE CHURCH OR NATION TO FASTING

*Gird yourselves, and lament, ye priests: howl, ye ministers of the altar: come, lie all night in sackcloth, ye ministers of my God: for the meat offering and the drink offering is withholden from the house of your God. Sanctify ye a fast, call a solemn assembly, gather the elders and all the inhabitants of the land into the house of the LORD your God, and cry unto the LORD (Joel 1:13-14).*

*Therefore also now, saith the LORD, turn ye even to me with all your heart, and with fasting, and with weeping, and with mourning: Gather the people, sanctify the congregation, assemble the elders, gather the children, and those that suck the breasts: let the bridegroom go forth of his chamber, and the bride out of her closet. Let the priests, the ministers of the LORD, weep between the porch and the altar, and let them say, Spare thy people, O LORD, and give not thine heritage to reproach, that the heathen should rule over them: wherefore should they say among the people, Where is their God? (Joel 2:12, 16-17).*

*"On a fast day...you shall read the words of the Lord" (Jer. 36:6).*

Usually, fasting is undertaken occasionally, as the believer deems it necessary, as a matter between him and God. Public fast is an exception to this notion. Sometimes situations arise in which a church, a group of people or a nation resorts to fasting to seek God's direction and intervention. This is a proclaimed fast.

## PROCLAIMED AND REGULAR FAST

There is generally a connection between public and regular fasts in that, almost all the regular fasts of the Bible were also public fasts, but not all the public fasts were necessarily regular.

Regular fasts were those prescribed by God to be observed at specific times of the year. A good example is the Day of Atonement, prescribed by the Mosaic Law. On this day, God required the Israelites to afflict their souls (Lev. 23:27, Psalm 35:13).

In addition to "a fast day" (Jer. 36:6) associated with the Day of Atonement, the book of Zechariah contains four other regular fast days:

> *"Thus saith the LORD of hosts; The fast of the fourth month, and the fast of the fifth, and the fast of the seventh, and the fast of the tenth, shall be to the house of Judah joy and gladness, and cheerful feasts; therefore love the truth and peace" (Zech. 8:19).*

We have clear indication of the observance of the regular fast (Day of Atonement) in the New Testament.

> *"Now when much time was spent, and when sailing was now dangerous, because the fast was now already past, Paul admonished them..." (Acts 27:9).*

This was no doubt, in reference to the Day of Atonement. And during the earthly ministry of Jesus, the Pharisees made an empty religious ritual out of this practice as typified by the story of Jesus in Luke 18:11, 12:

> *"The Pharisee stood and prayed thus with himself, God, I thank thee, that I am not as other men are, extortioners, unjust, adulterers, or even as this publican. I fast twice in the week, I give tithes of all that I possess."*

## THE DIFFERENT TYPES OF FASTS

Notice Jesus' teaching in verse 9:

*"Also He spoke this parable to some who trusted in themselves that they were righteous, and despised others."*

This is an apparent example of religious egotism; the Pharisees were known to despise others, even with their fasts. Fasting was used by the Pharisees at this period of time as an instrument of oppression against the poor, the needy, and the meek. They despised the very people they ought to be caring for in their seasons of fast (Isaiah 58:7). This was a prototype of the manner and spirit with which the Pharisees held regular fasts in the days of Jesus.

Despite these contemptuous practices by the Pharisees in relation to fasting, there was a revisiting of the practice of collective regular fasting in the second and third centuries. It was widely believed that regular fast was revived among the early Methodists by John Wesley. As a requirement for ordaining Priests in the Methodist Church, prospective candidates were required to fast weekly, Wednesdays and Fridays till 4.00 pm.

Arthur Wallis, however, remarks that while caution needs to be exercised not to allow regular fasting to become religious rituals, devoid of its spiritual intent, the practice should not be abandoned altogether. *"It needs to be stressed,"* he insists, *"that fasting, whether regular or occasional, is a matter between individual and God. Making it a requirement may lead to the same bondage in which the Pharisees were ensnared."*

The paramount purpose of a regular fasting is to provide a regular opportunity for spiritual examination and orientation. It is like spiritual medicine for the spirit, soul and body.

Generally, a proclaimed fast is for the purpose of bringing believers together for a special session of collective fasting and prayer. It operates on the principle of spiritual agreement as taught by Jesus in Matthew 18:18:

> "Again I say unto you, that if two of you shall agree on earth as touching anything that they shall ask, it shall be done for them of my Father which is in Heaven."

No doubt, greater power is released in fasting combined with prayer than in prayer alone. Proclaimed fast offers the believers the opportunity to move in the same direction of faith in one accord.

A wonderful, practical example of a proclaimed fast is found in 2 Chronicles 20:1-6.

> "It came to pass after this also, that the children of Moab, and the children of Ammon, and with them other beside the Ammonites, came against Jehoshaphat to battle. Then there came some that told Jehoshaphat, saying, There cometh a great multitude against thee from beyond the

## THE DIFFERENT TYPES OF FASTS

*sea on this side Syria; and, behold, they be in Hazazontamar, which is Engedi. And Jehoshaphat feared, and set himself to seek the Lord, and proclaimed a fast throughout all Judah. And Judah gathered themselves together, to ask help of the Lord: even out of all the cities of Judah they came to seek the Lord. And Jehoshaphat stood in the congregation of Judah and Jerusalem, in the house of the Lord, before the new court .And said, O Lord God of our fathers, art not thou God in Heaven? And rulest not thou over all the kingdoms of the heathen? and in thine hand is there not power and might, so that none is able to withstand thee?"*

During the reign of King Jehoshaphat, King of Judah, enemies from neighbouring nations invaded Judah. As stated, the Bible says "Jehoshaphat feared and set himself to seek the Lord, and proclaimed a fast throughout Judah."

This incident brought the people of Judah together to seek help of the Lord through prayer and fasting. Jehoshaphat prayed relying on the covenant of protection and deliverance God had given to Abraham and his descendants.

King Jehoshaphat's prayer as recorded in verse 12 is noteworthy:

*O our God, wilt thou not judge them? for we have no might against this great company that cometh against us; neither know we what to do:* **but our eyes are upon thee** *(emphasis added).*

In this scripture, what drove King Jehoshaphat into fasting was pretty apparent: *"no might against this great company that cometh against us…"* Judah was invaded by enemies too great for Jehoshaphat and his people to combat militarily; so, they resolved to fight the battle using spiritual weapons – prayer and fasting.

The nation of Judah expressed total and unwavering dependence on God in the midst of this terrible battle. They said, *"…our eyes are upon thee" (2 Chr. 20:12).* Here lies the secret to victory in any battle of life – absolute dependence in God. A fasting saint is saying to God, *'I have no might of my own, my eyes are upon you.'* God takes this degree of faith very seriously.

In yet another battle between the nations Israel and Judah, the later expressed profound trust in God for deliverance thus:

> "But as for us, the Lord is our God, and we have not forsaken him: and the priests, which minister unto the Lord, are the sons of Aaron, and the Levites wait upon their business:... And, behold, God himself is with us for our captain, and his priests with sounding trumpets to cry alarm against you. O children of Israel, fight ye not against the Lord God of your fathers: for ye shall not prosper" (2 Chr. 13:10,12).

Jesus was succinct when He said that certain situations could not be dealt with otherwise, but by prayer and fasting:

# THE DIFFERENT TYPES OF FASTS

*"Howbeit this kind goeth not out but by prayer and fasting"* (Matt. 17:21).

In relation to the nation of Judah and Jehoshaphat, while they were united in prayer and fasting, the Bible says:

> **It is like spiritual medicine for the spirit, soul and body.**

*"Then upon Jahaziel the son of Zechariah, the son of Benaiah, the son of Jeiel, the son of Mattaniah, a Levite of the sons of Asaph, came the Spirit of the LORD in the midst of the congregation..." (verse 14).* This is the tremendous power of a proclaimed fast! The spirit of God did not come upon Jehoshaphat – the leader, but on another person in the congregation – how beautiful!

*"And he said, Hearken ye, all Judah, and ye inhabitants of Jerusalem, and thou king Jehoshaphat, Thus saith the LORD unto you, Be not afraid nor dismayed by reason of this great multitude: for the battle is not yours, but God's" (verse 15).*

You can imagine how good that sounded to Judah. The Holy Ghost spoke the mind of God to the fasting nation! This was the very purpose of their fasting-based meeting. They, no doubt drew great comfort and solace from this apparent intervention of God, long before the battle was fought God had declared the people of Judah victorious! They could sense incipient relief building up.

# THE TRANSFORMATIONAL POWER OF FASTING

The effectiveness of a proclaimed fast rests in the unity and singleness of purpose it creates.

Kenneth Copeland observes that the paramount reason proclaimed fasting brings incredible results is down to the fact that it causes the people's minds to go in the same direction. That direction is toward God. They drop other things and centre their attention on Him. This brings the manifested presence in their midst; a view that finds consensus with Pius Quensnel who said, *"God is found in union and agreement. Nothing is more efficacious than this in prayer."*

Ezra likewise, exhorted the Jews to conduct a public (proclaimed) fast before their journey back to Jerusalem, with the precious things for the temple. They were returning from their seventy years Babylonian captivity to rebuild the temple (Ezra 8. 21-22); the result? *"So we fasted and besought our God for this: and he was intreated of us" (verse 23).* What a timely intervention!

Esther also proclaimed a fast among the Jews in order to avert an imminent danger - a total annihilation of the Jewish race as orchestrated by Haman- the Prime Minister of the Land. Esther gave the following instructions:

> Go, gather together all the Jews that are present in Shushan, and fast ye for me, and neither eat nor drink three days, night or day: I also and my maidens will fast likewise; and so will I go in unto the king, which is not according to the

*law: and if I perish, I perish (Est. 4:16).*

After this fast, God turned the situation that warranted the people to seek God with fasting, around. "The Jews," the Bible says, "had light, and gladness, and joy, and honour. And in every province, and in every city, whithersoever the king's commandment and his decree came, the Jews had joy and gladness, a feast and a good day. And many of the people of the land became Jews; for the fear of the Jews fell upon them" (Est. 8:16-17). The erstwhile gloomy and hopeless situation was reversed and became a testimony of "light, and gladness, and joy, and honour" (verse 8), because the people of Judah took it upon themselves to respond with fasting in the midst of a national crisis.

Furthermore, the Bible declares, *"…on the very day when the enemies of the Jews hoped to gain the mastery over them, the reverse occurred: the Jews gained mastery over those who hated them" (Est. 9:1).* And Haman, the perpetrator of the heinous crime against the Jews was *"hanged on the gallows that he had prepared for Mordecai" (Est. 7:10),* on the order of the king!

The New Testament example is found in Acts 13:1-2:

> *Now there were in the church that was at Antioch certain prophets and teachers; as Barnabas, and Simeon that was called Niger, and Lucius of Cyrene, and Manaen, which had been brought up with Herod the tetrarch, and Saul. As they ministered to the Lord, and fasted, the Holy Ghost said,*

*Separate me Barnabas and Saul for the work whereunto I have called them. And when they had fasted and prayed, and laid their hands on them, they sent them away.*

The Holy Ghost spoke in the midst of ordinary men, as they were fasting and ministering to the Lord. This set in motion a great move of God that literally changed the world. That assignment brought into being two-third of the New Testament. As instructed, they laid their hands on Saul and Barnabas and sent them forth. The result of their exploits was overwhelming.

For a proclaimed fast to be effective and achieve its desired purpose, it needs to be well planned, structured and executed. It is not enough to require a group of people or a church to observe a fast for, just the sake of it, without establishing a structure that ensures all the participants understand what is required of them at any given time, such as the prayer points for each day or prayer section, times of meetings for prayer, venue for prayer. If the fast being undertaken is not an absolute fast, the people need to know what type of fluids are allowed to be taken.

# 8

# PERSONAL FAST

The other type of fast is the personal fast. This is the most common. The general purpose of this type of fast is self-affliction and repentance. It may be observed in times of personal or communal crisis in order to seek God's divine intervention or, more commonly, as penitence for personal wrong doing. It could also be resorted to as a means of establishing a fasted-life - taking on fasting as a way of life.

It must be stressed, however, that you do not fast to impress God. Fasting changes you, not God. Sometimes, fasting is viewed as an attempt to twist God's arm or to win His approval; but God does not respond to pressure.

As Mckay explains it, *"Some would say that the sacrifice of fasting can "release" a blessing or answer that otherwise wouldn't have been granted — that, as in Jesus' parable of the woman and the unjust judge, God will listen to those who show persistent effort…The petitioner is blessed instead in simply receiving guidance in how to pray, and finding a deeper connection to God through deeper prayer."*

Whether or not fasting-strengthened prayer changes God's receptivity to supplications, both sides agree that it changes the receptivity of the supplicator to God's guidance. The physical emptiness of fasting clears the channels of communication so that spiritual intuitions can more readily be discerned.

Fasting therefore, cannot be used as an attempt to manipulate God. A group of people in the book of Acts tried to get God on their side through manipulative fasting:

> *"In the morning some of the Jews made a plan to kill Paul, and they took an oath not to eat or drink anything until they had killed him. They went to the leading priests and the older Jewish leaders and said, 'We have taken an oath not to eat or drink until we have killed Paul" (Acts 23:12,14).*

But God did not answer their prayer and their plan did not work. In essence, they fasted in vain. Using fasting in a manipulative way was done by the people in Jeremiah's day too. God said:

> *"Although they fast, I will not listen to their cry; though they offer burn offerings and grain offering, I will not accept them. I will destroy them with the sword, famine, and plague" (Jer. 14:12).*

Edith Schaeffer was emphatic when she said:

> "Is fasting ever a bribe to get God to pay more attention to the petitions? No, a thousand times no. It is simply a way to make clear that we sufficiently reverence the amazing opportunity to ask help from the everlasting God, the Creator of the universe, to choose to put everything else aside and concentrate on worshiping, asking forgiveness, and making our requests known–considering His help more important than anything we could do ourselves in our own strength and with our own ideas."

> **Fasting changes you, not God.**

# KEY POINTS TO NOTE ABOUT PERSONAL FAST

Generally, personal fasting is done in secret; a matter between the individual and God. However, this rule might be very difficult to observe in a household setting, where, for example, a wife is undertaking a fast but the husband is not.

In the first place, arrangement needs to be made for the family meals. Secondly, as between husband and wife, where only one of them is fasting, it is perfectly in order to let the other party be aware of your intention to observe a fast, and for what duration well ahead of time, as this could mean an abstention from marital relationship for the duration of the fast (1 Cor. 7:5).

It is also highly recommended for husband and wife to mutually agree to engage in the act of fasting together towards achieving a common goal; that then becomes a proclaimed fast.

In Matthew 6:16-18, in the Sermon on the Mount, Jesus devoted a great deal of time teaching on how to engage on a personal fast:

> *"Moreover when ye fast, be not, as the hypocrites, of a sad countenance: for they disfigure their faces, that they may appear unto men to fast. Verily I say unto you, They have their reward. But thou, when thou fastest, anoint thine head, and wash thy face: That thou appear not unto men to fast, but unto thy Father which is in secret: and thy Father, which seeth in secret, shall reward thee openly."*

It is evident that the scripture in context opens up a vast field of reflection and merits our careful consideration:

1. The fact that Jesus expects the believer to fast is very apparent from the wording of the said scripture, "when ye fast…" (Matt. 6:16).

2. Jesus warned against using fasting as a hypocritical religious exercise. During the Lord's earthly ministry,

fasting had become a very important part of the Jewish life; albeit an empty religious rite. Jesus condemned the "look-at-how-spiritual-I-am" attitude associated with fasting, as depicted by the attitude and motive of the Pharisee spoken of by Jesus in Luke 18: 10 – 14.

3. Hypocritical piety will always defeat the purpose and power of a fast. If you publicise your spirituality in order to gain the praise of men, you would have succeeded in exchanging the reward of God for the praise of men.

Let us now examine the story in depth:

> *"Two men went up into the temple to pray; the one a Pharisee, and the other a publican. The Pharisee stood and prayed thus with himself, God, I thank thee, that I am not as other men are, extortioners, unjust, adulterers, or even as this publican. I fast twice in the week, I give tithes of all that I possess. And the publican, standing afar off, would not lift up so much as his eyes unto Heaven, but smote upon his breast, saying, God be merciful to me a sinner. I tell you, this man went down to his house justified rather than the other: for every one that exalteth himself shall be abased: and he that humbleth himself shall be exalted."*

The Lord's verdict on fasting conducted with the wrong motive is swift and well delivered: *"...verily I say unto you, they have their reward." (Matt. 6: 16).* "But thou", says Jesus, *"when thou fastest, anoint thine head, and wash thy face;* **That thou appear not unto men to fast, but unto thy Father which**

***is in secret:*** *and thy Father, which seeth in secret, shall reward thee openly" (emphasis added).*

4. Jesus spoke of the rewards for fasting. Rewards for personal fasting are on two different levels: You have rewards from the admiration of men, as described above, and an open reward that comes from God when you fast in secret. Believe God for this reward as you go into a fast. Focusing on the reward lessens the burden of fasting on you. This makes fasting easy.

# 9
# NORMAL, PARTIAL AND ABSOLUTE FAST

The other categorisation of fasting revealed in the word of God includes the normal, partial and absolute fasts. These forms of fasting are essentially defined by the degree of abstinence involved in them. Zacharias Fomum alludes to these facts and affirms that fasting saints must consider adding some dimensions of withdrawal and total investment in waiting on God.

Generally, these three forms of fasting were substantially practiced in the Bible days under different circumstances.

# THE NORMAL FAST

The most common form of fast is generally known as the normal fast. There are very few rules about this fasting under the Old Testament. The normal fast was conducted on the Day of Atonement, and was from sunset of one day to sunset of the next (Lev. 16:29; 23:32).

However, what the normal fast entails is very clear from the 40 days fast of the Lord Jesus.

> *"He fasted forty days and forty nights and afterwards He was hungry"(Matt. 4:2).*

This type of Christian fast makes our definition of fasting ever more apparent which is, abstaining from all forms of food but not from water or fluid. It is very clear from the details given that Jesus' fast was the normal fast. The passage says, "He ate nothing" (Luke 4:2), 'not that He drank nothing.' Afterwards "He was hungry", and 'not that He was thirsty'. Again, satan tempted Him to eat bread, but not to drink. These all suggest that our Lord's fast was an abstention from food, not from water. It is also suggested that in a hot desert climate like the wilderness where Jesus fasted, people could die in twenty-four hours if they drank no water. And for many, their body could not survive forty days fast without food, unless they are being supernaturally sustained.

## FASTING AND SLEEP

Despite the broad definitions given to fasting by some, there is nothing to suggest that fasting involves abstention from sleep. God may require it as part of the sacrifice involved in fasting for some reasons, albeit for a short period of time, but not necessarily required as part of the overall activities we must be involved in during a fast. Paul speaks of "watchings" as distinct from "fastings" (2 Cor. 6:5; 11:27).

It is argued that if abstaining from sleep were a requirement of fasting, no long fast would ever be possible without some supernatural interventions, as the body craves sleep as much as water, and is bound to succumb to sleep at some point during the fast.

There is however, a strong indication in 1 Corinthians 7: 3-5 that, for married couples, fasting may involve an abstention from marital relationship:

> *"Let the husband render unto the wife due benevolence: and likewise also the wife unto the husband. The wife hath not power of her own body, but the husband: and likewise also the husband hath not power of his own body, but*

*the wife. Defraud ye not one the other, except it be with consent for a time, that ye may give yourselves to fasting and prayer; and come together again, that Satan tempt you not for your incontinency"*

Having established that the normal fast involves abstaining from all forms of food, but not from water, it must now be distinguished from the other two forms of fasts – the absolute and the partial fasts - which we must now consider.

## THE PARTIAL FAST

This type of fast is based on the fasting practice of Daniel as recorded in Daniel Chapters 1 and 10. There is no complete abstinence from food in this kind of fast. The emphasis here is on restriction of diet rather than complete abstention. This type of fast is highly recommended for beginners to the discipline of fasting, and those with health needs (having obtained their physician's permission to fast).

There are many forms partial fasts can take. The observer of this fast could take just one meal every twenty-four hours. A word of caution, though! The single meal should be light and not the size of three meals in style, which would be gluttony. Yet another type of partial fast is to drink, throughout the duration of the fast, fruit juice or milk. A classic example of this fast, as seen at the commencement of the Book of Daniel is with regards to Daniel and his three companions (Shadrach, Meshach and Abednego), who ate only vegetables and drank only water (Daniel 1:15). They had been selected from among the Hebrew exiles as a result of their noble birth and intellectual attainments for special training. They served before the King of Babylon.

These Hebrew men had resolved not to defile themselves with the King's meat or wine, as these would have first, been offered to the Babylonian gods. Instead, they requested for vegetables for food and water, instead of wine.

The steward over their affairs agreed to test the effect of this simple diet on them for ten days. The Bible says:

> *"...at the end of ten days their countenances appeared fairer and fatter in flesh than all the children which did eat the portion of the king's meat" (Daniel 1:15).*

Whether or not there was supernatural intervention in this particular fast is difficult to ascertain, however, it could be argued, especially from a nutritional perspective that a simple and wholesome diet is far more beneficial than a rich and elaborate one. It is also true that those who live where there is constant dining and wining are, often than not, beset with ailments. It is an instructive fact that all forms of fasting practiced in a sensible biblical manner are physically beneficial, as will be examined in detail later.

However, the value of partial fast, or any other fast, is not confined to the physical benefits. Later in the Book of Daniel, we read how this Prophet received a revelation from God about the future of his people Israel. He describes how he sought the Lord for the understanding of this vision:

> "In those days I Daniel was mourning three full weeks. I ate no pleasant bread, neither came flesh nor wine in my mouth, neither did I anoint myself at all, till three whole weeks were fulfilled" (Daniel 10:2,3).

While we are not told the reasons why he did not engage in a normal fast as we see him do in the previous chapter, there is, undoubtedly, a definite spiritual value in a special season of seeking God with such restricted diet. For Daniel, it resulted in a great spiritual victory over the powers of darkness as well as the unfolding of a transformational vision by an angelic messenger.

Something akin to a partial fast could be said to be the period of Elijah's spiritual preparation. At the Brook Cherith, the raven brought him bread and meat morning and evening, and he drank from the brook. Later, in the home of the widow of Zarephath, he was sustained with simple cakes made from meal and oil (1 Kings 17:6, 9).

The advantages of this kind of fast are numerous: First, it allows a great many variations which have been tried with tremendous benefits. Further, a partial fast is known to be beneficial where circumstances make it impossible or inconvenient to undertake a normal fast. It is also of tremendous benefits, and highly recommended for people who have health problems that prevent them from undergoing complete fasts. It has been seen as a stepping-stone to the normal fast by those who have never fasted before. A case for partial fast may also be made for people whose nature of jobs are very demanding, and consequently make long complete fasts impossible.

# THE ABSOLUTE FAST

This type of fast is one in which the person refrains from both food and water for an extended period of time. Usually this is never for more than three days, perhaps, because of the health implications associated with such abstention. The body can function many days, even weeks without food, and can be tremendously beneficial physically and medically; but the body can survive only for a very limited time without water - seventy-two hours being the maximum.

Let us now examine some biblical personalities that undertook this form of fast:

# QUEEN ESTHER

A pattern for the duration of absolute fasts (without food and fluid) could be said to have been set by Queen Esther in Esther 4: 15-16:

> *"Then Esther bade them return Mordecai this answer, Go, gather together all the Jews that are present in Shushan, and fast ye for me, and neither eat nor drink three days, night or day: I also and my maidens will fast likewise; and so will I go in unto the king, which is not according to the law: and if I perish, I perish."*

Esther decided to fast for three days, abstaining from both "food and water" both "day and night.

A critical situation warranted this measure.

According to Arthur Wallis, *"a crisis of the utmost gravity threatened the whole Jewish race with extermination. Even Esther herself could expect no immunity because she was queen. She called this absolute fast because desperate situations require desperate measures."*

Other patriarchs that resorted to this kind of measure in dealing with crisis of great magnitude include:

# PROPHET EZRA

Driven by overwhelming concerns over the shameful compromise of the Priests and Levites of his day, Ezra fasted absolute for three days (Ezra 9:3):

> *"And when I heard this thing, I rent my garment and my mantle, and plucked off the hair of my head and of my beard, and sat down astonished".*

This significant act is frequently mentioned in the sacred writings, and was common among all ancient nations. Shaving the head and beard were signs of excessive grief; much more so the plucking off the hair, which must produce exquisite pain. All these expressed his abhorrence, not merely of the act of taking strange wives, but of joining affinity with these strange women in their idolatrous practices. Also in Ezra 10:6 we see his deep abhorrence for the evil practices of his day expressed in the following words:

> *"...and when he came thither, he did eat no bread, nor drink water: for he mourned because of the transgression of them that had been carried away."*

The only way Ezra knew best to deal with these acts of apostasy among his people, and evoke God's intervention, was to seek God through fasting.

## SAUL OF TARSUS (PAUL)

Saul of Tarsus, the great persecutor of the Church, got supernaturally blinded with his encounter with Jesus, and the Bible says, *"And for three days he...neither ate nor drank" (Acts 9:9).* The outcome of this supernatural encounter marked a milestone, not just for his personal life, but for the Church as a whole.

## KING DAVID

David was another observer of the absolute fast. He fasted seven days as a plea to God to save the life of his illegitimate child with Bathsheba (2 Sam. 12:15-20):

> *"And Nathan departed unto his house. And the Lord struck the child that Uriah's wife bare unto David, and it was very sick. David therefore besought God for the child: and David fasted, and went in, and lay all night upon the earth. And the elders of his house arose, and went to him, to raise him up from the earth: but he would not, neither did he eat bread with them. And it came to pass on the seventh day that the child died. And the servants of David feared to tell him that the child was dead: for they said, Behold, while the child was yet alive, we spake unto him, and he would*

*not hearken unto our voice: how will he then vex himself, if we tell him that the child is dead? But when David saw that his servants whispered, David perceived that the child was dead: therefore David said unto his servants, Is the child dead? And they said, He is dead. Then David arose from the earth, and washed, and anointed himself, and changed his apparel, and came into the house of the Lord, and worshipped: then he came to his own house; and when he required, they set bread before him, and he did eat."*

# FASTING BEYOND THREE DAYS ABSOLUTE

Absolute fasts, of a protracted nature – extending beyond three or seven days, are also found in the Bible, but these exceptions were based upon direct guidance from God. Readers are, therefore, advised that the people involved in these fasts were supernaturally sustained, and loss of lives have resulted from long fasts that were not cautiously undertaken. You must not undertake a fast for periods longer than your body can survive!

Examples of the observers of these extreme fasts are:

## MOSES

On two separate occasions of forty days and forty nights, Moses was in the presence of God, neither eating nor drinking (Exod. 34:28, Deut. 9:9-18).

> *"And he was there with the Lord forty days and forty nights: he did neither eat bread, nor drink water. And he wrote upon the tables the words of the covenant, the Ten Commandments" (Exod. 34: 28).*

> *"I fell down before the LORD, as at the first, forty days and forty nights: I did neither eat bread, nor drink water, because of all your sins which you sinned, in doing wickedly in the sight of the LORD, to provoke him to anger" (Deut. 9:9-18).*

## ELIJAH

Another person who undertook a protracted fast, without food and water was Elijah (1 Kings 19:8):

> *"And he arose, and did eat and drink, and went in the strength of that meat forty days and forty nights unto Horeb the mount of God".*

## NORMAL, PARTIAL AND ABSOLUTE FAST

Arthur Wallis draws a striking parallel between these two distinguished Old Testament figures: while Moses was the law giver, Elijah was its restorer (Mal 4:4-6; Mark 9:12). Secondly, both had a supernatural ending to their lives, and hundreds of years after they died, both appeared on the mountain of transfiguration with Christ (Matt. 17:1-8). It is perfectly in order to attribute such deep encounters both of them had with God to the fasted life they lived.

Finally, as discussed, Jesus also exemplified a protracted fast:

> *"And Jesus being full of the Holy Ghost returned from Jordan, and was led by the Spirit into the wilderness. Being forty days tempted of the devil. And in those days he did eat nothing" (Luke 4:1,2).*

The length of the fast a believer observes is a matter between him and God, as said. However, due caution should be observed not to choose fasting of a duration too long that he cannot complete, or too gruesome to cause him harm.

# UNDERSTANDING JESUS' TEACHING ON FASTING

# 10

# WHAT JESUS TAUGHT ABOUT FASTING

*"WHEN YE FAST..." (Matt. 6:16).*

In the teaching of Jesus, there is an apparent assumption that Christians would fast, as clearly indicated by the phrase, "when you fast"... in Matthew 6:16. We can arrive at a logical conclusion that the fact that Jesus chose such a phrase and not the opposite – 'If you fast', indicates that the discipline of fasting has not been left at the discretion of the believer whether to fast or not. Jesus' words therefore, imply that fasting will be a regular practice in His followers' lives. Fasting is therefore, the duty of today's believer.

This finds consensus with the views expressed by Dietrich Bonhoeffer, "Jesus takes it for granted that His disciples will observe the pious custom of fasting. Strict exercise of self-control is an essential feature of the Christian life. Such customs have only one purpose — to make the disciples more ready and cheerful to accomplish those things which God would have done." And Wesley Duewel concurs, "You and I have no more right to omit fasting because we feel no special emotional prompting than we have a right to omit prayer, Bible reading, or assembling with God's children for lack of some special emotional prompting. Fasting is just as biblical and normal a part of a spiritual walk of obedience with God as are these others."

The Lord's teaching on fasting offers the present day church an explicit theological standard to adhere to in fasting.

Jesus admonishes:

> *Moreover when ye fast, be not, as the hypocrites, of a sad countenance: for they disfigure their faces, that they may appear unto men to fast. Verily I say unto you, They have their reward. But thou, when thou fastest, anoint thine head, and wash thy face; That thou appear not unto men to fast, but unto thy Father which is in secret: and thy Father, which seeth in secret, shall reward thee openly (Matt. 6:16-18).*

Analysis of the above scripture presents us with a great deal of understanding that can significantly revolutionise, not just our fasted life, but every facet of our relationship with God.

First, as said, Jesus in His "...when you fast..." choice of words in preference to "if you fast" appears to make fasting a necessary and vital condition for victorious Christian living. He implied by His choice of words that all who truly believe in Him would and should fast. This is a lesson of supreme importance.

## THE APPEARANCE OF THE FASTING SAINT

Further, in the said scripture, Jesus dealt with the vital and critical issue of how one should present oneself during a fast. In dealing with this significant matter, Jesus categorises the observers of fasts into two groups – the hypocrites and the Saints. The Lord's classification or grouping of the observers of fasts has huge implications, not least because fasting is not an automatic evidence of genuine spirituality, but because its practice is validated in all religions of the world – Islamic, Buddhism, Hinduism etc. These all fast for various reasons.

For the hypocrites, Jesus directed His comments at the Pharisees, and His remarks were without reservation:

> "Moreover when ye fast, be not, as the hypocrites, of a sad countenance: for they disfigure their faces, that they may appear unto men to fast. Verily I say unto you, They have their reward" (Matt. 6:16).

The reality is that there are no groups of people or nationals in modern world particularly tagged 'hypocrites'. Hypocrisy is a product of the mind!

How many times have you heard non - Christians joke about the hypocrisy of Christians? How many disillusioned people have you met that have been burned by fake Christians and Christian leaders, who preach one thing and practice another – the exact opposite.

Hypocrisy seems to touch a raw nerve in Jesus. Jesus did not just speak out against it; He went on a full-on assault against it. Jesus attacked it over and over again throughout His earthly ministry.

However, for far too many people, being Christians and being hypocrites go hand in hand. We could try to say that the outsiders just have misunderstood those in the church, but sadly, most of their perceptions are true.

Religious artificiality is a disease of the soul that can only be healed by having an authentic relationship with the great healer.

Let us examine the Old Testament on the same subject:

The Lord says:

> *"These people come near to me with their mouth and honor me with their lips, but their hearts are far from me. Their worship of me is made up only of rules taught by*

*men" (Isaiah 29:13).*

I have been around Christians my entire life; it is true that authenticity is rare.

In Ezekiel 33:30-32:

*"As for you, son of man, your countrymen are talking together about you by the walls and at the doors of the houses, saying to each other, 'Come and hear the message that has come from the LORD.' My people come to you, as they usually do, and sit before you to listen to your words, but they do not put them into practice. With their mouths they express devotion, but their hearts are greedy for unjust gain. Indeed, to them you are nothing more than one who sings love songs with a beautiful voice and plays an instrument well, for they hear your words but do not put them into practice" (NIV):*

Scary isn't it? God condemned them because they came, heard the words of the Lord, expressed devotion with their mouths but in their hearts nothing was changing, they put nothing into practice.

Do we act one way with some people and another with others?

Now, let us examine the passage in context.

At the time this was written, there were three significant disciplines among the Jews…giving, praying, and fasting.

We need to understand that Jesus did not dispute these as good works. He was all for giving, praying and fasting. His concern was that this had degenerated into a masking of evil motives. He was against, not the observance of these disciplines, but the motives for observing them.

Now, let us examine the relevant verses separately, and in some depth:

> "But when you give to the needy, do not let your left hand know what your right hand is doing..." (verse 3).

> "And when you pray, do not be like the hypocrites, for they love to pray standing in the synagogues and on the street corners to be seen by men..." (verse 5).

> "When you fast, do not look sober as the hypocrites do, for they disfigure their faces to show men they are fasting..." (verse 16)

When we give, pray, or fast, we are warned not to be hypocritical.

We are encouraged, for instance, to give generously (Luke 6:38), but it must be a matter between the believer and God. When you publicise it in your own way, no matter how subtle it may be, that is your reward. Motivations can be so deceiving. What is at the heart of your giving?

Praying is great. But when you pray, go into your room, close the door and pray! Take a look at your prayer life.

How much of it is real? In my view, it is almost insane to spend hours in prayer just to be noticed by men, and earn their admiration. Prophet Isaiah couldn't be more emphatic when he said, *"Come, my people, enter thou into thy chambers, and shut thy doors about thee: hide thyself as it were for a little moment, until the indignation be overpast" (Isaiah 26:20).* Jesus did not mince His words when He taught on the subject: *"And when you pray, do not be like the hypocrites, for they love to pray standing in the synagogues and on the street corners to be seen by others. Truly I tell you, they have received their reward in full. But when you pray, go into your room, close the door and pray to your Father, who is unseen. Then your Father, who sees what is done in secret, will reward you" (Matt. 6:5-6).*

At this juncture, let us examine some incredible lessons, on the basis of what we have learned under this heading so far:

1. Constantly evaluate your private life against your public life. If you are practicing any or all of these disciplines: giving, praying, or fasting in public only, something is wrong. Evaluate your heart. Why do you do the things you do? What is the motive behind it? Do not hide behind a mask. Be real. Ask for help. Admit your weaknesses. Jesus loves when we admit our weaknesses and ask for help but he hates hypocrisy.

2. Probe yourself of the result you desire to be the outcome of your engaging in any of the disciplines as

analysed - giving, praying, and fasting. If you cannot pinpoint any benefits flowing directly from God, then the motive is likely to be wrong. There would, undoubtedly, be some rewards, but they are likely to emanate from the wrong source – man.

3. Learn to give the glory to God. It does not matter how successful you think you are in this regard, learn to attribute it all to the grace of God.

4. Walk in humility before the Lord. Remember, "God resisteth the proud, and giveth grace to the humble" (1 Peter 5:5); in the next verse, we are given the responsibility of cultivating the virtue of humility in our lives, "**Therefore humble yourselves under the mighty hand of God**, that He may exalt you in due time" (1 Peter 5:6, emphasis added). It is therefore, our responsibility; not God's! We should truly spear ourselves the danger of God humbling us.

The Lord said in unequivocal terms to the second group – His saints:

> *"But thou, when thou fastest, anoint thine head, and wash thy face; That thou appear not unto men to fast, but unto thy Father which is in secret: and thy Father, which seeth in secret, shall reward thee openly" (Matt. 6:17-18).*

The fast of the Saints of God is to be different. They are to honour and please God with their fasting; never for personal aggrandisement. They are to wash and anoint their faces. Accordingly, their external appearance is to be given serious consideration, so that the fasting believer does not draw undue attention to himself. As seen, this has grave consequences. Believers who fast must pay special attention to their physical appearance. They should be clean. They should bathe at least twice a day. They should brush their teeth once every two hours. Fasting people have a special mouth odour. They cannot afford to burden other people with it.

# 11

# WHO SHOULD SEE AND REWARD THE FAST?

## WHO SEES THE FAST?

Another great lesson from Jesus's teaching on fasting has to do with who we should allow to see our fast. Here again, Jesus identifies two categories of people with different attitudes - the hypocrites and the Christians. The hypocrites fast in order to attract the attention of men. They put the admiration of men and personal glorification ahead of the legitimate objectives of fasting. They possibly think of a class of people who they want to impress with their fasting.

However, for the precious saints of Christ, they are to fast, not to be seen by men, but by the Almighty – who

> *...for the precious saints of Christ, they are to fast, not to be seen by men, but by the Almighty...*

alone rewards fasting. They are to fast as a sacrifice, offered on the altar of incense, to be seen and smelt by their Father who is in Heaven!

Can you see the enormous difference between fasting to attract the praise of men, and fasting in praise and honour to the Lord? If He is the Lord of your life, He is to be Lord over your fast!

> *"A son honoureth his father, and a servant his master: **if then I be a father, where is mine honour? and if I be a master, where is my fear?**" (Mal. 1:6, emphasis added).* God once enquired.

To the praise and Glory of the Lord, I have observed fasts of various lengths and durations; the longest so far being a forty day straight fast. Can you imagine how foolish it would have been to embark on a fast of such length, with the sole objective of letting men see what a 'fasting guru' I have become? God forbid!

The question of 'who sees the fast' carries with it an expensive price-tag, indeed, grave implications, when we consider the indispensable issue in relation to the outcome of the fast – reward!

## WHO REWARDS THE FAST?

The fourth vital issue in the passage under consideration raises the question of who rewards the observer of the fast. Jesus stated very categorically, "*... thou appear not unto men to fast, but unto thy Father which is in secret: and thy Father, which seeth in secret, **shall reward thee openly**" (Matt. 6:17-18 emphasis added)*. Two astounding logical conclusion can to be drawn from the above analysis.

First, *'whoever sees the fast rewards the fast'!* The hypocrites fast to catch the eye of man; so man is the rewarder of the fast of the hypocrites. Whoever fasts to be seen by man is a hypocrite! He receives his reward from the people who see his fast and sing his praise.

The Saints of the Most High, on the other hand, fast so as to be seen by their Father, who is in secret. He is Omnipresent! Nothing escapes His glorious eyes! David asks brilliantly:

> *Whither shall I go from thy spirit? or whither shall I flee from thy presence? If I ascend up into Heaven, thou art there: if I make my bed in hell, behold, thou art there. If I take the wings of the morning, and dwell in the uttermost parts of the sea: Even there shall thy hand lead me, and thy right hand shall hold me (Psalm 139: 7 - 10).*

Every transaction of man is within the watchful eyes of the all-knowing God. He sees your fast! Those who fast for His glory labour to ensure that their fasting is seen only by Him, so as to draw the reward He promised! For the hypocrites, God's verdict is that they receive their rewards by the 'congratulations' they receive from men. He received it when people looked at his disfigured face and exclaimed, "What a fasting expert!" Notice that he – the hypocrite receives his rewards instantaneously. But the righteous – the ones whose fasting are channelled to please and honour God, have their rewards both now and in the future.

Second, when speaking of fasting for the saints of God, Jesus said in unequivocal terms, that if conducted after the pattern as laid out in scriptures, and not after the conducts of the religious hypocrites, we shall be rewarded. It is important to note that our Heavenly Father's promised reward for the disciplined action would not be compared to the reward gained by the Pharisees, who are rewarded by mere men.

It is noteworthy that the word used by Jesus in relation to the reward accruable to the fasting of the believer has special significance. As R. Smith made abundantly clear, the Greek connotation of the word Jesus used in relation to the benefits the believer stands to receive in fasting suggests restoration over a period of time instead of an immediate reward which can be counted in earthly terms.

According to Smith, *"The word He [Jesus] chose to use (as presented in Greek) at the end of verse sixteen, in Matthew chapter six, is different from that used at the end of verse eighteen. The implication is that Pharisee fasting (praying and giving, also) has an immediate reward in the applause of men, but true Christian fasting need not have any apparent benefits straight away. The Father's recompense has an eternal value; basically this recompense is spiritual even though it creates physical features also. In other words, the benefits of fasting are 'added extras' which come to Christians 'by the way'. There is no doubting the fact that if we fast to honour God, and for reasons that are grounded in the word of God, as argued, we shall be recompensed. Bible-based fasts, if rightly conducted, will without fail, be rewarded by the God who sees in secret, openly."*

## THE BELIEVERS FASTING ACCOUNT IN HEAVEN

Zachariah Fomum takes this discussion, in my view, to a new dimension that elevates the subject in context beyond the limits of the rewards that are accruable to fasting while on this side of eternity. He affirms, *"There is a reason for fasting that has nothing to do with the current age or getting things from God now but has to do with the age to come."* He adds, *"when the Lord comes He will reward His servants according to their works. His book shall be opened.*

> Fasting is to be a natural outcome of discipleship.

*There shall be the book of prayer, the book of giving to the Lord, the book of self-denial, the book of fasting, the book of obedience, etc, and believers shall be reward according to what has been recorded in those books. My dear brother and sister the book of fasting shall be opened.*

*What do you have recorded in that book against your name?*

*Is there anything at all? Are there only partial fasts?*

*Are there only a few complete fasts?*

*Are there any absolute fasts? Are there any long fasts?*

*Are there any fasts that satisfy the heart of God?*

*It is possible to know now so that no one will be surprised on that day. There will be no reward for any fast by any believer that was carried out to draw attention to himself. God does not record such fasts, since the fasting person has already received his reward from the one whose attention he drew to his fasting. This should make believers think. There will be rewards only for those whose fasts were meant to catch the eye of God alone. What does this all mean? I think that the first thing that it means is that any reward that may be received now, like power for service, divine visitation, etc., is only a foretaste of what will be in the future. The central issue will be the reward*

## WHO SHOULD SEE AND REWARD THE FAST?

*by the One Who sees in secret. Those who may not receive any visible reward for their fasting in time need not be discouraged. The Lord is keeping their reward for the judgment Day."*

What a prophetic insight into the glorious reward God has in store for those who worship the Master with fasting. Something serious to think about, no doubt!

Finally, some fast with the intention of drawing the attention of God and man at the same time? It is clear from our teaching so far that God does not record such fasts, because He cannot be involved in a mixture. It is either entirely God's or man's. God will not share His glory with any man!

Between verses 17 and 18 of Matthew chapter 6, Jesus continued His inspiring teaching on how to engage in biblical fasting:

> "Moreover when ye fast, be not, as the hypocrites, of a sad countenance: for they disfigure their faces, that they may appear unto men to fast. Verily I say unto you, They have their reward. But thou, when thou fastest, anoint thine head, and wash thy face: That thou appear not unto men to fast, but unto thy Father which is in secret: and thy Father, which seeth in secret, shall reward thee openly."

Further, in His response to the seeming accusation levied by the Pharisees against His disciples' refusal to fast, an apparent violation of the Jewish custom, Jesus referred to a time when, after the departure of the Bridegroom (referring to the post - ascension era), the disciples would see fasting as a divine obligation placed on them. Jesus said to them:

> *"...Can the children of the bridal chamber fast, while the bridegroom is with them? As long as they have the bridegroom with them, they cannot fast. But the days will come, when the bridegroom shall be taken away from them, and then shall they fast in those days" (Mark 2:19-20).*

Accordingly, after the Lord's death, His disciples frequently fasted as of necessity, and went through much deprivations and trials. In essence, this prophetic word, as it were, had found fulfilment in the lives of His 'immediate disciples, and should also for the His present day 'disciples', until He returns to take to Himself His bride, when there will be a glad and everlasting feasting.

Fasting is to be a natural outcome of discipleship. We are to fast for the same reason we pray. This does not, by any means, indicate that we are to fast every time we pray!

Jesus addressed fasting in association with both prayer and almsgiving. He declared *"when you give alms" (Matt. 6:2), "when you pray" (Matt. 6:6),* and *"when you fast" (Matt. 6:16).* The logical conclusions from these texts are: though the Bible is silent as to how often we should fast, Jesus intends fasting to be undertaken by the believer as a discipline. Just as He expects us to pray and give alms, Jesus expects us to fast.

In addition, in the Sermon on the Mount, when Jesus spoke about prayer and fasting, He used similar phrases in addressing both subjects. The main difference, however, is that in relation to prayer; he included a structure of prayer often referred to as 'the Lord's Prayer'.

# 12

# EXCEPT BY PRAYER AND FASTING

*Howbeit this kind goeth not out but by prayer and fasting (Matt. 17:21).*

Another significant statement made by Jesus about fasting is contained in the passage of scripture referenced above. However, the backdrop to that scripture is strategically important. A number of significant events preceded this statement which deserves our attention. For this reason, let us examine the applicable portions of Matthew 17:14-21:

*And when they had come to the multitude, a man came to Him, kneeling down to Him and saying, Lord, have mercy on my son, for he is an epileptic and suffers severely; for he often falls into the fire and often into the water. So I brought him to Your disciples, but they could not cure him.*

*Then Jesus answered and said, O faithless and perverse generation, how long shall I be with you? How long shall I bear with you? Bring him here to Me. And Jesus rebuked the demon, and it came out of him; and the child was cured from that very hour. Then the disciples came to Jesus privately and said, Why could we not cast it out? So Jesus said to them, Because of your unbelief; for assuredly, I say to you, if you have faith as a mustard seed, you will say to this mountain, 'Move from here to there,' and it will move; and nothing will be impossible for you.* **However, this kind does not go out except by prayer and fasting** *(NKJV, emphasis added).*

In this incident, a man took his epileptic son to the Lord's disciples, so that they might heal him. When they could not heal him, the father took him to the Lord. Jesus gave instant healing to the boy. The disciples were puzzled! Why could they not heal this young boy? The Lord told His disciples that they were hindered in their work because of their own unbelief!

Perhaps in trying to heal this boy, they really did not think they could do it. The Lord puts the blame squarely on the disciples – their unbelief. Today's so-called 'faith healers' will blame the one desiring healing for lack of faith, if they cannot procure healing for them. Here, the Lord put the blame on those attempting to do the healing.

Mark's recording of this event tells us that the disciples asked the Lord in private why they were not able to heal this boy. It must have been embarrassing and disappointing to them when they could not heal the boy. We read in Mark 9:28-29, *"And when He had come into the house, His disciples asked Him privately, "Why could we not cast it out? So He said to them, "This kind can come out by nothing but prayer and fasting."* Faith is required to function effectively as God's servant, in every area of our calling.

In the statement under consideration, Jesus referenced two vital disciplines in Christianity as faith-booster for tremendous exploit in the kingdom. These are prayer and fasting.

Jesus' message here is very clear: "Howbeit, this kind ..." (Matt. 17:21) means this kind of devils - this kind of captor. Where they have had long possession of their captives, and have produced such painful, fixed, and alarming effects, they can only be expelled with prayer and fasting.

The phrase, "Goeth not out but by prayer and fasting" (Matt. 17:21), means in order to work miracles of this kind, to cast out devils in cases as obstinate and dreadful as this, faith of the highest kind is necessary. That faith is produced and kept vigorous only by much fasting.

According to the book of Ephesians 6:12 *"... we wrestle not against flesh and blood, but against principalities, against powers, against the rulers of the darkness of this world, against spiritual wickedness in high places."*

Demons are different according to their rankings and wickedness. Jesus' teaching took cognisance of this fact in addressing the disciples on this crucial subject; the fact that some high-ranking demons can only be dislodged with a higher degree of faith. Fasting helps the believer overcome unbelief and builds stronger faith. Fasting is a supernatural weapon *"mighty to the pulling down of stronghold..." (2 Cor. 10:5),* Jesus gave His disciples. Some tough situations take the combination of prayer and fasting to yield, there are no other ways around it as alluded to by Bill Bright who, so accurately describes this potent weapon as, *"the spiritual atomic bomb that our Lord has given us to destroy the strongholds of evil and usher in a great revival and spiritual harvest around the world."* John Eckhardt agrees, *"there are those kind of demons that just don't give up. They are strong, proud, arrogant, and defiant...Sometimes you have to do something unusual, extraordinary, and beyond the norm to see breakthrough. Normal church, normal Christianity, normal preaching, and normal praying are not going to get the job done. Some little sweet prayer is not doing to do... It is going to take the anointing that destroys the yoke. When you fast the anointing increases in your life because you are into the spirit...extraordinary situations requires extraordinary measures. Sometimes it only happens when you get desperate – when you are so tired of being defeated and hindered in an area...you have to get so tired of the devil that you say, "Enough is enough. If I have to turn my plate down to get a breakthrough in this area, I won't eat."*

# 13

# THEY SHALL FAST

*"And then they shall fast..." (Matt. 9:15).*

Yet, another remarkable statement made by Jesus with regards to fasting was a prediction to a return to fasting by His disciples - Jesus' disciples, past and present! This further strengthens the argument or submission that there was an apparent expectation in the mind of Jesus that His followers would take up fasting as part of their Christian discipline.

> *Then came to him the disciples of John, saying, Why do we and the Pharisees fast oft, but thy disciples fast not? And Jesus said unto them, Can the children of the bridechamber mourn, as long as the bridegroom is with them? but the days will come, when the bridegroom shall be taken from them, and then shall they fast (Matt. 9:14-15).*

The highly significant statement Jesus made concerning fasting was in response to the question the disciples of John the Baptist and the Pharisees asked Him: *"Why,"* they enquired, *"do we and the Pharisees fast, but your disciples do not fast?" (Matt. 9:14)*. The first thing to be noted about this question is that, though directed at Jesus, it was not about Jesus not fasting. They did not say Jesus did not fast. They were rather perturbed that the disciples of Jesus were not fasting. They knew that Jesus authenticated the discipline of fasting by engaging in the act Himself. They regarded the disciples' attitude in this regard as a flagrant violation of the Jewish tradition.

To this important question, Jesus gave a powerful and intriguing answer:

> "When the Bridegroom is taken from them... then they will fast" (Matt.9:15).

On the surface, this answer seems straightforward and simple, yet more has been written on this incident than about any other New Testament reference on the practice of fasting.

In Matthew's account, the question was asked by the disciples of John the Baptist. Luke attributed the question to the Pharisees (Luke 5:30, 33), and Mark wrote that the questions came from both groups (Mark 2:18).

Whereas Matthew and Mark record a question that calls for an answer, Luke's account records a simple statement that has the force of a question. In all three accounts, there was a clear assumption, by human judgement, that Jesus' disciples were doing something wrong.

An important explanation, however, is that Jesus and His disciples did not conform to the common customs of traditional Judaism. Their conduct reveals a clear-cut breach with existing religious practice. This issue concerning fasting brought into focus the whole question of Jesus' attitude toward the Jewish tradition. This is also evident in the two following analogies of placing a new patch on old cloth and putting new wine in old wineskins (Matt. 9:16-17; Mark 2:21-22; Luke 5:36-38). Christ's teaching could not be blended with rabbinic traditions.

Fasting was embarked upon as a religious duty among the Jews in the days of Jesus' earthly ministry. However, both the Pharisees and the disciples of John the Baptist were appalled that while they observed the traditional rites of the time (fasted, according to the Jewish tradition), the disciples of Jesus did not. They decided to confront Jesus with the matter.

As often His custom, Jesus responded to this important question by way of a parable. He spoke of three significant issues: the "bridegroom," "children of the "bride-chamber," and the appointed "time to fast."

All three are remarkably important:

## THE TRANSFORMATIONAL POWER OF FASTING

In the first place, as always in the New Testament, the bridegroom is Christ Himself. The children of the bridechamber are the disciples of Jesus (now present day believers).

While this is perhaps the most crucial statement as recorded in the New Testament on the subject of fasting, however, the question remains, what period could Jesus be referring to? It is very clear that the days of His absence indicated by the words "when the Bridegroom is taken away from them," refer to the period of this present church age, from the time of His ascension to the Father, until His return to rapture His Bride. Arthur Wallis held the conviction that *"Fasting . . . in this age of the absent Bridegroom is in expectation of His return. Soon there will be the midnight cry, 'Behold, the bridegroom! Come out to meet him.' It will be too late then to fast and to pray. The time is now."*

That was undoubtedly, the way His disciples understood Him. It was after His Ascension to the Father that we read of them fasting (Acts 13:2,3; 14:23).

So, the days of fasting are finally upon us! The departure of the bridegroom signals the beginning of this glorious discipline. Since the prophecy of the "bridegroom being taken away" has been fulfilled, the accompanying responsibility vested on the Saints to engage in fasting as a result, must be fulfilled also. However, before the Bridegroom left, He promised to return to receive the believers unto Himself. While the Church awaits His glorious return, fasting must continue. The time is now!

Now, how far have the disciples fulfilled the Lord's prophecy in relation to fasting?

# THE EARLY CHURCH FULFILLED THE PROPHECY

The Bible says,

> *"Now there were in the church that was at Antioch certain prophets and teachers: as Barnabas, and Simeon that was called Niger, and Lucius of Cyrene. As they ministered to the Lord, and fasted" (Acts 13:1-2).*

No doubt, Christ's answer to the said question is also deeply pertinent to much broader question of whether fasting is relevant to the believer today. He asks, "Can the wedding guests mourn as long as the Bridegroom is with them?" (Matt. 9:15). Then, quite prophetically, He added, "But the days will come when the bridegroom is taken away from them, and then they will fast." In His statement, Jesus viewed fasting as a sign of mourning, which is inconsistent with the joy of the bridegroom's presence.

Whereas, there were times when Jesus and His disciples went hungry; times when, due to the heavy demands of

Kingdom assignments, they had no time to eat. A very glaring example is in Mark 11: 12 – 14:

> *"The next day as they were leaving Bethany, Jesus was hungry. Seeing in the distance a fig tree in leaf, he went to find out if it had any fruit. When he reached it, he found nothing but leaves, because it was not the season for figs. Then he said to the tree, "May no one ever eat fruit from you again." And His disciples heard Him."*

However, there is no evidence of Jesus and His disciples undertaking a definite voluntary fast together. (Jesus, of course, fasted forty days and nights in the wilderness before His public ministry). Reason? The Bridegroom was still with the wedding guests! The occasion called for feasting, not fasting, rejoicing, not mourning. Although the disciples would fast when the bridegroom was taken from them, it would be for a different purpose and in a different spirit from that which characterised the fasting of the Pharisees. There would be no return to the legalism of the old order. However, by and by, fasting would be replaced by feasting (Rev. 22:17,20):

> *"And the Spirit and the bride say, Come. And let him that heareth say, Come. And let him that is athirst come. And whosoever will, let him take the water of life freely. He which testifieth these things saith, Surely I come quickly. Amen. Even so, come, Lord Jesus."*

As said, Jesus wanted John's disciples along with His own disciples to realise that while He was with them, it was a time of joy. This was not a time of mourning or fasting or weeping. It is simply inappropriate to fast at a wedding feast. No, a wedding feast is a time of celebration. But as bold as this statement is about Jesus' presence altering everything, we also find a hint that His death will alter everything, and this time, in a painful way. The point: Jesus' presence conditions the time; it changes everything; it determines our joy.

In Martin G. Collins' view, the bridegroom's friends would not think of fasting while He was with them. For them, it was a time of festivity and rejoicing—mourning was not appropriate. When the bridegroom left them, their festivities would end, and the proper time for fasting and sorrow would begin.

While Christ, the Bridegroom, was with His disciples, it was a time for joy. Expressing grief by fasting would have been inappropriate at that time. In addition, since Jesus was with them, they had no need to draw closer to Him through fasting. After Christ died, the disciples fasted when appropriate.

It is noteworthy however, that Jesus in His response did not tell the disciples of John that their question was wrong – which could have given the indication that there was no reason to fast in the ministry of the believers. He rather said that it was a matter of timing. There would be a time when the true disciples of Jesus would need no reminding of their Heavenly duty to serve the lord with fasting. That time, according to Jesus would be after His ascension, because at the moment, the 'bridegroom' was still very much here. Fasting, while He was with us would be very inappropriate. The Lord Jesus clearly taught that when He would be taken away from the disciples, they would begin to fast and continue until He came back for them. From His very inspiring teaching on the subject, the period between the death of the Lord Jesus and His return to take the Church, His bride unto Himself, would be a fasting period for all believers.

We know that the Lord died and rose again around A.D 34. We also know for certain that He has not come yet to take His church unto Himself. We are therefore, in the period the Lord promised the disciples of John that the diligent disciples of Jesus would fast. The question then is: are the disciples fulfilling their Heavenly duties? Are the disciples fasting? The Bridegroom has departed, shall we fast now?

# A GRAVE MISINTERPRETATION OF THE STATEMENT IN CONTEXT

Some have inaccurately attributed this statement to the period between Christ's death and Resurrection, or between His death and the day of Pentecost. Impliedly contending that from the decent of the Holy Spirit until this present day there has been no need for fasting, since the Lord has been with His church in the same way that He was with the first disciples. The above line of reasoning is fallacious in many respects, not least, the fact that it makes the biblical accounts of fasting in the Acts of Apostle and in the ministry of Paul unaccounted for. Why did they fast if there was no need to do so? I hold firmly to the view that the early Christians did appoint some fast days in commemoration of the passion and crucifixion of Jesus. And I submit without reservation, that they did this with reference to the Lord's words in context: *"when the bridegroom shall be taken from them, and then shall they fast" (Matt. 9:15)*. Jesus was most vehement when he said at His exit from the world's scene His followers would fast. The early believers as recorded in the book of Acts, and the churches as chronicled in the epistles fulfilled this prediction to the later!

# 14

# JESUS EMPOWERED THROUGH FASTING

Jesus not only taught fasting, as discussed, He validated the practice by fully engaging in the act. Immediately after His baptism, Jesus was led by the Holy Spirit to spend forty days and nights fasting in the wilderness:

> *"Jesus being full of the Holy Ghost returned from Jordan, and was led by the Spirit into the wilderness. Being forty days tempted of the devil. And in those days he did eat nothing: and when they were ended, he afterward hungered" (Luke 4:1-2).*

However, there is a significant difference in the recording of Luke about Jesus, both before and after His fast. Luke's record of Jesus before the fast was: *"And Jesus being full of the*

*Holy Ghost returned from Jordan…" (Luke 4:1)*. However, at the end of the fast, Luke 4:14 asserts, "Then Jesus returned in the power of the Holy Spirit to Galilee, and news of Him went out through all the surrounding region."

When Jesus went into the wilderness, He was already "full of the Holy Spirit." That was outstanding! In other words, He started out 'full' of the Holy Spirit. But look at verse 14. At the end of the wilderness experience - the 40 days fast, He became empowered by the Holy Spirit! Of course, how could Jesus have performed the astonishing miracles we read about, throughout His earthly ministry?

In the light of the evidence such as this, Derek Prince concludes:

*"It would appear that the potential of the Holy Spirit is power, which Jesus received at the time of his baptism in Jordan, only came forth into full manifestation after He had completed his fast. Fasting was the final phase of preparation through which he had to pass, before entering into His public ministry."*

There is therefore, a significant difference between being filled with the Spirit and operating in the power of the Spirit. For Jesus, a transformation took place; a transition that took Jesus from being filled with the Spirit, to walking in the Spirit. He got empowered with that which had possessed Him.

## MOVING BEYOND THE "IN-FILLING" PROCESS

This has been clearly demonstrated to us by Jesus. Being filled with the Spirit alone does not guarantee empowerment.

The way to empowerment involves a process; never by accident! And there are no short-cuts involved. In the life and ministry of Jesus, we see a clear-cut process, right from His baptism at river Jordan, "And it came to pass in those days, that Jesus came from Nazareth of Galilee, and was baptized by John in the Jordan And immediately coming up out of the water, he saw the Heavens opened, and the Spirit like a dove descending upon him"(Mark 1:9 -10), to another phase where He was led by the Spirit into the Wilderness, and was "full of the Holy Spirit." (Luke 4:1). And, of course, to the final and ultimate phase of His empowerment – being the stage where he began to perform breath-taking miracles, signs and wonders (Luke 4:14). This was precipitated by a remarkable event that bridged the earlier phases with the ultimate phase, and that was His forty days fast!

# JESUS' DISCIPLES AND THE DIVINE PROCESS

The same spiritual law that applied in Christ's ministry was evident in the ministry of His disciples. In John 14:12, Jesus said, "He that believeth on me, the works that I do shall he do also." By these words, Jesus opened the way for His disciples to follow through on the pattern He had set in His own ministry. If fasting was a necessary part of Christ's preparation for ministry, it must play a vital part also in the disciple's execution of their ministerial mandate.

Having adequately demonstrated this in His own ministry, Jesus went on to stress the significance of fasting in achieving spiritual breakthroughs, when prayer by itself proved inadequate (Matt. 17:21): He said to His awe-stricken disciples: *"...this kind goeth not out but by prayer and fasting."*

What a lesson! No one had ever taught them that before. Neither had experience in ministry led them that way before this time. However, with this revelation about the incredible power of fasting as impacted by the Master, the disciples had been given the one secret they needed, like their Master, to have success in the ministry – a piece of armoury that would significantly impact their lives and ministry forever. If they were ever going to "make full proof of [their] ministry" (2 Tim. 4:5), and make their *"calling and election sure" (2 Peter 1:10)*, it would undoubtedly, be with the help of this great revelation about the incredible power of fasting they had just been given.

Similarly, the disciples were with Jesus for a period of three years, during which they were trained, and impacted. The life and ministry of Jesus was replicated in them. Yet it was not until after the Upper room experience, with the combined ministry of prayer and fasting, coupled with the painful experience of having the bridegroom taken away from them that they pressed into both the in-filling and the empowerment stages of their ministry.

Signs and wonders authenticated this process! Pandemonium hit the streets of Jerusalem like a thunderbolt on the Day of Pentecost! The disciples were visited with the most amazing power of the Holy Spirit, amidst extra-ordinary demonstration of the same power that shaped and defined their ministry thereafter.

The early church suddenly became a force to reckon with. The outburst of the power that resulted from the empowerment process could not be curtailed, not even by the Sanhedrin Council. (The Sanhedrin was the supreme council, or court, in ancient Israel).

Outstanding miracles were a living proof of this incredible outpouring of the Spirit of God in, not just the Antioch Church, but in Jerusalem and beyond. This was the birth-place of the unprecedented move of God which flames spread and engulfed the whole world.

This power is available today! It belongs to our time and generation! However, the secret key that opens the reservoir of power – the floodgate of Heaven - is fasting and prayer! The combined effect of prayer and fasting is adorable, astonishing and startling! They produce undeniable results.

Have you noticed that men may criticise methods and principles, but are never able to deny or critique results? It is often said that if you do not appreciate your harvest, all you need to do is to change your seed. Fasting is a tremendous seed that yields astonishing dividends in the life of the believer.

# THE FASTING MINISTRY OF JESUS

# 15

# JESUS IN THE MINISTRY OF FASTING

Jesus taught the subject of fasting extensively – not only the need to fast, the benefits (rewards) of fasting, and how to engage in the act of biblical fasting, but more significantly, He validated fasting by engaging in the act Himself. Jesus' fast immediately followed His baptism (Matt. 3:13), which inaugurated Jesus' public ministry. Matthew 4:1–2 says that Jesus was led by the Holy Spirit into the wilderness to fast for forty days and nights. During that time of fasting, Jesus was repeatedly tempted by the devil. This testing time prepared Him for the three-year ministry that would change the world.

During those forty days, when Jesus' flesh was at its weakest, He endured relentless temptation from the devil. Satan offered Him several alternatives to God's agenda, alternatives that would have satisfied His natural appetite no doubt, given the condition of abstinence He was in at the time, but would have dealt a deadly blow to His very identity as the Son of God (Matt. 4:3). Jesus used the Word of God, not His own strength, to defeat those temptations and remains victorious over sin. He demonstrated for us that fasting can strengthen us spiritually when we use it to draw closer to God.

After Jesus' fast, the devil left Him and "angels came and ministered unto him" (Matt. 4:11). Luke 4:14 concludes the account of this testing time by saying, "Jesus returned to Galilee in the power of the Spirit." He had conquered temptation and was ready to embrace the purpose for which the Father had sent Him. He would not rely on His humanity to perform miracles, deliver the oppressed, or defeat death. Fasting was a way to declare mastery over His human nature so that He would live every moment directed by the "power of the Spirit" (Luke 10:21). He set the example for us who "are not in the realm of the flesh but are in the realm of the Spirit" (Romans 8:9). If the Son of God did not rely on His flesh to live in obedience to God, then we can't either.

The practice of fasting was extremely common in the ancient world, and is still commonplace today as a means of preparation, cleansing, focusing, and penitential prayer. But this is an act practiced by believers who recognise their own sinful nature and their need of mercy and grace. Jesus, however, being sinless, would have no need of penitence. Why then, did He fast?

## WHY DID JESUS FAST?

Although the answer seems simple, let us dig deeper to discover more of why Jesus fasted.

Jesus knew the positive value of prayer and fasting, and was confident that they were the only means to the end that He sought. Jesus received the Holy Spirit, but this did not seem sufficient. It required fasting and prayer to operate fully in the Holy Ghost. After fasting forty days and forty nights Jesus began to manifest Himself as the Son of God with all powers, sighs and wonders. There was such an awakening! As Franklin Hill explains it, *"fasting is the most powerful means at the disposal of every child of God. Fasting literally becomes prayer to the praying Christian, prayer that is as different as an atomic bomb compared to an ordinary bomb. Prayer alone is like the ordinary bomb, and the fast with prayer, is comparable to the Super-Atomic Bomb."*

# JESUS FASTED TO ESTABLISH A CLOSER WALK WITH THE FATHER

The gospels record Jesus fasting for 40 days before undergoing an intense confrontation with the devil (Matt. 4:1-11; Luke 4:1-13). Jesus' own words reveal that the purpose of His fasting was to draw near to God for help. When satan tempted Him, asking Him to turn stones into bread, He responded quoting Deuteronomy 8:3, *"Man shall not live by bread alone, but by every word that proceeds from the mouth of God."* By fasting, Jesus demonstrated His faith in the fact that true nourishment comes from God. In doing so, He acknowledged God as the sole source of His strength rather than relying on Himself; an ageless lesson for the believer!

On one occasion, Jesus was questioned as to why His disciples did not regularly fast, since the Pharisees, the disciples of John, and other devout religious people of the day regularly fasted. Jesus confirmed that His disciples would not fast while He was with them, but that they would do so after His death and ascension (Luke 5:33-35). This firmly establishes that fasting should be an ongoing practice for the believers today.

Given the understanding that fasting draws a person closer to God for help, and considering the substantial physical stresses that Jesus faced on a daily basis, it would not be surprising if Jesus fasted regularly, even though it was not recorded. As disciples of Jesus Christ, fasting is a spiritual tool that we can and should use to strengthen our relationship with God. Just as Jesus fasted to prepare for and ultimately won His spiritual battle with satan, we can also draw near to God, acknowledge that victory comes by His power rather than our own, and learn to better overcome sin in our lives.

## JESUS FASTED TO LAUNCH HIS PUBLIC MINISTRY

According to Jentezen Franklin, when Jesus was on earth, He was all God and all man in one form. That is the reason He is called "Son of Man" (Matt. 24:30), and "Son of God" (Luke 1:35) in the Bible. But even though He was God's son and He and the Father were one (John 10:30), Jesus fasted. Why? He knew He would face every difficulty known to mankind and that He needed to fast to have the strength to overcome in every situation. Jesus fasted to show us that we did not have to be controlled by our appetites. As the writer of Hebrew puts it, "... *we have not an high priest which cannot be touched with the feeling of our infirmities;* **but was in all points tempted like as we are,** *yet* *without sin (Heb. 4:15, emphasis added).* In Hebrews 5:8-9, we see greater emphasis placed on the fact that Jesus suffered just as we do, *"Though he were a Son, yet learned he obedience by the things which he suffered; And being made perfect, he became the author of eternal salvation unto all them that obey him."* As a matter of fact, He was made perfect by the things He suffered (verse 9).

He fasted to be our example of how to be an overcomer regardless of what we face in life. If Jesus was led to fast, doesn't it make sense that it is really important for us to fast?

Before Jesus began His ministry on earth, He fasted. "After his baptism, as Jesus came up out of the water, the heavens were opened and He saw the Spirit of God descending like a dove and settling on him. And a voice from heaven said, 'This is my dearly loved Son, who brings me great joy.' Then Jesus was led by the Spirit into the wilderness to be tempted there by the devil. For forty days and forty nights He fasted and became very hungry." (Matt. 3:16-4:2).

With the water of the Jordan River still running down His face and clothes, God declared how pleased He was with Jesus. What better time to launch a public ministry than when God Himself publicly proclaims His approval! But instead of capitalising on the publicity, Jesus went into total isolation for 40 days, eating nothing and being tempted by the devil. Jesus fasted in the desert before He preached one sermon, before He healed anyone, and before He called any disciples. When Jesus successfully completed His fast, He was prepared for the spiritual battles ahead, as He stepped out into His destiny on earth.

The Lord Jesus knew that the three and a half years of ministry that were before Him were critically important. He had been preparing for it in the last thirty years. He knew that generation to come depend on it. Part of His preparation for the big occasion was His water baptism, having the Holy Spirit come upon Him and having the approval of His father!

He needed more time of waiting before His Father in prayer. He was led by the Holy Spirit to wait on the Lord God Almighty in prayer and fasting.

Deep things must have been received from His Father as He waited in fasting.

Before the fast, Jesus was said to be full of the Holy Spirit, *"And Jesus being full of the Holy..." (Luke 14:1)*. However, after the fast, the Bible says, "And Jesus returned in the power of the Spirit into Galilee: and there went out a fame of him through all the region round about" (Luke 4:14). So, He went into the fast full of the Holy Spirit and after the forty days of the fast, He was clothed with the power of the Holy Spirit, that equipped Him for public ministry. Gleaning from the Scripture, there was no record of Jesus performing any miracles before His forty-days fast. Indeed the Bible refers to Christ's "beginnings of miracles" (John

2:11), at the wedding of Cana. This was three days after His baptism through which He was revealed. Not only that, His public ministry received public acclaim. The Bible says, "…and there went out a fame of him through all the region round about" (Luke 4:14).

After praying and fasting for forty days and forty nights, Jesus began to manifest Himself as the Son of God with all power, signs and wonders.

The writer of Hebrews states unequivocally,

> *"God also bearing them witness, both with signs and wonders, and with divers miracles, and gifts of the Holy Ghost, according to his own will?" (Heb. 2:4).*

There was such an awakening! Jesus and His public ministry 'exploded.'

This time of fasting and enduring temptation prepared Jesus for His three years public ministry in which He delivered the oppressed, performed miracles, and defeated death (Acts 10:38).

## JESUS FASTED TO DEMONSTRATE HIS HUMANITY

Jesus' time of physical fasting would have put His humanity in the weakest possible position. But it was there, in His extreme weakness, that He faced the tempter. But in that moment, instead of physical food, Jesus fed on God's Word, the only thing that sustained Him against the prince of darkness.

This is another example of how Jesus truly can identify with us in our weakness. When we pray in Jesus name, especially in times of personal weakness and desperation, we have an intercessor who knows the kind of physical weakness we possess.

Should we choose to fast today, this month, this year, or anytime, we can know that we have an advocate with the Father, Jesus Christ the Righteous, who Himself fasted for 40 days and nights, who knows us wholly, truly, and promises to not leave us or forsake us (Deut. 31:6), even in moments of despair. And in our time of fasting and prayer, we can feast upon His Word, allowing the Lord to do His work in us and preparing us to be ministers in His Kingdom. Therefore, let us keep the fast, and may we learn to rely, not on our own strength, but to take the time in prayer and supplication to feed on the Word of God.

## JESUS FASTED TO LEAVE AN ETERNAL LEGACY FOR THE WOULD-BE DISCIPLES

Jesus fasted as an example to those who would believe in Him. He had said with absolute certainty:

> "...but the days will come, when the bridegroom shall be taken from them, **and then shall they fast**" (Matt. 9:15, emphasis added).

At the time of Jesus' ministry, the Pharisees and the disciples of John the Baptist fasted regularly as an exercise of self-denial and self-discipline; also as a sign of repentance for sin, which implied a mood of sorrow.

By contrast, Jesus indicated that His disciples did not engage in such fasting, since doing so would have been as inappropriate as the friends of a bridegroom fasting at His wedding occasion, which was meant to be a time of celebration. However, Jesus predicted a time period, following His ascension, when His disciples would incorporate fasting in the full expression of their earthly ministry, and they did! *"And when they had fasted and prayed, and laid their hands on them, they sent them away" (Acts 13:3).* The true disciples of Jesus have taken on fasting, among other things, as true expression of their love and reverence to the Lord Jesus.

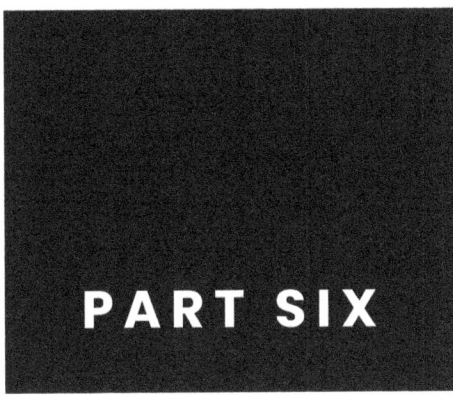

# PART SIX

# UNDERSTANDING THE GUIDELINES FOR PERSONAL AND COLLECTIVE FASTS

# 16

# GUIDELINES FOR PERSONAL AND COPORATE FASTINGS

This section aids the believer in laying the right foundation for his fast. It is like laying the foundation of a house; the bigger and higher the structure, the stronger and deeper the foundation! So it is with fasting, it must never be without adequate preparation in place before you start. In actual fact, the success of your fasting depends greatly on the preparation you put in place before you set out.

Prepare your heart, mind and body for fasting. Fasting is not a spur of the moment practice. It needs to be planned, unless on very rare occasions, God instructs the believer to fast as a matter of urgency. Every great endeavour starts with good preparation. Preparation is critical; ask great achievers! See what the Bible says about the value of preparation: *"So Jotham became mighty, because he prepared his ways before the Lord his God" (2 Chr. 27:6).* As a matter of fact, fasting must be declared – the beginning and duration of any particular fast - must be pre- planned and pre-determined.

First, make sure you are medically able to fast before attempting it. Hear the insightful caution of St John Chrysostom:

*"If you cannot go without eating all day because of an ailment of the body, beloved one, no logical man will be able to criticise you for that. Besides, we have a Lord who is meek and loving (philanthropic) and who does not ask for anything beyond our power. Because he neither requires the abstinence from foods, neither that the fast take place for the simple sake of fasting, neither is its aim that we remain with empty stomachs, but that we fast to offer our entire selves to the dedication of spiritual things, having distanced ourselves from secular things... because human nature is indifferent and gives itself over mostly to comforts and gratifications, for this reason the philanthropic Lord, like a loving and caring father, devised the therapy of the fast for us, so that our gratifications would be completely stopped and that our worldly cares be transferred to spiritual works..."*

Some people may be able to undertake a one-day partial fast with juice, perhaps, because of a medical condition. God understands their unique situations and would not expect them to harm their "temple" (1 Cor. 6:19) in order to be spiritual.

# DECIDING THE PARAMETERS OF YOUR FAST

## STEP 1: SET YOUR OBJECTIVE

*"Holy and lawful fasting has...objectives. We use it either to weaken and subdue the flesh that it may not act wantonly, or that we may be better prepared for prayers and holy meditations, or that it may be a testimony of our self-abasement before God when we wish to confess our guilt before him"* - **John Calvin**.

Determine the Purpose of the fast. The need to set an objective for fasting cannot be over-emphasised. If the Lord leads us to fast, He will always burden our hearts with an objective – reason for the sacrifice, reason to seek Him beyond the threshold of daily devotional prayer. We should prayerfully ascertain what that is, so that our efforts can be channelled to achieving such goals.

Accordingly, you need to ask yourself, *'Why am I fasting?'* Is it for spiritual renewal, for guidance, for healing, for the resolution of problems, for special grace to handle a difficult situation? Ask the Holy Spirit to clarify His leading and objectives for your fasting. This will enable you to pray more specifically and strategically. The position is not in any way different with corporate fasts as Bruce Clarke explains, *"Why are we fasting as a church? As we start the year, we ask for... Repentance – we need to seek God about growing in holiness (Dan. 9). Wisdom – we need to seek God for the future directions of the church (Acts 13:1-3). Renewal – we need to seek God for him to renew our first love of him (2 Chr. 7:14 & Rev 2:4-5), Spiritual Power – we need to seek God for him to fill us by his Spirit so that we are empowered for ministry. (Luke 4:1-14). Gospel Growth & Mission - we need to seek God for the lost being found this year and many coming to Christ (Acts 13:1-3)."* So, set an objective for your fast. Fasting without a clear objective is like flying an airplane without any particular destination. You can well imagine what the outcome is likely to be!

## STEP 2: MAKE YOUR COMMITMENT

Here is where you take your fast to the "drawing board" like an Architect, and get a structure for the journey. It is where, among other things, you decide the following upfront: what type of fast you will be undertaking, the duration of the fast, what physical and spiritual activities you will restrict, for example, freeing yourself from some of your usual daily and weekly activities (TV movies, video, and games), for the duration of the fast.

Further, you will have to decide how much time each day, you will devote to prayer and Bible reading. Making these commitments ahead of time will help you sustain your fast when physical temptations and life's pressures tempt you to violate it (Matt. 6:16-18; 9:14-15).

## STEP 3: PREPARE YOURSELF SPIRITUALLY

1. Enter into a fast with a positive faith. Begin your time of fasting and prayer with an expectant heart, believing God to reward you. God requires positive faith from all those that seek Him, *"But without faith it is impossible to please him: for he that cometh to God must believe that he is, and that he is a **rewarder of them that diligently seek him**"* (Heb. 11:6, emphasis added).

Biblical fast, no doubt, helps us in our fervent and desperate search for God. We are also warned that *"...whatsoever is not of faith is sin" (Romans 14:23)*. If you determine to seek God diligently by fasting, you have the scriptural right to expect that God will reward you. Jesus promised *"thy Father, which seeth in secret, shall reward thee openly" (Matt. 6:18)*. As Bill Bright puts it, if you sincerely humble yourself before the Lord, repent, pray, and seek God's face; if you consistently meditate on His Word, you will experience a heightened awareness of His presence (John 14:21). The Lord will give you fresh, new spiritual insights. Your confidence and faith in God will be strengthened. You will feel mentally, spiritually, and physically refreshed. You will see answers to your prayers. However, it must be acknowledged that a single fast is not a spiritual cure-all. Just as we need fresh in-fillings of the Holy Spirit daily, we also need new times of fasting before God. A 24-hour fast each week has been greatly rewarding to many Christians. It takes time to build your spiritual fasting muscles. If you fail to make it through your first fast, do not be discouraged. Withdraw and refresh yourself, and undertake another fast as soon as possible, until you do succeed. God will reward your faithfulness.

2. More significantly, in the insightful writings of Kenneth Copeland, we learn, "As you embark on the quest for the rewards of fasting, be sure you have met the conditions required to see results. Before you begin a spiritual fast, get rid of all strife, gossip or anything else that is out of the love walk. You MUST be operating in the love of God to see results from a fast. These conditions prevent satan from coming in and destroying the effectiveness of the fast. If you are not operating in love, your fasting will not profit you." Therefore, forgive all who have hurt you and seek forgiveness from all whom you have offended, and (Mark 11:25; Luke 11:4; 17:3, 4). This is because fasting, being such a spiritual exercise, nothing in the physical must be allowed to corrupt or contaminate the process.

3. Read good books on fasting, especially those that contain testimonies of people who have had amazing

breakthroughs through fasting. I particularly find this very helpful when I am fasting. Study scriptures on fasting; major on God's miraculous intervention through fasting. Such scriptures as 2 Chronicles 20, Esther 4, Ezra 8, Luke 4 and whole lot of others will strengthen you greatly.

4. Meditate, go for a walk, take lots of naps, keep journal, and listen to inspirational music, take warm bathes and relax, above all, be sensitive to the Spirit of God.

5. Avoid distractions at all cost. Disconnect from television, radio, newspapers and the Internet for the duration of your fast. This will help you stay focused on the Lord, His word, and the object of your fast.

6. Take a retreat. Though fasting is not necessarily a holiday in the true sense of the word, experience has nonetheless shown, that if maximum benefits are to be derived from any period of fasting, time needs to be taken away from people and the daily routine of life that has dominated our lives, to spend time in quietness and stillness with the lord; gazing at His love, might, glory, beauty and power.

7. Fasting is a time to study God's Word, meditate and pray. To achieve this, have a structured plan for prayer and Bible study. Spend quality time talking to God and allow Him to reveal Himself, His will and purpose to

you in His Word. Meditate on the attributes of God, His love, sovereignty, power, wisdom, faithfulness, grace, compassion, and others (Psalm 48:9,10; 103:1-8, 11-13).

8. Finally, given that the very foundation of fasting and prayer is repentance, attention must be paid to our spiritual state of mind. Unconfessed sin will hinder your prayers. Here are several things you can do to prepare your heart: Confess every sin that the Holy Spirit calls to your remembrance and accept God's forgiveness (1 John 1:9). Make restitution as the Holy Spirit leads you. Ask God to fill you with His Holy Spirit according to His word in Ephesians 5:18 and His promise in 1 John 5:14, 15. Surrender your life fully to Jesus Christ as your Lord and Saviour; refuse to obey your worldly nature (Romans 12:1,2).

## STEP 4: PREPARE YOURSELF PHYSICALLY

Fasting requires reasonable precautions. Consult your doctor first, especially if you take prescription medication or have a chronic ailment. Some people should never fast without professional supervision.

Physical preparation undoubtedly, makes the drastic change in your eating routine a little easier so that you can turn your full attention to the Lord in prayer. Do not rush into your fast. Prepare your body. Eat smaller meals before starting a fast. Avoid high-fat and sugary foods. Eat raw fruit and vegetables for at least, two days before starting a fast. In addition:

1. It is wise to abstain from strong stimulants such as caffeinated and sugary drinks during a fast, including the artificial sweeteners found in diet drinks. Also, avoid soy protein drinks, which have been known to cause health problems during a fast.

2. Begin with short fasts and gradually move to longer periods of fasts if you desire. If you have never fasted before, you need to start gradually. Do not start with a long fast. There is a wealth of wisdom in starting a life of fasting with a moderate approach. The idea behind it is to prepare or condition the body slowly before moving towards a higher level.

3. Do not be put off by negative reactions such as dizziness, headache, or nausea in the early stage of your fast. Most people have never gone without food for longer than a few hours; this causes some negative reactions in the early days of their fasting. Further, nausea and headaches, during a fast can also result from caffeine withdrawal. So, I recommend, if you are a heavy soda or coffee drinker, start withdrawing about a week before the start of your fast. This should make it much easier, at the same time, less headaches to grapple with. Headaches during early days of fasting are also indication that you have left fasting for too long.

## DURING THE FAST

4. Drink sufficient water after the fast begins. The loss of fluids during the fast takes a toll on the body and creates problems in completing the fast successfully. Of course, if you are to derive maximum health benefits from your fasting, you must drink adequate amount of water in order to get rid of toxins. The use of natural diuretics (substance that reduces the body's water volume by increasing the kidneys' urine production and output) helps in losing the excess fluids, which in turn helps in losing body weight. Ginger has been found to be very useful for this purpose. Thus, using the natural diuretics forms one of the important tips to lose weight fast.

5. If you are on a juice fast, drink raw fruit juices such as apple, grape and pineapple, which are excellent sources of necessary natural sugar to stabilise blood sugar and keep energy levels up. Orange and grapefruit juice are also good, but these are not recommended for arthritis or allergy sufferers. Monitor juice acidity carefully as it can cause canker sores (mouth ulcers). Raw vegetable juices such as carrot, celery, beet or green vegetable combinations are excellent as well. Fresh fruit and vegetable juices can be made in a juice extractor or purchased ready-made (be sure to buy juices without any added sugar). Some of the benefits of drinking raw juice versus bottled ones are that it

does not stimulate digestion (hunger) and it maintains all of its enzymes and nutritional value.

6. Take adequate rest before and during a fast. The smaller the responsibilities and work pressure you are involved in during a fast the better for the journey and ultimate successful completion of the fast. This also helps you to be focused on the assignment at hand.

7. Some people experience vast mood swings during a fast. One moment they are totally focused on God and the next they are wallowing in self-pity, and depression. Knowing that this is likely to happen will help you react properly. Learning to refocus on God and His goodness during this tough emotional time will help when your fast is over and you experience similar emotions.

> *...when we stop feeding the body, the suppressing factor of food is eliminated from the equation and many hidden feelings can often surface…..*

Most of us use food to stay alive physically, but also eat to cover up frustration, anger, stress and other negative emotions. So, when we stop feeding the body, the suppressing factor of food is eliminated from the equation and many hidden feelings can often surface that you were not fully aware of. But it may not be limited to anger. You may also feel a lot of sadness, fear and even sorrow.

The solution is learning to always refocus on God. You must also rely on the Holy Spirit to strengthen you at this crucial time. Generally, these could be signs of the enemy's revenge. Stand your ground, be resolute, and continue with your fast. Note that the devil would do everything possible to cause you to give up, as he feels uncomfortable with your fast.

## STEP 5: PUT YOURSELF ON A SCHEDULE

For maximum spiritual benefits, set aside ample time to be alone with the Lord. Listen to His leading. The more time you spend with Him, the more meaningful your fast will be.

Here is a rough guide you can follow:

**Morning**

Dedicate your fast to the Lord, ask for His leading.

Begin your day with praise and worship.

Read and meditate on God's Word.

Pray fervently concerning the object of the fast. Pray the Word!

Invite the Holy Spirit to work in you to will and to do His good pleasure in you. (Phil. 2:13).

# GUIDELINES FOR PERSONAL AND COPORATE FASTINGS

Invite God to use you. Ask Him to show you how to influence your world, your family, your church, your community, your country, and beyond.

Pray for His vision for your life and the anointing of the Holy Ghost, to do His will.

**Noon**

Return to prayer and God's Word. Study faith-building and lifting-scriptures, especially, relating to the reason of your fast.

**Take a short prayer walk.**

Spend time in intercessory prayer for your church, community's and nation's leaders, for the world's unreached millions, for your family or special needs.

Pray again, even with greater intensity concerning the object of your fast, engage in warfare against all oppositions concerning the subject-matter of the fast.

**Evening**

Get alone for an unhurried time of "seeking His face."

If others are fasting with you, meet together for prayer.

When possible, begin and end each day with your spouse for a brief time of praise and thanksgiving to God. Longer periods of time with our Lord in prayer and study of His Word are often better spent alone.

Avoid caffeinated drinks. And avoid chewing gum or mints, even if your breath is bad. They stimulate digestive action in your stomach. Feed your journal.

## STEP 6: END YOUR FAST GRADUALLY

However, it must be emphasised that the way you begin and conduct your fast will largely determine your success. By following these seven basic steps to fasting, you will make your time with the Lord more meaningful and spiritually rewarding.

Break a prolonged fast gradually with meals that are light and easy to digest, preferably, raw vegetables, fruit, or light soup. Trying to eat too much following a fast will only make you sick and leave you with an unpleasant memory of fasting, and could nullify the physical benefits of the fast. The longer the fast, the more careful you need to be in breaking the fast.

Begin eating gradually. Do not eat solid foods immediately after your fast. Suddenly reintroducing solid food to your stomach and digestive tract will likely have negative, even dangerous, consequences.

## STEP 7: EXPECT RESULTS

God has committed Himself to answer the prayers of His praying saints (Psalm 65:2, 1 John 5:14).

The Bible says in addition, *"... God [will] avenge his own elect, which cry day and night unto him, though he bear long with them?* ***I tell you that he will avenge them speedily"*** *(Luke 18:7-8a, emphasis added).*

If you sincerely humble yourself before the Lord, repent, pray, and seek God's face; if you consistently meditate on His Word, you will experience a heightened awareness of His presence (1 Chr. 7:14, John 14:21). The Lord will give you fresh, new spiritual insights. Your confidence and faith in God will be strengthened. You will feel mentally, spiritually, and physically refreshed. You will see answers to your prayers. Jesus promised unequivocally, that the fasting of the believer shall be rewarded (Matt. 6:16-18). You can count on it.

# GUIDELINES FOR COLLECTIVE FASTING

For a proclaimed or collective fasting, all the guidelines examined under personal or individual fasting apply, including the following:

1. Explain to all participants the objective(s) of the fast.

2. Make sure everyone in the group is willing to fast. Never super-impose fasting on anyone.

3. If you are leading a group of people to undertake a fast, it is always a good idea to spend time teaching a series on the subject. For instance, you could teach on such topics as the meaning of fasting, God's purpose for fasting, the power of fasting, and reward of fasting, well ahead of time.

4. Explain to the fasting candidates some unpleasant reactions they could experience in the course of the fast such as, dizziness, weakness, headaches and sleeplessness.

5. If at all possible, ask all the participants to assemble both mornings and evenings for corporate prayers. Share scriptures about God's intervention through fasting at such meetings, for example, Esther 4:16, 2Chronicles 20.

6. Explain the different types of fast there are: absolute, normal and partial fast; and inform the group what type of fast is being undertaking at any given time.

7. If the fast goes beyond 72 hours, do stress the need for the fasting candidates to take as much fluid as

possible – i.e., if the fast being observed is an absolute one.

8. Create an atmosphere of faith throughout the period of fasting.

9. Teach the participants how to break a fast successfully, especially a fast that goes beyond three days. Emphasise the danger of breaking a fast wrongly.

10. Expose participants to good books on fasting. This has the advantage of helping them learn more about fasting while engaging in the act.

# PART SEVEN

# UNDERSTANDING THE RELATIONSHIP BETWEEN PRAYER AND FASTING

# 17

# THE RELATIONSHIP BETWEEN PRAYER AND FASTING

*We observe that in the scriptures, fasting almost always is linked with prayer. Without prayer, fasting is not complete fasting; it's simply going hungry* -**Joseph B. Wirthlin**.

A connection between prayer and fasting is not specifically explained in scripture. However, a common thread connecting the two seems to run throughout the Bible. It appears that fasting with prayer had to do with a sense of need and dependence, and of abject helplessness in the face of actual or anticipated calamity. Prayer and fasting are combined in the Old Testament in times of mourning, repentance, and deep spiritual need.

The first chapter of Nehemiah describes Nehemiah praying and fasting, because of his deep distress over the news that Jerusalem had been desolated. His many days of prayer were characterised by tears, fasting, confession on behalf of his people, and pleas to God for mercy. So intense was the outpouring of his concerns that it was almost inconceivable he could "take a break" in the middle of such prayer to eat and drink, *"And it came to pass, when I heard these words, that I sat down and wept, and mourned certain days, and fasted, and prayed before the God of Heaven,"* (Neh. 1:4).

The devastation that befell Jerusalem also prompted Daniel to adopt a similar posture: *"So I turned to the Lord God and pleaded with him in prayer and petition, in fasting, and in sackcloth and ashes"* (Dan. 9:3). Like Nehemiah, Daniel fasted and prayed that God would have mercy upon the people, saying, "We have been wicked and have rebelled; we have turned away from your commands and laws" (verse 5).

In several instances in the Old Testament, fasting is linked with intercessory prayer. David prayed and fasted over his sick child (2 Sam. 12:16), weeping before the Lord in earnest intercession (verses 21-22). Esther urged Mordecai and the Jews to fast for her as she planned to appear before the king (Est. 4:16). Clearly, fasting and petition are closely linked. Arthur Wallis shared this conviction, "Fasting is calculated to bring a note of urgency and importance into our praying, and to give force to our pleading in the court of Heaven. The man who prays with fasting is giving Heaven notice that he is truly in earnest".

There are instances of prayer and fasting in the New Testament, but they are not connected with repentance or confession. The prophetess Anna *"never left the temple but worshiped night and day, fasting and praying" (Luke 2:37)*. At the age of 84, her prayer and fasting were part of her service to the Lord in His temple as she awaited the promised Saviour of Israel. Also in the New Testament, the church at Antioch was fasting in connection with their worship when the Holy Spirit spoke to them about commissioning Saul and Barnabas to the Lord's work. At that point, they prayed and fasted, placed their hands on the two men and sent them off. So, we see in these examples that prayer and fasting are components of worshipping the Lord and seeking His favour. Fasting with prayer gives an indication of the sincerity of the people praying in relation to the critical nature of the situations in which they find themselves (2 Chr. 20).

The more critical the situation, the more appropriate it is to fast and pray. In Mark 9, Jesus casts a demon from a boy. The disciples had been unable to deliver the child, although they had previously been given authority over unclean spirits (Mark 6:7). Later, the disciples asked Jesus why they failed in their attempts to free the boy from the demon, and Jesus said, *"This kind can come out only by prayer" (Mark 9:29)*. Matthew's account adds the words "and fasting" (Matt. 17:21). In this particular case, the demon was exceptionally intransigent and obdurate (Mark 9:21-22). Jesus seems to be saying that a determined foe must be met with an equally determined faith. Prayer is a ready weapon in the spiritual battle (Eph. 6:18), and fasting helps to focus prayer and give it resolve.

In His discourse, Jesus spoke of fasting with the same expression He employed in speaking about prayer. He said, *"When you pray," (Matt. 6:16)*.

Secondly, the theme of His teaching on both subjects centred on motive:

> *Moreover when ye fast, be not, as the hypocrites, of a sad countenance: for they disfigure their faces, that they may appear unto men to fast. Verily I say unto you, They have their reward. But thou, when thou fastest, anoint thine head, and wash thy face; That thou appear not unto men to fast, but unto thy Father which is in secret: and thy Father, which seeth in secret, shall reward thee openly (Matt. 6:16-18).*

The theology of fasting is a theory of priorities in which believers are given the opportunity to express themselves in an intensive and undivided devotion to the Lord and to the concerns of their spiritual lives. This devotion will be expressed by abstaining for a short while from such normal and good things as food or food and drink, so as to enjoy a time of uninterrupted communion with our Father. Our confidence to enter the Most Holy Place by the blood of Jesus (Heb. 10:19), whether fasting or not, is one of the most delightful parts of that "better thing" which is ours in Christ. Prayer and fasting should not be a burden or a duty but rather, a celebration of God's goodness and mercy to His children.

# DIVERGENCE OF OPINION

It has been argued by some that Jesus dealt with fasting as a spiritual exercise distinct from prayer, contending that though fasting and prayer are often linked in scriptures and experience, both stand as distinct disciplines. In other words, they contend that fasting stands on its own ground and may, occasionally, serve a spiritual purpose of its own. They insist that fasting and prayer are two distinct weapons; two instruments of spiritual warfare that can work independently.

According to the proponents of this argument, just as there may be praying without fasting, there may, on occasions, be fasting, truly acceptable to the Lord without praying – at least in the sense of intercession. They argue there was no mention of prayer accompanying the fasts recorded in the book of Esther, for instance. The prophets and teachers in Antioch, they contend, were worshipping and ministering unto the Lord with fasting, rather than with prayer and fasting combined (Acts 13:2). Therefore, they conclude, 'the fact that one is not able to give oneself to long prayers during a long period of fast does not mean that the period not accompanied by prayer is devoid of spiritual power'.

Undoubtedly, this line of reasoning is striking; given that at the height of a lengthy fast is a common experience of physical weakness that makes lengthy and fervent prayer impossible on occasions. But how safe are we, treating the disciplines of prayer and fasting as distinct from each other?

Thomas Ryan was convinced that *"In every culture and religion in history, fasting has been an instinctive and essential language in our communication with the Divine."* McKay agrees, *"While this purpose for fasting obviously only applies to theists, it's quite central for those who do believe in God; in religious scriptures, whenever fasting is mentioned, it's almost always connected with prayer."* In his view, Fasting intersects with and intensifies prayer in several ways; not least the fact that accompanying prayer with fasting shows sincere intention; a view that found acceptance with R. Smith's notion on the subject. He contends, *"These go together; a praying Christian should fast sometimes and a fasting Christian should pray often. It is useless to emphasis one and neglect the other. Jesus said: 'This sort goeth not out*

# THE RELATIONSHIP BETWEEN PRAYER AND FASTING

*but by prayer and fasting'. Much of fasting must be with prayer. If you decide to devote a weekend to fellowship with God in fasting, you must spend the time in prayer and Bible reading. If you determine to fast until God gives you the desire of your heart, you must pass those days in waiting upon God in prayer."* Fasting is calculated to bring a note of urgency and importance into our praying, and to give force to our pleading in the court of Heaven. The man who prays with fasting is giving Heaven notice that he is truly in earnest.

As Lynne M. Baab puts it, *"The fast is somehow a declaration: This thing I'm praying for is so important that I'm willing to set aside my every life — including food — to focus on praying for it."* Second, spiritual fasters will often choose a particular purpose for their fast (a question in need of guidance; a loved one in need of healing) and then use the hunger pangs induced by fasting as a reminder to pray for it; whenever they notice the gnaw of their appetite, they offer up a supplication. Physical hunger also intensifies the urgency of one's prayers. If fasting *"provides physical sensations that point to spiritual realities,"* the desire for food heightens the desire to make known one's deeper needs. Petitioning becomes pleading. Finally, because fasting removes the need to eat, the time one would have used for meals can be used for prayers, which further amplifies their frequency and focus.

It is my earnest opinion that situation that would cause one to forego the pleasures of life, albeit for a period of time, to seek God beyond the limit of prayer, would warrant the engagement of as many weapons of warfare as possible to overcome it. Accordingly, it is my deep conviction that prayer should be 'found' where fasting exists, but not necessarily the other way round.

In the case of lengthy fasts, as stated, direct communication with God should still be maintained in whatever form: both the short prayers that are uttered in short and disjointed phrases throughout the day and night, and the groanings which cannot be uttered (Romans 8:26), still serve as booster rocket, lifting our prayers beyond the boundaries of earth into the Heavenlies. That said, it must be stressed, however, that fasting accompanied with prayer have stronger power to undermine the enemy's stronghold than either of them distinctly.

It is to be noted that fasting without the study of the word of God and communication with God through prayer, is an exercise void of its full potential. Stripped of these disciplines, fasting ceases to be a fast, in my view, but a hunger strike.

# PART EIGHT

# UNDERSTANDING THE BENEFITS OF BIBLICAL FASTING

# 18
# REWARDS AND BENEFITS OF BIBLICAL FASTING

*Well, if God does not reward fasting because we create it and offer it to him to get a recompense, why does he reward it? If, in fact, God himself is the Creator and Sustainer of fasting, why is it that he has appointed this act as an occasion of his reward? The answer is that God is committed to rewarding those acts of the human heart that signify human helplessness and hope in God. Over and over again in Scripture God promises to come to the aid of those who stop depending on themselves and seek God as their treasure and help* – **John Piper.**

The spiritual benefits of fasting are undeniable. God rewards fasting; we have seen that throughout this book, the strongest indication being the word of Jesus in

Matthew 6: 18, *"...and thy Father, which seeth in secret, shall reward thee openly."*

In the words of Marilyn Hickey, *"Fasting and Prayer put you into the Best Possible Position for a Breakthrough. That breakthrough might be in the realm of the spirit. It may be in the realm of your emotions or personal habits. It may be in the realm of a very practical area of life, such as a relationship or finances. What I have seen repeatedly through the years- not only in the Scriptures but in countless personal stories that others have told me -- is that periods of fasting and prayer produce great spiritual results, many of which fall into the realm of a breakthrough. What wasn't a reality . . . suddenly was. What hadn't worked . . . suddenly did. The unwanted situation or object that was there . . . suddenly wasn't there. The relationship that was unloving . . . suddenly was loving. The job that hadn't materialized . . . suddenly did..."*

Any fast undertaken must be done with spiritual wholeheartedness and wisdom. When dealing with our physical body, we must count the cost honestly, and honour the temple of the Holy Spirit.

Let us now examine the various benefits of biblical fasting.

# ANSWERED PRAYER

*"The Lord is near to all who call on him, to all who call on him in truth. He fulfils the desire of those who fear him; he also hears their cry and saves them" (Psalm 145:18-19). "And call upon me in the day of trouble: I will deliver thee, and thou shalt glorify me" (Psalm 50:15).*

Most assuredly, God will reward our fasting with specific response to our specific request (s), if we seek Him with the right motive and in accordance with Scripture. God would answer the request (s) that drove us into fasting, in the first place. Rees Howells firmly believes that the meaning of [seeking] is answer. He held the conviction that prayer which did not procure its answer was meaningless.

The writer of Hebrews declares, *"... God is not unrighteous to forget your work and labour of love, which ye have shewed toward his name..." (Heb.6:10)*. In 2 Chronicles 14:7, King Asa instructed the people of Judah:

*"... Let us build these cities, and make about them walls, and towers, gates, and bars, while the land is yet before us;* **because we have sought the Lord our God, we have sought him, and he hath given us rest on every side. So they built and prospered"** *(emphasis added)*. And in the following chapter – 2 Chronicles 15:1, the Spirit of the Lord spoke through His Prophet and put the position succinctly: "And the

Spirit of God came upon Azariah the son of Oded: And he went out to meet Asa, and said unto him, Hear ye me, Asa, and all Judah and Benjamin; The Lord is with you, while ye be with him; and if ye seek him, he will be found of you; but if ye forsake him, he will forsake you."

God has committed Himself to reward the secret fasting of His fasting saints, openly (Matt. 6:18).

This is a very special honour reserved, only for His fasting believers; so long as they fast with the right motive.

The writer of Hebrews lays a basic principle for approaching God and desiring anything from Him.

Hebrews 11:6 states:

> But without faith it is impossible to please him: for he that cometh to God must believe that he is, and that he is a rewarder of them that diligently seek him.

We are required to approach God on the basis of faith; the only place where answers to prayer are guaranteed and procured; especially, in areas of critical and urgent needs in our lives that have defiled every erstwhile solution. The Psalmist once lamented, *"Deep calls to deep in the roar of your waterfalls; all your waves and breakers have swept over me" (Psalm 42:7).* In this typically beautiful poetry, Psalm 42 expresses a cry from the heart of God's people during a time of trouble. Here, the Psalmist portrays his distress

## REWARDS AND BENEFITS OF BIBLICAL FASTING

figuratively: it is as if waves and breakers were sweeping over him, as they sometimes do!

"Many," the Bible says, "are the afflictions of the righteous," (Psalm 34:19). For the Psalmist, trouble was surging, with one overwhelming swell coming after another. The "deep" trials he faced kept coming, wave after wave, deep after deep.

James Smith and Robert Lee's work on the subject was insightful. They alleged, *"The deep of man's need calleth unto the deep of God's fullness; and the deep of God's fullness calleth unto the deep of man's need. Between our emptiness and His all-sufficiency there is a great gulf. . . . Deep calleth unto deep. The deep mercy of God needs our emptiness, into which it might pour itself. . . . Nothing can fully meet the depth of our need but the depth of His Almighty fullness."* Fasting then becomes the instrument that helps us to reach out to God's fullness in the midst of our emptiness and deepest needs.

In fasting, we acknowledge that our human needs are great, but the riches of God are greater. Our wisdom is shallow, but His knowledge and judgments are unsearchable (Romans 11:33–34). The height, breadth, and depth of God's resources are without measure.

From the depth of his despair, the psalmist found help in the depth of God's goodness, and he was able to say in conclusion, "Why am I discouraged? Why is my heart so sad? I will put my hope in God! I will praise him again—

my Saviour and my God!" (Psalm 42:11, NLT). What a sudden turn of event. Even though we were not told that David fasted in this instance, he relied on God as fasting would have us do, with greater focus.

If there is ever a generation that needs the kind of faith that procures answers to fasting, it's ours; in what Charles Price calls, "meeting our saviour in the garden of answered prayer." However, be warned! The thing we most long for- answered prayer- is the very thing the enemy is most resisting in our time of seeking. You must therefore, be resolute; stand your ground, "...and having done all," stand! (Eph. 6:13). Moreover, it is the nature of God to answer prayers; as an expression or demonstration of His fatherly love to the believer. In Psalm 102:17, the scripture assures us that God "... regards the prayer of the destitute and does not despise their prayer."

God, in His sovereign power, has guaranteed to answer the prayers of His children. He gives the invitation, "Call unto me and I will answer you and show you great and mighty things which thou knoweth not" (Jer. 33:3); and fasting shows Him just, how desperate we are concerning our requests.

John affirms, *"...this is the confidence that we have in him, that, if we ask any thing according to his will, he heareth us: And if we know that he hear us, whatsoever we ask, we know that we have the petitions that we desired of him" (1 John 5:14-15, emphasis added).* The confidence we have in

Him, as a God that answers prayer (v14), is what propels, motivates and induces us to His presence. The Psalmist explains it this way, "O thou that hearest prayer, unto thee shall all flesh come" (Psalm 65:2). God's testimony serves as a divine incentive to His presence. David understood the eternal blessings of staying close to God; in Psalm 16:11, he says, "You will show me the path of life; **In Your presence is fullness of joy**; At Your right hand are pleasures forevermore" (emphasis added). Jabez called on the God of Israel, and "**God granted him that which he requested**" (1 Chr. 4:10, emphasis added).

However, with fasting, we are often rewarded with far greater blessings than we desire; fringe benefits, I call it! As Prophet Isaiah puts it:

"...*they that wait upon the Lord shall renew their strength; they shall mount up with wings as eagles; they shall run, and not be weary; and they shall walk, and not faint*" (Isaiah 40:31). Notice the almost endless list of blessings accruable to those that set everything aside to 'wait' upon the Lord.

In his prayer for the Ephesians Christians, Paul said:

> "Now to him that is able to do exceeding abundantly **above all that we ask or think**, according to the power that woks in us" (Eph. 3:20, emphasis added).

Among the blessings God promised Solomon was, "***And I have also given thee that which thou hast not asked***, *both* *riches, and honour: so that there shall not be any among the kings like unto thee all thy days"* (1 Kings 3:13, emphasis added). For the Corinthian Christians, Paul prayed, "And God is able to make all grace abound toward you; that ye, always having all sufficiency in all things, may abound to every good work" (2 Cor. 9:8).

Unarguably, God has His bonuses for His saints that honour and serve Him with fasting and prayer. He will bless and reward them beyond solving the specific problem that drove them into fasting. He will hear their prayers (Jer. 33:3), but He will give them some extra benefits!

On this note, I encourage you to look up and look beyond. Look beyond your suffering, your sickness, your pain, beyond the affliction, oppression or issue that drove you into fasting. In the words of another, "life is too short to start your today with the broken pieces of yesterday; it will definitely destroy your wonderful today and ruin your great tomorrow." Therefore, begin to live in anticipation of answers to your prayers, the glorious benefits the Lord has reserved for His fasting believers, and the great future ahead of you. If you do, the Lord will turn your mid-night into sunshine.

# FASTING STRENGTHENS INTIMACY WITH GOD

*Almost everywhere at all times fasting has held a place of great importance since it is closely linked with the intimate sense of religion. Perhaps this is the explanation for the demise of fasting in our day. When the sense of God diminishes, fasting disappears* – **Edward Farrell.**

God craves for man's intimacy. No place was this more vividly demonstrated than in the Garden of Eden. The desire of God to establish close relationship with man has not waned ever since. Fasting inflames our Spirit-man to hunger for God. George Pitt reflects, *"Every time I fasted, I establish a new spiritual dimension in my life and had new spiritual authority with people."*

Since the beginning of time, God has longed to enjoy a close relationship with His children. This is why in the Old Testament; the Israelites were instructed to build the Tabernacle; God wanted a dwelling place amongst His people. A place where they could meet with Him and receive a portion of His power and presence.

However, because our sin created a separation between us and God, there were certain regulations and restrictions involved upon entering the Tabernacle—and only the

High Priests were allowed access into the Holy Place. Even still, it was only through the blood sacrifice of animals that the High Priests could receive God's pardon for their sins and the sins of their nation.

This was merely a symbolic representation, a foreshadowing, of what was to come.

Hebrews 9:11-12 says,

> *"But when Christ came as high priest of the good things that are now already here, he went through the greater and more perfect tabernacle that is not made with human hands, that is to say, is not a part of this creation. He did not enter by means of the blood of goats and calves; but he entered the Most Holy Place once for all by his own blood, thus obtaining eternal redemption."*

Jesus poured Himself out as our blood offering to pay for our eternal salvation, to restore mankind back to the Father, and to grant us access into God's powerful and cleansing presence. When He died, the veil was torn. Thus, it is only in Jesus' name that we inherit the gift of salvation.

Hebrews 9:22-24 says,

> *"In fact, the law requires that nearly everything be cleansed with blood, and without the shedding of blood there is no forgiveness. It was necessary, then, for the copies of the Heavenly things to be purified with these sacrifices, but*

*the Heavenly things themselves with better sacrifices than these. For Christ did not enter a sanctuary made with human hands that was only a copy of the true one; he entered Heaven itself, now to appear for us in God's presence."*

I thank God for the finished work of the cross! It is because of that great demonstration of love that we now have this immense privilege of communing with God—at any place and any time. Because of this sacrifice, we can trust that Jesus' name alone ushers us into God's presence and empowers us with these precious benefits of our salvation.

This reality is vitally important to understand. As Christians, we want to experience intimacy with God. It is not just to have our needs met; it is a sign of maturity and sonship in Christ. Those who know the Lord have a sense of desperation for fellowship with Him. He has become our 'daily bread'.

The Psalmist exhibited this fervent love for oneness with Him when he said, "One thing have I desired of the Lord, that will I seek after; that I may dwell in the house of the Lord all the days of my life, to behold the beauty of the Lord, and to enquire in his temple" (Psalm 27:4). And Paul's exuberant quest for intimacy with the Lord was coded in his unweaning hunger for Him. *"That I may know him, and the power of his resurrection, and the fellowship of his sufferings, being made conformable unto his death"* (Phil. 3:10).

The Scriptures show us that God is intimate with those who trust Him. The more we trust God, the more intimately we come to know Him. A felt distance from God is often due to a disruption in trust, such as a sin or disobedience.

The secret of drawing near to God and having Him draw near to us is revealed clearly in the Bible: we draw near to God through faith in Christ who alone gives us access to Him (Heb. 4:14–16, 7:25, Phil. 3:9), and we put our trust in all of His "precious and great promises" (2 Peter 1:4, 2 Cor. 1:20). God is impressed with our faith, not our feats. Where faith is lacking, He is not impressed with our intelligence or the quality of our aesthetic events. *"Without faith it is impossible to please him, for whoever would draw near to God must believe that he exists and that he rewards those who seek him" (Heb. 11:6).* When God sees a believer, whose heart fully trusts His promises and lives by them, He comes to strongly support him and manifests Himself to him.

> *For the eyes of the Lord run to and fro throughout the whole earth, to shew himself strong in the behalf of them whose heart is perfect toward him. Herein thou hast done foolishly: therefore from henceforth thou shalt have wars. (2 Chr. 16:9).*

REWARDS AND BENEFITS
         OF BIBLICAL FASTING

# FASTING BRINGS VICTORIES IN DIFFICULT SITUATIONS

As seen in the life of Jesus, and other cases that would be considered shortly, fasting brings great victories in difficult situations. Author Wallis contends that *"fasting is important – more important, perhaps, than many of us have supposed… when exercised with a pure heart and a right motive, fasting may provide us with a key to unlock doors where other keys have failed; a window opening up new horizons in the unseen world; a spiritual weapon of God's providing, "mighty, to the pulling down of strongholds" (2 Cor. 10:4)"*.

In the first chapter of Joel, we read,

> *"The vine is dried up and the fig tree is withered; the pomegranate, the palm and the apple tree – all the trees of the field- are dried up. Surely the joy of mankind is withered away. Put on sackcloth, O priests, and mourn; wail, you who minister before the altar. Come; spend the night in sackcloth, you who minister before my God; for the grain offerings and drink offerings are withheld from the house of your God. Declare a holy fast; call a sacred assembly. Summon the elders and all who live in the land to the house of the LORD your God, and cry out to the LORD" (Joel 1:12-14).*

## THE TRANSFORMATIONAL POWER OF FASTING

In the passage in context, we are presented with a very gloomy situation that had engulfed and overwhelmed the nation. Indeed, a very depressing situation, only reminiscent of the times we live in now. Everything that could go wrong had, indeed, gone wrong. Israel was in a crisis situation: acute lack, famine, despondence, and bewilderment, all accurately described the situation in the land. Notice, there was no solution anywhere, humanly-speaking.

However, the Lord pointed the people in the right direction - as a way out of their predicament. - The Lord told the people to *"...sanctify a holy fast..." (Joel 2:15)*. Indeed, at such a time that it appears that the Heavens are closed, and all you can see and feel are the very elements that result from a closed Heaven, be rest assured that the supernatural holds the answer! The supernatural must be scaled and accessed for solution in times of crisis, be it in personal life, family, business, church or, as in this case, the nation. The lesson is very clear in this passage: when things are tough, and nothing seems to be working for you in life, or the devil seems to be making a ridicule of you and your destiny, God says, "stop everything and fast." You may have prayed all kinds of prayers, but to no avail. Jesus says, *"... this kind goeth not out but by prayer and fasting" (Matt. 17:21)*. The nation of Israel said, "... Our bones are dried, and our hope is lost: we are cut off for our part..." (Ezek. 37:11). Does this describe your situation today? Have you been praying and believing

## REWARDS AND BENEFITS OF BIBLICAL FASTING

God for certain breakthroughs in life for a long while? You have done everything humanly possible, but there does not seem to be any notable breakthrough, or at best, you are constantly faced with solutions that 'appear for a while and disappear'; Jesus offers fasting as a solution to overcoming such situations. This is consistent with the instruction God gave Israel in Joel 2: 12-13:

> *"Even now," declares the LORD, "return to me with all your heart, with fasting and weeping and mourning. Rend your heart and not your garments. Return to the LORD your God, for he is gracious and compassionate, slow to anger and abounding in love, and he relents from sending calamity."*

Then in Joel 2: 18-32, we have a long list of what God promised to do in response to the fasting of His people, Israel:

> *"Then will the Lord be jealous for his land, and pity his people. Yea, the Lord will answer and say unto his people, Behold, I will send you corn, and wine, and oil, and ye shall be satisfied therewith: and I will no more make you a reproach among the heathen: But I will remove far off from you the northern army, and will drive him into a land barren and desolate... Fear not, O land: be glad and rejoice: for the Lord will do great things. Be not afraid, ye beasts of the field: for the pastures of the wilderness do spring, for the tree beareth her fruit, the fig tree and the vine do yield their strength. Be glad then, ye children of Zion, and*

*rejoice in the Lord your God: for he hath given you the former rain moderately, and he will cause to come down for you the rain, the former rain, and the latter rain in the first month. And the floors shall be full of wheat, and the vats shall overflow with wine and oil. And I will restore to you the years that the locust hath eaten, the cankerworm, and the caterpiller, and the palmerworm, my great army which I sent among you. And ye shall eat in plenty, and be satisfied, and praise the name of the Lord your God, that hath dealt wondrously with you: and my people shall never be ashamed. And ye shall know that I am in the midst of Israel, and that I am the Lord your God, and none else: and my people shall never be ashamed. And it shall come to pass afterward, that I will pour out my spirit upon all flesh; and your sons and your daughters shall prophesy, your old men shall dream dreams, your young men shall see visions: And also upon the servants and upon the handmaids in those days will I pour out my spirit. And I will shew wonders in the Heavens and in the earth, blood, and fire, and pillars of smoke. The sun shall be turned into darkness, and the moon into blood, before the great and terrible day of the Lord come. And it shall come to pass, that whosoever shall call on the name of the Lord shall be delivered: for in mount Zion and in Jerusalem shall be deliverance, as the Lord hath said, and in the remnant whom the Lord shall call"* (Joel 2:18-32).

This is amazing! If you have been brought low through personal defeat; if there is a call in your soul to a deeper walk with the Lord, to a renewed consecration; if there is the challenge of some new task for which you feel ill-equipped, then it is time to separate yourself unto Him in fasting.

## FASTING HELPS US DISCOVER GOD'S WILL

If we expect God to reveal His direction for our lives, we must put Him first. Often, this means putting aside the fulfilment of our physical appetites, so that we can focus our attention on Him. We find a clear example of fasting for direction in 2 Chronicles 20:1-30. Three nations were coming against Judah to destroy them. King Jehoshaphat, the king of Judah, proclaimed a fast for the whole nation and they asked the Lord what they should do. God moved as a result of their prayer and fasting, and gave the people prophetic direction! God told them what to do.

Acts 13:2 is another example of direction given by God to His fasting saints. Here, we find the leaders of the church of Antioch worshipping and fasting. The Holy Spirit used this occasion to tell the church leaders to choose Paul and Barnabas from among their group and send them out to spread the gospel among the Gentiles. So fasting is one of the ways through which we seek God's guidance and direction for our lives.

# FASTING INTENSIFIES THE POWER OF PRAYER

*Fasting is designed to make prayer mount up as on eagles' wings. It is intended to usher the supplicant into the audience chamber of the King and to drive back the oppressing powers of darkness, thereby loosening their hold on those being prayed for. Fasting definitely will give an edge to (a person's) intercession and power ...petition* - **Leonard Le Sourd remarks.**

R.A Torrey concurs *"...If we would pray with power, we should pray with fasting..."*

Fasting supercharges prayer. It ignites and enables the believer to pray with greater fervency, focus and intensity. Fasting restores and amplifies prayer power. It is an effective aid to meaningful prayer. Through fasting, prayer is intensified, spirituality is sensitised, and ministry is more powerfully effective. If prayer is the fire, fasting is the high-octane fuel that makes that fire rage! Fasting deepens and strengthens your prayer life.

It makes you a better intercessor. It enables you to engage in more serious, heart-felt intercessory prayer. (Neh.1:3-4).

In the words of Hallesby:

# REWARDS AND BENEFITS OF BIBLICAL FASTING

*"Fasting gives us that inner sense of spiritual penetration by means of which we can discern clearly, the reasons why the spirit of God would have us pray in exceptionally difficult circumstances. Unceasing, incessant prayer is essential to the vitality of your relationship with the Lord, and your ability to function in the world."*

In the Old Testament, God said:

> "Command Aaron and his sons, saying, This is the law of the burnt offering: It is the burnt offering, because of the burning upon the altar all night unto the morning, and the fire of the altar shall be burning in it" (Lev. 6:9).

Further, we read in the law that the fire on the altar should burn incessantly! After God has lighted the fire, the priest was to ensure that the fire burned always, and never extinguished. How did the priest discharge this onerous responsibility? He was to *"...burn wood on [the altar] every morning, and lay the burnt offering in order upon it; and he shall burn thereon the fat of the peace offerings.* ***The fire shall ever be burning upon the altar, it shall never go out"*** *(Lev. 6:12-13, emphasis added).*

When your prayer life needs revitalisation, embrace the grace of fasting. Your heart will be touched more easily, your spirit will soar higher, and your awareness of His presence will increase. Without prayer and fasting, every Christian will more or less mark time and fail in their purpose.

> *...spiritual reality is more easily discernible through fasting...*

If the power of the spirit is developed to a degree by many through the use of the most powerful agent known to man - prayer and fasting, we will witness the greatest invasion of Heaven on earth. Without a fasting life, prayer becomes ineffective.

In the words of Oswald Sanders, "*... many who practice [fasting] from right motives and in order to give themselves more unreservedly to prayer testify that the mind becomes unusually clear and vigorous. There are a noticeable spiritual quickening and increased power of concentration on the things of the spirit.*"

This means that spiritual reality is more easily discernible through fasting. In a long fast, you are so overwhelmed with His presence that the desires of the flesh are significantly reduced and the spirit rises and soars controlling the soul. In fact, the things of the world become absolutely meaningless. One cannot but agree with Oswald Sanders' view that one of the values of fasting lies in the fact that its discipline "helps us keep the body in its place. It is a practical acknowledgment of the supremacy of the spiritual."

Fasting is still God's chosen way to deepen and strengthen prayer. Without it, your prayer life lacks the requisite vitality and 'fire' to confront the gate of hell, and put the enemy to flight! Answers to prayer, guidance, direction, insight – all flow more freely when fasting is freely and willingly embraced with grace in the heart. Fasting will remove road-blocks and distractions in your prayer life and thus, will intensify your prayer life, drawing you closer to God, to hear Him clearly.

Fasting has established a new spiritual dimension in my life, lifting me to a higher plane of spiritual authority.

# FASTING NOURISHES OUR FAITH

*It is well known that nothing on earth is so desirable as great faith. Many people may wish to have it and may pray for it, and yet there are few who come to possess it* – **Andrew Murray**.

Faith is an indispensable possession of any saint that must live a victorious Christian life. Next to salvation in my view, is faith; and whatever gives life to such a significant component of a believer's life must be held in high esteem.

The Bible says, *"For whatsoever is born of God overcometh the world:* **and this is the victory that overcometh the world, even our faith**" *(1 John 5:4, emphasis added).*

> **Fasting will remove road-blocks and distractions in your prayer life...**

When it comes to faith, what matters is not the size, but the genuineness and pureness of the trust it conveys.

Faith, as small as a mustard seed, can accomplish great things, if it is placed on a great and mighty God. Charles Spurgeon gives a fascinating analogy of the working of faith thus: *"The eye cannot see itself. Did you ever see your own eye? In a mirror you may have done so, but that was only a reflection of it. And you may, in like manner, see the evidence of your faith, but you cannot look at the faith itself. Faith looks away from itself to the object of faith, even to Christ."*

## AN AID TO MORTIFICATION

Fasting mortifies the flesh, and enables our members to break free from bondage (Col. 3:5). The strongholds of the flesh are pulled down, so that faith has no real barriers (2 Cor. 10:3:5). Fasting casts down reasoning, so that we will not listen to the evidence that our senses convey but sets faith loose. It is certain that waiting on God is a richer experience when accompanied with fasting, because fasting subdues the flesh and gives freedom to the spirit.

# REWARDS AND BENEFITS OF BIBLICAL FASTING

As Charles Hodge pointed out *"all eminently pious persons have been more or less addicted to fasting"* proves its undeniable personal spiritual value.

As you live a fasted life, you will not be flesh-ruled, and the power to commit sin is broken! Why? Because when you fast, you are bringing your body into submission. In other words, we find freedom from the passions of the flesh by mortifying them, through fasting. Fasting helps us to tame the wild impulses of our flesh and bring them under the bridle of self-control.

This has the consequent effect of causing the believer to develop and produce the fruit of the Spirit, according to Galatians 5:22.

Eating is something we must do for survival – we have to eat. However, if we can on a periodic basis, incorporate self-denial in our life schedule, then we surely will be able to train our flesh in other areas. Paul said, *"I discipline my body and bring it into subjection, lest, when I have preached to others, I myself should become disqualified" (1 Cor. 9:27 NKJV)*. He said all those who are able to train the flesh would be granted an incorruptible crown as reward for their discipline. The same Paul spoke so articulately about the need to have mastery over the dictates of the flesh. In 1 Corinthians 6:12, he contends, *"All things are lawful unto me, but all things are not expedient: all things are lawful for me,* **but I will not be brought under the power of any"** *(emphasis added).*

Fasting is a way of bringing the flesh under control. It is an exercise of self-denial. Jesus said, *"If any man will come after me, let him deny himself, and take up his cross daily, and follow me" (Luke 9:23 KJV).*

If we can deny ourselves food and drink for a period of time, we should be able to deny our flesh in the realm of sinful desires and in the disciplines of the Christian life such as prayer. When the disciples were asked by Jesus to stand with Him in prayer, they fell asleep, and Jesus said, *"Could you not watch with Me one hour? Watch and pray, lest you enter into temptation. The spirit indeed is willing, but the flesh is weak" (Matt. 26:40-41 NKJV).* If we can gain mastery over the flesh in the area of eating then, we sure are able to control it in every other area of life.

Deeply embedded addictions can be reversed by starving the flesh. We are not powerless. We give control to either the flesh or the Spirit. James 4:5 reminds us that our spirit has "envious yearnings." Do we yield to these yearnings, or do we give in to the pull of the flesh? We will crave more of what we feed. Fasting silences the voice of the flesh.

REWARDS AND BENEFITS OF BIBLICAL FASTING

# FASTING HELPS SUSTAIN THE ANOINTING

Fasting plays a vital role in releasing and sustaining the anointing. Fasting has a direct link with the measure of the grace of God that operates in a believer's life. This is because fasting helps the believer to tune into the spirit realm where his inheritance already exists. When the believer feels dry spiritually or needs a fresh release of the unction of God, fasting is the secret key that unlocks the flood-gate of Heaven and releases such level of grace that nothing else can. Fasting is for spiritual empowerment; without fail it releases astonishing power for outstanding achievements, and great exploits in the kingdom. This is the secret of excelling in the work of the kingdom. The surpassing power of God is available to everyone who desires it and can pay the price for it. Fasting is one infallible means of obtaining it. As said, Jesus the son of God fasted for forty days and nights. If Jesus could have accomplished all His earthly assignment without fasting, why should He do it?

The son of God fasted because He knew there were supernatural blessings, indeed, unction for exploits that could not be obtained any other way. How much more should fasting be a common practice in our lives? Fasting takes the believer from the ordinary realm to

> **Fasting takes the believer from the ordinary realm to the extraordinary.**

the extraordinary. Walking in favour is not a product of luck and coincidence! Breaking free from satanic forces, and life of miseries, agony, mischief, shame and reproach, to the enviable life God has destined for you, takes more than prayer. This was the lesson the Master conveyed to the disciples who could not heal a demon possessed boy, when He said *"...this kind goeth not but by prayer and fasting"* (Matt. 17:20-21). Jesus says, *"If you will lose your life for my sake you will find it" (Matt. 10:39).* The Greek text says, "If you will up that low life, you will find the high life." Fasting is one of the tools that help you shed the low life. As you begin to live a fasted life, the spirit of God begins to change your taste in life, urging you to reach out for that high place in God; the place of excellence, perfection, abundance, and uncommon breakthrough! How does it work? You see, prayer and fasting will cause you to be much more spiritually sensitive to the Lord and His direction for your life.

REWARDS AND BENEFITS
OF BIBLICAL FASTING

# FASTING DEEPENS OUR UNDERSTANDING OF THE WORD OF GOD

In Isaiah 33:6, the prophet declared, *"And wisdom and knowledge shall be the stability of thy times..."* This scripture is as applicable today as it was when Isaiah first spoke it concerning the sins that plagued Judah centuries ago. The situation is even worse now!

Today, the threat of a global pandemic, murder, acts of terrorism, and nuclear mishaps dominates our media headlines and tries to instil fear in our hearts. We live in a time of heightened fear, heightened anxiety and uncertainty as never before. It is comforting to know that God has promised to provide stability in these precarious times through knowledge and wisdom.

One of the personal rewards of fasting as promised by God is: *"Then [after you have fasted] shall thy light break forth as the morning..." (Isaiah 58:8).*

The Bible says,

> "The entrance of thy word giveth light, and giveth understanding to the simple" (Psalm 119:130).

> **With fasting, there is so much more depth to Scripture than what readily meets the eye without it.**

Bible revelations come as a result of a conscious 'downloading' from the source – God, through His word. The word of God has the power to change us!

Revelation 1:3, pronounces a blessing upon "... *he that readeth, ... and hear the words of this prophecy, and keep those things which are written therein...*" All you have to do to be blessed is to just read the book and keep what you have read. Those who understand this truth have an unwavering devotion to the study of the word of God. Moreover, we are instructed that, "***All scripture is** given by inspiration of God, and is **profitable** for doctrine, for reproof, for correction, for instruction in righteousness*" (2 Tim. 3:16, emphasis added). In other words, every portion of the Bible is profitable to the reader. You can see why Paul repeatedly instructed his protégée – Timothy on the value of building his life and ministry on the power and unparalleled wisdom of the word of God. In the first instance, he admonished Timothy, "Till I come, give attendance to reading..." (1 Tim. 4:13). Later, he enjoined him to, "***Study to shew thyself approved unto God***, *a workman that needeth not to be ashamed, rightly dividing the word of truth*" (2 Tim. 2:15, emphasis added).

# REWARDS AND BENEFITS OF BIBLICAL FASTING

Fasting gives an edge, greater understanding, and weight to the word of God. As you get intimate with God through fasting, your spirit-man is ignited to receive deeper insight, and such profound revelation from God that you would not receive otherwise. With fasting, there is so much more depth to Scripture than what readily meets the eye without it. Some truth will never be discovered until you study the word of God with fasting.

It was while Moses was settling the destiny of Israel with God through fasting that God gave him a powerful revelation that became known as – the Ten Commandments. Fasting lightens up your inner-man to hear and receive from God with clarity. I am always amazed at the depth of insight, illumination and revelations I receive from the word of God as I take time to sit and stare at the text, carefully considering its contents and application, while undergoing a fast.

*"One of the greatest spiritual benefits of fasting"* according to Elmer Towns, *"is becoming more attentive to God – becoming more aware of our own inadequacies and His adequacy, our own contingencies and His self-sufficiency – and listening to what He wants us to be and do…"*

This impacts not only your ability to receive revelations from God, but also your delivery of same. Fasting puts you in the realm where you practically "rightly divide the word of truth" (2 Tim. 2:15). Fasting sharpens you to better deliver the word of God as His divine mouthpiece.

Here, we are not talking about eloquence or fluent and persuasive speaking. No, we are about something far more serious! Paul puts it this way,

> "And I, brethren, when I came to you, came not with excellency of speech or of wisdom, declaring unto you the testimony of God. Howbeit we speak wisdom among them that are perfect: yet not the wisdom of this world, nor of the princes of this world, that come to nought: But we speak the wisdom of God in a mystery, even the hidden wisdom, which God ordained before the world unto our glory: Which none of the princes of this world knew: for had they known it, they would not have crucified the Lord of glory. But as it is written, Eye hath not seen, nor ear heard, neither have entered into the heart of man, the things which God hath prepared for them that love him.
>
> But God hath revealed them unto us by his Spirit: for the Spirit searcheth all things, yea, the deep things of God. For what man knoweth the things of a man, save the spirit of man which is in him? even so the things of God knoweth no man, but the Spirit of God. Now we have received, not the spirit of the world, but the spirit which is of God; that we might know the things that are freely given to us of God. **Which things also we speak, not in the words which man's wisdom teacheth, but which the Holy Ghost teacheth; comparing spiritual things with spiritual** (I Cor. 2:1, 6-13, emphasis added).

According to Ecclesiastes 10:10, *"If an axe is dull, And one does not sharpen the edge, then he must use more strength…"*

Fasting gives you that cutting edge of the anointing for kingdom service.

Speaking of fasting, Jesus said, *"And no man putteth new wine into old bottles: else the new wine doth burst the bottles, and the wine is spilled, and the bottles will be marred: but new wine must be put into new bottles"* (Mark 2:22), indicating that fasting plays a significant role in preparing old wineskins to once again receive new wine. Fasting has a powerful purging and shaping effect upon the vessel, preparing it for the release of the new wine of God.

## FASTING DEFINES AND EQUIPS THE VESSEL OF GOD

Fasting makes the man and woman of God! It is God's equipping tool! It shapes and defines the vessel of God. Hear Paul on this matter: In 2 Corinthians 6:3-10, he writes:

> *"…But in all things approving ourselves as the ministers of God, in much patience, in afflictions, in necessities, in distresses, In stripes, in imprisonments, in tumults, in labours, in watchings, in fastings; By pureness, by knowledge,*

> *by long suffering, by kindness, by the Holy Ghost, by love unfeigned, By the word of truth, by the power of God, by the armour of righteousness on the right hand and on the left, By honour and dishonour, by evil report and good report: as deceivers, and yet true; As unknown, and yet well known; as dying, and, behold, we live; as chastened, and not killed; As sorrowful, yet alway rejoicing; as poor, yet making many rich; as having nothing, and yet possessing all things (emphasis added).*

In this instance, Paul listed the various ways through which he had proved himself as a true minister of God. It is noteworthy that in verse 5, two of the factors identified by Paul are: 'watchings and fastings.'

Further, in 2 Corinthians 11: 23-27, Paul recounts:

> *Are they ministers of Christ? (I speak as a fool) I am more; in labours more abundant, in stripes above measure, in prisons more frequent, in deaths oft. Of the Jews five times received I forty stripes save one. Thrice was I beaten with rods, once was I stoned, thrice I suffered shipwreck, a night and a day I have been in the deep; In journeyings often, in perils of waters, in perils of robbers, in perils by mine own countrymen, in perils by the heathen, in perils in the city, in perils in the wilderness, in perils in the sea, in perils among false brethren; In weariness and painfulness, **in watchings often, in hunger and thirst, in fastings** often, in cold and nakedness" (emphasis added).*

In verse 27, Paul again joined watching with fasting. More significantly, the phrase "in fastings often," was indicative of Paul's devotion to the sacrificial life of self-denial. Paul saw fasting, not just as a power-booster, but as a means of drawing closer to God and enhancing intimacy with the Father.

This is a clear example for today's disciples of Jesus to emulate.

George Liddell was famous for saying, *"Give me a man – one man, One mighty prophet of the Lord, And I will give you peace on earth, Bought with a prayer and not a sword."* Real leaders, close to the heart of God are in short supply.

Throughout the Bible, God searched for such leaders, and He still does today. In Jeremiah 5:1, God instructs, *"Go up and down the streets of Jerusalem, look around and consider, search through her squares. If you can find but one person who deals honestly and seeks the truth, I will forgive this city."* Also in (1 Sam. 13:14), "…The Lord has sought out a man after his own heart and appointed him ruler of his people, because you have not kept the Lord's command." Finally, God said, *"… I sought for a man among them, that should make up the hedge, and stand in the gap before me for the land, that I should not destroy it: but I found none"* (Ezekiel 22:30).

The Bible teaches that when God does find a vessel that is ready to be used and embraces the sacrifice of self-denial, that vessel is used to the limit.

In His insightful writing, Paul says:

> *"In a great house there are not only vessels of gold and of silver, but also of wood and of earth; and some to honour, and some to dishonour. If a man therefore purge himself from these,* **he shall be a vessel unto honour, sanctified, and meet for the master's use, and prepared unto every good work** *(2 Tim. 2:20-22, emphasis added).*

The Church is painfully in need of such vessels!

Closely linked to one of the points just discussed, is the fact that fasting is the gateway to receiving deep revelations from God. In God, we grow in revelation and our ability to relate with, understand, interpret and retain spiritual knowledge.

> *"Then [when you have fasted] your light will break out like the dawn, and you will be healed quickly" -Isaiah 58:8 (CEB).*

When you fast, "your light", meaning, divine revelation, insight, illumination will break through. The Bible says, "The entrance of your word gives light…" (Psalm 119:130). In other words, when you fast, you begin to receive revelations from the light of His Word. God gives you new insight and understanding—all of which will strengthen your faith to receive from Him.

# REWARDS AND BENEFITS OF BIBLICAL FASTING

Bob Sorge sums it up, *"One of the prime benefits of self-denial [fasting] is that it empowers us to hear more clearly from God. Answers, guidance, direction, insight – all seem to flow more freely when self-denial is freely and willingly embraced with grace in the heart."*

Fasting helps you to tune into the spirit realm where healing and all of your inheritance that already belong to you exist. Spiritual fasting will shut down the influences of the five physical senses, so you can walk in the spirit. Your healing, your victory, your strength, your faith and the power of God are all in the spirit realm.

Therefore, when you fast, you prepare your spirit-man to receive revelations. It may be to understand something from the Word which you know God has been trying to reveal to you, but you have not been able to grasp.

As you fast, expect to hear from God—expect revelations from Him. As you do this, remember that fasting is laying things aside just to be with God.

We see throughout the Bible, instances where people needed to fast to gain spiritual insight. It wasn't that God wasn't speaking; it was simply because the circumstances had become louder than His still, small voice. When Daniel fasted from luxurious foods offered to him by the king, he had heightened spiritual insight. Before Jesus embarked on His earthly ministry, He went on a 40-day fast to subdue His flesh and strengthen the power of the Holy Spirit within Him.

Martin Luther once said:

*"It is right to fast frequently in order to subdue and control the body. For when the stomach is full, the body does not serve for preaching, for praying, for studying, or for doing anything else that is good. Under such circumstances God's Word cannot remain."*

When you get in an atmosphere of fasting, praying and listening to God, you are giving Him opportunity to speak. You are making room for Him to move and change things.

In fact, if you enter into a spiritual fast by the leading of the Holy Spirit, you will often find that in the process, you are not hungry because your spirit man has become the dominant force. Your body just cannot scream as loud because your spirit is in control. That is why when Jesus fasted for 40 days, He was only "afterword hungry" (Matt.4:2)

The fact that fasting subdues the flesh so you can better hear from God, might just be all that you need for your desired breakthrough. As Kenneth Copeland puts it, *"Fasting shuts down the influence of the body, so the spirit man can dominate. As you stay in The WORD and in fellowship with God, you will not be flesh-ruled. You will glorify God in your body."*

REWARDS AND BENEFITS
OF BIBLICAL FASTING

# FASTING IS A CATALYST FOR SPIRITUAL GROWTH

*Our seasons of fasting and prayer at the Tabernacle have been high days indeed; never has Heaven's gate stood wider; never have our hearts been nearer the central Glory* – **Charles Spurgeon.**

When you fast, you feed your spirit-man to grow. If you must operate in power, fasting should be a common practice in your life. Indeed, those who seek God through the discipline of fasting are open to the reservoir of God's power, because fasting creates a deep hunger for God. When you get hungry for God, He gets closer to you. Spiritual hunger moves God, and causes doors to open. How hungry are you for God? Notice, I did not ask how hungry you are for His blessings and provisions, but how hungry you are for Him; His face, not just His hands! Does your soul long and faint for the presence of the Lord? We very much need to be hungry if we are going to see God move in our lives.

David shared a deep sentiment for genuine hunger for God:

"… My soul yearns, yes, even pines and is homesick for the courts of the Lord; my heart and my flesh cry out and sing for joy to the living God... For a day in Your courts is better than a thousand [anywhere else]; I would rather be a doorkeeper and stand at the threshold in the house of my God than to dwell [at ease] in the tents of wickedness" (Psalm 84:1,2,10; Amp.). Also in Psalm 42:1, he writes, "As the deer pants for streams of water, so my soul pants for you, my God" (NIV).

Deep hunger for God shuts down the influence of the flesh, so that the Holy Spirit can take His dominant place in your lives.

## FASTING TURNS DEFEAT TO TRIUMPH

In the book of Judges we find an account of Israel engaging in a battle with the tribe of Benjamin for its atrocity. God gave the rest of the tribes of Israel directives to fight against the tribe of Benjamin.

The children of Israel asked God, *"Which of us shall go up first to battle against the children of Benjamin? And the LORD said, Judah shall go up first" (Judges 20:18).*

Mysteries unfolded in this battle. Even though Judah went into battle with the tribe of Benjamin at the express instruction of God, the former faced a woeful defeat in the hands of their enemies. Scripture records that the children of Benjamin killed twenty-two thousand men of the Israelites (verse 21). Those who survived the onslaught or massacre had a story to tell! However, with bitter tears, they enquired again from God, *"Shall I go up again to battle the children of Benjamin my brother? And the LORD said, Go up against him"* (verse 23).

With God's approval, they headed for battle again, *"And Benjamin went forth against them out of Gibeah the second day..." (v24).*

Sadly, this battle ended with Israel being defeated again with great loss of lives – this time - eighteen thousand men (v 25).

Israel had lost a total of forty thousand military men in just two days. At the second defeat, and in a desperate move to avert this national disaster, Israel decided to seek God with fasting. The Scripture says,

> "Then all the children of Israel, and all the people, went up, and came unto the house of God, and wept, and sat there before the LORD, **and fasted that day until evening**, and offered burnt offerings and peace offerings before the LORD" (Judges 20:26 KJV, emphasis added).

> "Then all the Israelites, including its army, went up from there to Bethel and wept, remaining there in the LORD's presence, **fasting throughout the day until dusk**, when

they offered burnt offerings and peace offerings in the LORD's presence" (Judges 20:26 NIV, emphasis added).

There is great power in *"remaining ...in the LORD's presence..."* until victory is obtained. With fasting, Israel did something rather different from the two previous occasions; their desperation had led them to set everything aside to seek the Lord, all day with fasting.

One of the leaders stood before the Ark of the Covenant and asked God:

*"Shall I yet again go out to battle against the children of Benjamin my brother, or shall I cease? And the LORD said, Go up; for tomorrow I will deliver them into thine hand" (verse 28).*

Notice there was something different with the response Israel received from God, after they had sought Him with fasting. God, not only gave Israel permission to go to battle, as in the two previous occasions, but He gave them a firm assurance of victory over their enemies! Further, God told them precisely, when the battle would be won. Fasting will always make God's mind clearer in any situation, to you. With this assurance, the Israelites braced themselves for the greatest supernatural intervention they had had in battle for a long time. Fasting made the difference! God kept His promise. The Word says, *"The Lord smote [defeated] Benjamin before Israel" (verse 35).*

They should have known to fast in the first place, yet they waited until two catastrophic defeats before they saw the need to fast for deliverance. In adverse situations believers do everything, but the very thing that is needed to overcome the problem - fasting. On their first two attempts, the Israelites tried to fight the battle by themselves. They suffered defeat, they encountered loses! But when they fasted, the story changed - the Lord won the battle for them! Warfare cannot be engaged in casually. Neither can carnal weapons be employed in fighting spiritual battles. Paul says,

> *"For the weapons of our warfare are not carnal, but mighty through God to the pulling down of strongholds (2 Cor. 10:4, KJV).*

As we use these weapons, we are guaranteed victory in whatever situation we are in.

## FASTING AVERTS GOD'S IMPENDING JUDGMENT

*"The Ninevites believed God. They declared a fast, and all of them, from the greatest to the least, put on sackcloth. When the news reached the king of Nineveh, he rose from his throne, took off his royal robes, covered*

*himself with sackcloth and sat down in the dust. When God saw what they did and how they turned from their evil ways,* **he had compassion and did not bring upon them the destruction he had threatened**" *(Jonah3:5, 10 NIV, emphasis added).*

The power to turn an imminent crisis around was never more clearly demonstrated in the Bible than when a pronouncement of divine judgement – *"Yet forty days,"* declared Jonah, *"and Nineveh shall be overthrown!" (Jonah 3:4)* – was averted through repentance, prayer and fasting. The trio still offer profound deliverance in the face of seemingly hopeless situations today. Far more than the prayer and fasting, I strongly believe, that the people' show of remorse and utter repentance moved God to change His mind in relation to His judgement.

The reaction of the Ninevites was spontaneous; God viewed this as a sign of repentance too. It is baffling how modern believers fast and pray in the face of apparent sins without any move whatsoever to repent of their sins. They expect God to be bought over with their fasts. Repentance and restitution are subjects, in my view, that should be taught in our Churches with unflinching, determined and uncompromising emphasis. Repentance still delivers high premium; and fasting softens the heart and puts it in the right mode to easily want to repent of any wrong done.

The Ninevites' repentance expressed through fasting, moved God to repent of the judgement He had anticipated to bring upon them.

Jonah's message of impending judgment was therefore, averted by the repentance of the people of Nineveh. This is very much in keeping with the nature of God. God has already guaranteed:

> *"At what instant I shall speak concerning a nation, and concerning a kingdom, to pluck up, and to pull down, and to destroy it; If that nation, against whom I have pronounced, turn from their evil, I will repent of the evil that I thought to do unto them" (Jer. 18:7, 8).*

The position of God on the subject is very clear, when man repents from his sins; God repents in respect of His judgment. The repentance of man provokes God's repentance concerning judgment! The Old Testament abounds with instances of this kind. It therefore, stands to reason that whenever God finds *'a faithful few'* who stand in the gap, even in the eleventh hour, and humble themselves with prayer and fasting, He is ever ready to change His mind in relation to any judgment He might have intended to execute. This is vividly demonstrated in the conversation Abraham had with God about the impending judgment on Sodom and Gomorrah:

> *The men turned away and went toward Sodom, but Abraham remained standing before the Lord. Then*

*Abraham approached him and said: "Will you sweep away the righteous with the wicked? What if there are fifty righteous people in the city? Will you really sweep it away and not spare the place for the sake of the fifty righteous people in it? Far be it from you to do such a thing—to kill the righteous with the wicked, treating the righteous and the wicked alike. Far be it from you! Will not the Judge of all the earth do right? (Gen.18:22-25).*

*The Lord said, "If I find fifty righteous people in the city of Sodom, I will spare the whole place for their sake" (verse 26).*

*"Then Abraham spoke up again: Now that I have been so bold as to speak to the Lord, though I am nothing but dust and ashes, what if the number of the righteous is five less than fifty? Will you destroy the whole city for lack of five people? If I find forty-five there, he said, I will not destroy it. Once again he spoke to him, What if only forty are found there?" He said, For the sake of forty, I will not do it. Then he said, May the Lord not be angry, but let me speak. What if only thirty can be found there? He answered, I will not do it if I find thirty there. Abraham said, "Now that I have been so bold as to speak to the Lord, what if only twenty can be found there? He said, For the sake of twenty, I will not destroy it. Then he said, May the Lord not be angry, but let me speak just once more. What if only ten can be found there? He answered, For the sake of ten, I will not destroy it. When the Lord had finished speaking with Abraham, he left, and Abraham returned home" (Gen. 18:27-33).*

All that God was looking for was a man. If He could find more than one that is even better (Deut. 32:30), that would make up the hedge, and stand in the gap before God for the land, that He would not destroy it (Ezekiel 22:30). We can see that clearly demonstrated in these accounts.

A condition for not destroying the land was God finding people (intercessors) to stand in the gap, pleading for mercy from God for the land. God has already covenanted, "If my people, which are called by my name, shall humble themselves, and pray, and seek my face, and turn from their wicked ways; then will I hear from Heaven, and will forgive their sin, and will heal their land (2 Chr. 7:14).

This no doubt, speaks of the nature and character of God, and it is profoundly encouraging and of immense benefit in the midst of an impending judgment!

However, Arthur Wallis takes this subject to a significant dimension, and argues, *"This action on the part of God presents us with a theological problem. God is revealed as omniscient, as One Who seers the end from the beginning. His foreknowledge is complete and infallible. His character and counsel are immutable. 'I the Lord do not change.'"* He insists that scripture affirms that these are the attributes of the Almighty, and our common sense tells us that without them God would not be God. And he asks *"Why, then, do so many Old Testament Scriptures affirm that 'The Lord repented' or changed His mind?"*

God no doubt, foreknew when He sent Jonah, that Nineveh would repent and His judgment would be averted. This then appears to be God's purpose for sending him, that He might extend mercy towards them. This nature of God is sufficiently demonstrated in 2 Peter 3:9:

> "...but is longsuffering toward us, not willing that any should perish, but that all should come to repentance" (KJV).

## FASTING HELPS TO STIR THE GIFTS OF GOD IN THE BELIEVER

This section has two important dimensions: First, is the realisation that every child of God has spiritual gifts invested in him:

> "For I say, through the grace given to me, to every man that is among you, not to think of himself more highly than he ought to think; but to think soberly, according as God has dealt to every man the measure of faith" (Romans 12:3).

According to Jamieson-Fausset-Brown Bible Commentary:

> "Faith...is the inlet to all the other graces, and so, as the receptive faculty of the renewed soul—that is, "as God hath

*given to each his particular capacity to take in the gifts and graces which He designs for the general good."*

The truth here is that God has given to every man "the measure of faith" (spiritual gifts); so we should consider what gifts, abilities, and knowledge we have, not of ourselves, but from God.

The second dimension has to do with the deployment, utilisation or usage of the grace which we have received of the Lord. It makes sense to argue that the deployment of the grace of God in our lives only comes into play when we realise that we have been endued with such grace.

In 1 Timothy 4:6-14, we see Paul admonishing his spiritual son – Timothy, along those lines. In it, he turned the spotlights on the issue of Spiritual Gifts.

> "Neglect not the gift that is in you, which was given you by prophecy, with the laying on of the hands of the presbytery" (verse 14).

Notice, after a very lengthy admonition, Paul did not forget the all-important matter of spiritual gifts – drawing Timothy's attention to this vital issue he needed to fulfil his ministry. He said to him in the succeeding verse:

*"Meditate on these things; give yourself wholly to them;* **that your profiting may appear to all**" *(verse 15, emphasis added).*

If this matter was of such importance to Timothy, it should be for us today.

# FASTING BRINGS DELIVERANCE

*And Jesus rebuked the devil; and he departed out of him: and the child was cured from that very hour. Then came the disciples to Jesus apart, and said, Why could not we cast him out? And Jesus said unto them, Because of your unbelief: for verily I say unto you, If ye have faith as a grain of mustard seed, ye shall say unto this mountain, Remove hence to yonder place; and it shall remove; and nothing shall be impossible unto you. Howbeit this kind goeth not out but by prayer and fasting (Matt. 17:18-21).*

*"Is this not the fast I have chosen? To loose the bands of wickedness...."—Isaiah 58:6 (KJV)*

We have been delivered from the power of darkness through the sacrifice of Jesus. The price has been paid! If there is any oppressive yoke, the believer can and should be freed from it. Yet, anyone failing to receive deliverance from bondage is being held back by one thing—unbelief.

This was what happened to Jesus' disciples. Jesus had given them power to cast out the devil, *"Behold, I give unto you power to tread on serpents and scorpions, and over all the power of the enemy: and nothing shall by any means hurt you" (Luke 10:19).* And they even exercised some of that power, *"And the seventy returned again with joy, saying, Lord, even the devils are subject unto us through thy name" (verse 17).* But in Matthew 17: 18-21, we find them stumped by a particularly tough situation when they were unable to drive a demon out of a young boy. When they later asked Jesus why they had failed, He said, *"This kind can come out by nothing but prayer and fasting" (verse 21, NKJV).*

Now, fasting in this instance would not have changed God. No doubt, it would have changed the disciples' position, and the overall outcome of the disciples' encounter with the sick boy! Jesus had already directed the disciples to cast the demon out. The demon was undoubtedly, stubborn and when he resisted, the disciples slipped into unbelief. Had they been fasting and praying, they would have been far more spiritually equipped to deal with the situation; doing exactly what Jesus did in the circumstance —cast the demon out! (See John 14:12.).

If you are born again, and you face attacks, oppositions, and temptation to submit to darkness, start fasting. Delve into the word of God as never before, until you gather enough faith to launch an attack, and prevail against the forces of darkness that are contending with your destiny. Remember, *"…the weapons of our warfare are not carnal, but mighty through God to the pulling down of strong holds;" (2 Cor. 10:4).*

Beyond the fasting, Jesus has already obtained deliverance through the completed work of Redemption. The Holy Spirit who lives inside you knows how to pray in order to bring the deliverance. Fasting simply brings the spirit man, which is in union with the Holy Spirit into ascendance over the flesh. It also limits the influence of the physical appetites, so you can more effectively hear from and respond to the Holy Spirit.

## FASTING QUICKENS YOUR SPIRIT

Wesley Duewel maintains that *"fasting can deepen hunger for God. Spiritual hunger and fasting have a reciprocal power. Each deepens and strengthens the other. Each makes the other more active. All of the most intense forms of prevailing prayer can be deepened, clarified, and greatly empowered by fasting."* Allene Van Oirschot agrees and explains that *"fasting empties the stomach and the mind; freeing up space to refuel our bodies with the Bread of Life…"* Fasting, he insists, *"not only fills the body, but it also renovates a Christian physically and mentally."*

Fasting ignites and empowers the spirit of man, as it regenerates the mind and Spirit. In what Ronnie Floyd likens to the 'Holy Spirit conducting an orchestra into a beautiful symphony' through fasting, your spirit gets enflamed and stands in attention and alertness to the Holy Spirit. The book of Proverbs teaches that the *"spirit of man is the candle of the LORD, searching all the inward parts of the belly" (Prov. 20:27)*. Further, Paul contends, *"For what man knoweth the things of a man, save the spirit of man which is in him? even so the things of God knoweth no man, but the Spirit of God" (1 Cor. 2:11)*. The Holy Spirit works in conjunction with the spirit of man. This spiritual phenomenon happens when you pray and fast. Your life 'gets it together' even in the midst of enormous challenges. All of your members (mind, will, emotions and body), become subject to the Spirit's leadership who has made your spirit more alive than ever before. When this dynamics happens, you can face the future boldly with God. That is where you enter into a new dimension of life; you rise to a new level in life and scale new horizon to pursue God; because you understand that sometimes, a perceived obstacle is just an opportunity in disguise. In the words of Henry Ford, *"When everything seems to be going against you, remember that the airplane takes off against the wind, and not with it."* In order to succeed in life, your desire for success should be greater than your fear of failure.

No doubt, God does the work, but your submission to Him in prayer and fasting discharges and projects you like a rocket launcher to heights in life.

# FASTING PRECIPITATES THE LATTER RAIN AND SERVES AS A GATEWAY TO RESTORATION

Fasting is a pre-condition for the latter rain. God promises that He would send His people the much needed former and latter rain, in response to the united prayer and fasting of His people. In a spiritual application of the rain, God says:

> *And it shall come to pass afterward, that I will pour out my spirit upon all flesh;* and your sons and your daughters shall prophesy, your old men shall dream dreams, your young men shall see visions: And also upon the servants and upon the handmaids in those days will I pour out my spirit (Joel 2:28-29 emphasis added).

Notice the word "afterward" in verse 28, which indicates that something happened as an aftermath of a previous action. The obvious question is: after what? After we have consecrated a fast, call a solemn assembly, seek God with corporate prayer and fasting. Then God promises, not only to avert the crises the nation faces, but commissions the ministry of the Holy Spirit, whose work it is to outlast the immediate generation that Prophet Joel served.

# REWARDS AND BENEFITS OF BIBLICAL FASTING

On the day of Pentecost, Apostle Peter addressing the crowed that assembled made reference to the prophecy of Prophet Joel, indicating that the phenomenon of the outpouring of the Holy Spirit that was seen on the day of Pentecost, was a fulfilment of the prediction (prophecy) of Prophet Joel:

> *"But this is that which was spoken by the prophet Joel: And it shall come to pass in the last days, saith God, I will pour out of my Spirit upon all flesh: and your sons and your daughters shall prophesy, and your young men shall see visions, and your old men shall dream dreams: And on my servants and on my handmaidens I will pour out in those days of my Spirit; and they shall prophesy: And I will shew wonders in Heaven above, and signs in the earth beneath: blood, and fire, and vapour of smoke"(Acts 2:16-18).*

So, here we see God not only seeking a fast as a remedy to the present predicament of the people, but as a springboard to letting loose the floodgate of Heaven, the beginning of the release of the most powerful presence of God on earth, through the ministry of the Holy Spirit. Fasting opens the great door of the supernatural, the place where the Church is better positioned to exercise power, dominion and authority!

The position of the Church today is reminiscent of the days in which Elijah prophesised rain upon earth, after a long period of draught. At first, it seemed as though there was not going to be a response whatsoever from Heaven, but thank God, he persisted, kept praying, banging on the gate of Heaven, and believing God. Eventually, his resilience paid off.

The Church must show the same level of commitment, dedication and devotion.

After a long period of draught in the Church, we must set our minds on using the key God has given the Church to finally unlock the Heavens in order to experience the "abundance of rain" again upon the earth, in the Church, and in our nation!

> *"And Elijah said unto Ahab, Get thee up, eat and drink; for there is a sound of abundance of rain. So Ahab went up to eat and to drink. And Elijah went up to the top of Carmel: and he cast himself down upon the earth, and put his face between his knees, And said to his servant, Go up now, look toward the sea. And he went up, and looked, and said, There is nothing. And he said, Go again seven times. And it came to pass at the seventh time, that he said, Behold, there ariseth a little cloud out of the sea, like a man's hand. And he said, Go up, say unto Ahab, Prepare thy chariot, and get thee down that the rain stop thee not. And it came to pass in the meanwhile, that the Heaven was black with clouds and wind, **and there was a great rain**..." (I Kings 18: 41-45, emphasis added).*

The Church would not only hear the *"sound of the abundance of rain"* as a result, but would move swiftly; in the spirit of

God, to overcome the onslaught of the Jezebel of our time that wants to vex and limit the church of God.

# FASTING AS A MEANS OF MINISTERING TO THE LORD

*And there was one Anna, a prophetess, the daughter of Phanuel, of the tribe of Aser: she was of a great age, and had lived with an husband seven years from her virginity; And she was a widow of about fourscore and four years, which departed not from the temple, but served God with fastings and prayers night and day. And she coming in that instant gave thanks likewise unto the Lord, and spake of him to all them that looked for redemption in Jerusalem. And when they had performed all things according to the law of the Lord, they returned into Galilee, to their own city Nazareth. And the child grew, and waxed strong in spirit, filled with wisdom: and the grace of God was upon him (Luke 2: 36-40).*

Fasting is not, in the least, limited to asking for things from the Lord. It can be a vehicle to reaching out to God in active and unrestricted worship. Anna, in the passage above, spent at least fifty years in the temple, worshipping the Lord, day and night with fasting. Yet, she was not fasting because of any particular situation in her life; she needed the Lord's intervention for. What a devotion! The act of using fasting as a means of ministering to the Lord was exemplified by the leaders of the Church in Antioch:

> "Now there were in the church that was at Antioch certain prophets and teachers; as Barnabas, and Simeon that was called Niger, and Lucius of Cyrene, and Manaen, which had been brought up with Herod the tetrarch, and Saul. **As they ministered to the Lord, and fasted, the Holy Ghost said, Separate me Barnabas and Saul for the work whereunto I have called them.** And when they had fasted and prayed, and laid their hands on them, they sent them away" (Acts 13:1-3, emphasis added).

This is no doubt, a pattern worth emulating.

The question is: how far can we take worship in our relationship with God? Throughout Scripture we see worship mentioned in both the Old and New Testaments, in significant ways. The clear instruction of the Holy Spirit notwithstanding, the Church did not rush to send Saul and Barnabas off to the mission field; they further prayed and fasted before they were released. Why? Because their assignment was a significant spiritual affair. Notice the Bible speaks of them as *"being sent forth by the Holy Ghost..."* (Acts13:4). How different this practice is from what we see in the Church today. Clearly, the Bible admonishes, "... *whatsoever things were written aforetime were written for our learning, [instruction NASB] that we through patience and comfort of the scriptures might have hope*" (Rom. 15:4).

A careful look at modern missionary zeal, depth, spirituality, commitment, spiritual authority, ambition, and fruit would leave one to think that for most of them, fasting and prayer was not part of their preparation and send-off. How sad!

# FASTING HELPS TO TURN THE BATTLE AGAINST THE ENEMY

*When the devil, the foe and the tyrant, sees a man bearing this weapon [fasting], he is straight-away frightened and he recollects and considers that defeat which he suffered in the wilderness at the hands of the Saviour; at once his strength is shattered and the very sight of this weapon, given us by our Commander-in-chief, burns him* –**Isaac of Syria.**

The weapons we fight satan with are not physical (2 Cor. 10:4); they are spiritual! The weapons should therefore, match the warfare! satan cannot be eliminated with an AR-15 rifle, but we can fast and pray. Those two high calibre spiritual bullets do substantial damage. Open the Word of God, pray, meditate, and worship for the fatal blow: "Not by might nor by power but by My spirit,' sayeth the Lord" (Zech. 4:6 KJV).

When Israel fought against the tribe of Benjamin, in one day, Israel lost thirty-two thousand soldiers, then they set aside a day to fast and pray:

> *"Then all the children of Israel, and all the people, went up, and came unto the house of God, and wept, and sat there before the LORD, and fasted that day until even, and offered burnt offerings and peace offerings before the Lord" (Judges 20:26).*

This singular act changed the dynamics of the battle; it made Israel to gain an upper hand against their erstwhile enemies - the tribe of Benjamin.

In 2 Chronicles 20, fasting produced a similar outcome. Through fasting, Jehoshaphat defeated the Moabites, Ammonites and their allies:

> *"It came to pass after this also, that the children of Moab, and the children of Ammon, and with them other beside the Ammonites, came against Jehoshaphat to battle. Then there came some that told Jehoshaphat, saying, There cometh a great multitude against thee from beyond the sea on this side Syria; and, behold, they be in Hazazontamar, which is Engedi" (2 Chr. 20:1-2).*

How did Jehoshaphat react to the enemy's invasion? The Bible says:

> *"And Jehoshaphat feared, and set himself to seek the Lord,* **and proclaimed a fast throughout all Judah.** *And Judah gathered themselves together, to ask help of the Lord: even out of all the cities of Judah they came to seek the Lord… O our God, wilt thou not judge them? for we*

*have no might against this great company that cometh against us: neither know we what to do: but our eyes are upon thee" (verses 3-4,12 emphasis added).*

Judah was invaded by enemies too powerful for her military might to contend with physically, so she resolved to fight the battle using spiritual weapons – prayer and fasting. The nation of Judah had expressed total and absolute dependence on God in the midst of the battle, through fasting. A fasting Saint is saying to God, "Lord, help me in this battle; I cannot deliver myself!" God takes this level of trust very seriously. The Bible says, "He will keep the feet of His saints, and the wicked shall be silent in darkness; for by strength shall no man prevail (1 Sam. 2:9). The outcome of this simple trust in God was astonishing:

*"For the children of Ammon and Moab stood up against the inhabitants of mount Seir, utterly to slay and destroy them: and when they had made an end of the inhabitants of Seir, every one helped to destroy another. And when Judah came toward the watch tower in the wilderness, they looked unto the multitude, and, behold, they were dead bodies fallen to the earth, and none escaped" (2 Chr. 20:23).*

We can be confident in our time of crisis if we let our great need drive us to prayer and fasting before God. In verses 1-4, we see the great need of the people of Judah; in verses 5-13, Jehoshaphat's prayer revealed the greatness of their

God in battle; verses 14-30 predicated their faith in God and the victory He brought about.

Queen Esther also proclaimed a fast to avert an imminent danger – a total annihilation of the Jewish race as orchestrated by Haman being the Prime Minister of the Persian Empire. The situation was bleak and inexorable! With the persuasion of her uncle, Mordecai, to take action necessary to avert the ruthless and atrocious situation, Esther could not think of any solution more efficacious to dealing with the impending danger than fasting.

She instructed:

> *"Go, gather together all the Jews that are present in Shushan, and fast ye for me, and neither eat nor drink three days, night or day: I also and my maidens will fast likewise; and so will I go in unto the king, which is not according to the law: and if I perish, I perish" (Est. 4:16).*

The fast not only thwarted the enemy's plot, but God used it to make Haman the sole victim of his heinous and vicious plan. The Bible says the king ordered Haman to be hanged *"on the gallows that he had prepared for Mordecai"* (Est. 7:10).

In the place of shame, fear, frustration, despair and bitterness that the Jews had been subjected to for so long in the hands of Haman and his accomplices, the Bible says, "The Jews had light, and gladness, and joy, and honour"

(Est. 8:16). The record is even more intriguing, and far more encouraging in Esther 9:1, *"On the thirteenth day of the twelfth month, the month of Adar, the edict commanded by the king was to be carried out. On this day the enemies of the Jews had hoped to overpower them,* **but now the tables were turned and the Jews got the upper hand over those who hated them***" (NIV, emphasis added).*

Finally, in 1 Samuel 7, the Philistines posed a grave threat to Israel. It was a dreadful and atrocious time. Consequently, Samuel called Israel to fasting and prayer.

> *"And Samuel said, Gather all Israel to Mizpeh, and I will pray for you unto the Lord. And they gathered together to Mizpeh, and drew water, and poured it out before the Lord,* **and fasted on that day,** *and said there, We have sinned against the Lord. And Samuel judged the children of Israel in Mizpeh. And when the Philistines heard that the children of Israel were gathered together to Mizpeh, the lords of the Philistines went up against Israel. And when the children of Israel heard it, they were afraid of the Philistines. And the children of Israel said to Samuel, Cease not to cry unto the Lord our God for us, that he will save us out of the hand of the Philistines" (I Sam. 7: 5-8, emphasis added).*

What was the outcome of the people response to the enemy's threat?

The Bible says,

*"...Samuel cried unto the Lord for Israel; and the Lord heard him. And as Samuel was offering up the burnt offering, the Philistines drew near to battle agains Israel: but the Lord thundered with a great thunder on that day upon the Philistines, and discomfited them; and they were smitten before Israel. And the men of Israel went out of Mizpeh, and pursued the Philistines, and smote them, until they came under Bethcar. Then Samuel took a stone, and set it between Mizpeh and Shen, and called the name of it Ebenezer, saying, Hitherto hath the Lord helped us. So the Philistines were subdued, and they came no more into the coast of Israel: and the hand of the Lord was against the Philistines all the days of Samuel. And the cities which the Philistines had taken from Israel were restored to Israel, from Ekron even unto Gath; and the coasts thereof did Israel deliver out of the hands of the Philistines. And there was peace between Israel and the Amorites" (verses 9-14).*

It is fitting, at this stage, to outline the various spiritual weapons Israel used against their enemy, according to the scripture in context,

**1. Repentance** – *"And Samuel spake unto all the house of Israel, saying, If ye do return unto the Lord with all your hearts, then put away the strange gods and Ashtaroth from among you, and prepare your hearts unto the Lord, and serve him only: and he will deliver you out of the hand of the Philistines. Then the children of Israel did put away Baalim and Ashtaroth, and served the Lord only...and said there, We have sinned against the Lord" (Verses 3,4,6).*

**2. Unity Prayer** – And Samuel said, Gather all Israel to Mizpeh, and I will pray for you unto the Lord. "**And they gathered together to Mizpeh,** and drew water, and poured it out before the LORD, and fasted on that day, and said there, We have sinned against the LORD. And Samuel judged the children of Israel in Mizpeh. And when the Philistines heard that the children of Israel were gathered together to Mizpeh, the lords of the Philistines went up against Israel…" (Verses 5-7, emphasis added). Pius Quensnel observed "God is found in union and agreement. Nothing is more efficacious than this in prayer." Mahesh Chavda agrees, and contends, "…When the corporate prayers of many joined in the name of [Jesus] are mounted on the booster rocket of our corporate fasting, our prayers suddenly take on a supernatural power that few on earth have ever seen! You can be sure that satan fears this holy combination as no other. Every time God's people have dared to lay aside their differences or personal concerns long enough to seek God in prayer and fasting together in one mind and one accord, terrible things have happened to his dark kingdom, while wonderful and miraculous things have happened to mankind".

**3. Prayer** – *"And Samuel said, Gather all Israel to Mizpeh, and I will pray for you unto the Lord…And the children of Israel said to Samuel, Cease not to cry unto the Lord our God for us, that he will save us out of the hand of the Philistines"* *(Verses 5, 8).*

**4. Fasting** – *"And they gathered together to Mizpeh, and drew water, and poured it out before the Lord, and fasted on that day..." (verse 6).*

**5. Sacrifice** – *"And Samuel took a sucking lamb, and offered it for a burnt offering wholly unto the Lord..." (verse 9).*

It is evident that this consideration opens up a vast field for reflection. We shall give consideration to one or two of the many directions in which it applies:

First, none of the other spiritual weapons, as stated, would have had the effect of bringing the enemy to defeat, had Israel not repented of her sinful ways before the Lord, first. Under the leadership of Samuel, Israel prioritised repentance! Sin would have simply rubbed the other spiritual weapons of their potency. What a lesson!

Certainly, *"...the LORD'S hand is not shortened, that it cannot save; neither his ear heavy, that it cannot hear: "But your iniquities,"* insists the Lord's prophet, *"have separated between you and your God, and your sins have hid his face from you, that he will not hear" (Isaiah 59:1-2).* Indeed, "... sin is a reproach to any people" (Prov. 13:34).

Second, this biblical account demonstrates the supremacy of spiritual power over carnal powers. While the Philistines relied on carnal weapons (the arm of flesh), Samuel and his people utilised spiritual weapons. This was vividly demonstrated in yet, another battle the children of Israel were involved in. Reminiscent of the account in context, God again assured His people victory over their enemies ahead of the battle. God told His people:

> *"Be strong and courageous, be not afraid nor dismayed for the king of Assyria, nor for all the multitude that is with him: for there be more with us than with him: With him is an arm of flesh: but with us is the Lord our God to help us, and to fight our battles. And the people rested themselves upon the words of Hezekiah king of Judah" (2 Chr. 32:7-8).*

David remarks, *"Some trust in chariots, and some in horses: but we will remember the name of the Lord our God."* What is the outcome of where they placed their trust? *"... we are risen, and stand upright" (Psalm 20:7-8).*

The two passages quoted above highlight the outright superiority of spiritual weapons over carnal (physical weapons), and the outcome of Israel battle with the Philistines clearly demonstrated this. In 2 Corinthians 10:4, Paul says, *"... the weapons of our warfare are not carnal, but mighty through God to the pulling down of strongholds".* Notice, according to Paul, spiritual weapons are formidable because God is involved in their usage. They are applied through God.

# 19

# THE HEALING VALUE OF FASTING

*Fasting will detoxify your body, including your bloodstream, organs, and brain. With this detox you will see huge energy bursts. You will be able to think more clearly as the "brain fog" clears. Fasting has been shown to build immunity...*
-Dr J. Harold Smith.

The practice of fasting is as old as humanity. More than two thousand years ago, fasting was a custom advocated by the school of the natural philosopher, Aslepiades for curative purpose. It was used for religious purposes, and as a method for restoring health.

If done correctly, fasting has powerful and long-lasting health benefits. Part of the benefits God promises those that fast is:

*"...thine health shall spring forth speedily..." (Isaiah 58).*

God has a passion to see us walk in health, and has made adequate provisions for that:

*"Surely he hath borne our griefs, and carried our sorrows: yet we did esteem him stricken, smitten of God, and afflicted. But he was wounded for our transgressions, he was bruised for our iniquities: the chastisement of our peace was upon him; and with his stripes we are healed" (Isaiah 53:4, 5).*

Also, the Bible says,

*"How God anointed Jesus of Nazareth with the Holy Ghost and with power: who went about doing good, and **healing all that were oppressed of the devil**; for God was with him" (Acts 10:38, emphasis added).*

These are some key healing provisions in the Bible we can rely on in times of health challenges. In 1 Peter 2:24, the Bible attributes the healing of our bodies to the finished work of Jesus on the Cross, and it says:

*"Who his own self bare our sins in his own body on the tree, that we, being dead to sins, should live unto righteousness: **by whose stripes ye were healed**" (emphasis added).* A conviction also shared by the Psalmist, "Who forgiveth all thine iniquities; who healeth all thy diseases; Who redeemeth thy life from destruction..." Indeed, we have

been redeemed from sicknesses, from diseases, from pain and destruction" (Psalm 103:3).

Our bodies are capable of instigating their own healing if we allow them the opportunity. Fasting is such an opportunity. Fasting instigates powerful therapeutic processes that can help people recover from mild to severe health conditions. Some of the most common ones are high blood pressure, asthma, allergies, chronic headaches, inflammatory bowel disease and a host of others.

The reason fasting has such a powerful effect on healing the body, it has been alleged, is because in the fasting state, the body scours for dead cells, damaged tissues, fatty deposits, tumours and abscesses, all of which are burned for fuel or expelled as waste. Diseased cells are dissolved in a systematic manner, leaving healthy tissue. There is a remarkable redistribution of nutrients in the body through fasting.

To start with, the process of digestion involves many bodily functions. In most cases, the blood which is often required in the process of digestion is now liberated to work in other areas of the body. This gives the body more energy, given that so much energy is not being utilised in the digestion process. Consequently, a great deal of energy is released into your immune system as it works to detoxify your body, rebuild and refurbish your system.

Secondly, during an extended fast, you are not taking in foods that contain toxins. As a result the body has less foreign matters to grapple with. Fasting provides a period of concentrated physiological rest during which time the body can devote its self-healing mechanisms to repairing and strengthening damaged organs. The process of fasting also allows the body to cleanse cells of accumulated toxins and waste products.

It is amazing, the Bible says in Isaiah 58:8 that with fasting *"your health shall spring forth…"* Healing springs forth "speedily," from within our bodies, without any external interventions.

Dr Don Colbert, MD who is an expert in the field of nutritional health contends:

"Fasting allows your body to heal by giving it a rest. All living things need to rest, including you. Even the land must rest, which was a principle God gave to the ancient agrarian Jewish nation regarding their fields. Every seventh year they were not permitted to grow any crops at all. They had to let the land lie fallow so that it could re-establish its own mineral and nutrient content (Leviticus 25:1-7) … Every winter many animals will hibernate or rest for a season. Every night when you sleep, you give rest to your body and mind. Blessed rest is as much a law of the universe as gravity. It is also a powerful principle of healing. Think about it: when an animal is injured or sick, what does it do? It finds a resting place where it can lap up water, and it quits eating while it heals. This is natural, instinctual wisdom that God has placed within the animal Kingdom." Dr Frank McCoy alluded to these facts: *"I have made a most exhaustive study of every method of cure, from mind cure to modern surgery and gland therapy, and I have never found a single method that could approach even closely, in its results, the benefits which come from some form some of the fasting cure."*

Generally, fasting is associated with the following:

• Helps you lose weight and keep it off.

• Cleanses your body of metabolic wastes and toxins.

• Improves your skin tone and health, making you looks younger.

• Stimulates new cell growth, making you feel younger.

• Strengthens your immune system and natural defences.

• Improves glandular health and hormonal balance.

• Increases mental clarity.

• Enhances your moods, enjoy a more positive outlook.

• Gives you more energy and enthusiasm.

• Enhances your spiritual connection.

- Rests to the digestive track.

- Rejuvenates physically, mentally and spiritually.

- Energises cells.

## THE PSYCHOLOGICAL BENEFITS OF FASTING:

There are some psychological benefits that are derivable from fasting. These include a calming effect, the ability to focus on priorities and a generalised improvement in mental functioning. Studies have shown that fasting leads to positive psychological experiences, such as increased sense of reward and achievement. Through fasting, the symptoms of many mental illnesses have improved tremendously, and in some cases, disappeared altogether.

# 20

# THE OPEN REWARD OF THE SECRET FAST OF THE BELIEVER

*Moreover, when you fast, do not be like the hypocrites, with a sad countenance. For they disfigure their faces that they may appear to men to be fasting. Assuredly, I say to you, they have their reward. But you, when you fast, anoint your head and wash your face, so that you do not appear to men to be fasting, but to your Father who is in the secret place; and your Father who sees in secret will reward you openly (emphasis added, Matt. 6: 16-18).*

There is a dimension to this scripture that is noteworthy, and needs to be explored. Whereas we fast to achieve specific blessings from the Lord, we see from the scripture in context, that God has His reward for those that fast.

This is beyond and in addition to the specific issues that drove us into fasting. No doubt, the Lord will answer your prayer concerning the subject-matter of your fast; the very thing that warranted the fast, but, as said, He has His own reward for you in addition - just for fasting. This is my firm conviction; that those that fast have a special reward from God, apart from God's commitment to reward them also with whatever motivated them to fast. "Shall reward them openly" is an emphatic promise of the Master to those that fast, whatever be the reason (s) for the fast, as long as it is within the confines of the word of God, and with the right motive.

According to Kenneth Copeland, reward for personal fast is on two different levels:

*One is from the admiration of men… [but] "an open reward comes from God when you fast in secret." You can believe for this reward when you go into the fast. Be specific about its purpose. If you believe for the reward from the onset, the pressure on your physical body will lessen.*

Notice that these rewards also apply to proclaimed fast. You can fast as a congregation and claim the benefits (rewards) of fasting for that congregation. God calls us to fast to bring the spirit of man in authority over the flesh. This enhances intercession and sets the captive free.

In Zechariah 8:19, God pronounced a blessing on the people for their dedication and devotion to fasting:

*Thus saith the LORD of hosts: The fast of the fourth month, and the fast of the fifth, and the fast of the seventh, and the fast of the tenth, shall be to the house of Judah joy and gladness, and cheerful feasts; therefore love the truth and peace.*

These blessings are still available today to the people of God that worship and honour Him with fasting.

## PERSONAL REWARD FOR FASTING ACCORDING TO PROPHET ISAIAH

In the 58th chapter of his book, Prophet Isaiah dealt comprehensively with the rewards that are accruable to the people (believers) who set time aside, to fast with the right motive.

In verse 6, he spelt out the attitude and motive that characterise the fasting that is pleasing to God:

*Is not this the fast that I have chosen? To loose the bands of wickedness, to undo the heavy burdens, and to let the oppressed go free, and that ye break every yoke?*

Indeed, as earlier established, there are many bands of wickedness that cannot be undone, many yokes that cannot be broken, and many oppressed that cannot be set free, until believers take their God-given position of authority and deal with these manifestations of the devil, through prayer and fasting. Certainly, satanic strongholds that have dominated and held lives bound, and destroyed such institutions as marriages, families, and wreak havoc on erstwhile great and enviable destinies can be terminated!

The Psalmist prayed:

> "Oh let the wickedness of the wicked come to an end..." (Psalm 7:9).

Isaiah continues by describing the attitude that is required by the fasting believer towards people – especially toward the needy and the oppressed, as stated:

> Is it not to deal thy bread to the hungry, and that thou bring the poor that are cast out to thy house? When thou seest the naked, that thou cover him; and that thou hide not thyself from thine own flesh? (verse 7).

You see, fasting is man getting into a very serious business with God! Every fast must be God-ward (towards God). Therefore, if it must have the approval of God and attract the desired reward, it has got to be done God's way – with the right commitment, motive and attitude. On the contrary, if we do as we please when we fast, like the Pharisees in Jesus' day, God will ask the same question he put to the Israelites in Prophet Zechariah's day:

> "... When ye fasted and mourned ... those 70 years, did ye at all fast unto me, even to me?" (Zech. 7: 5-6).

Fasting of the kind that God is pleased with must be associated with sincere and practical charity in our relationships with those close to us – especially the poor and needy – those that need our help in material and financial matters.

In subsequent verses, Isaiah once again re-visited the issue in relation to the attitudes associated with the "God kind of fast", and contrasted these attitudes with genuine practical charity:

> ...If thou take away from the midst of thee the yoke, the putting forth of the finger, and speaking vanity: And if thou draw out thy soul to the hungry, and satisfy the afflicted soul... (Verse 9-10).

This is very crucial, and must be adhered to if our fasting will achieve the desired result.

*"The yoke, the putting forth of the finger, and speaking vanity"*, according to Derek Prince could be *"summed up in three words: legalism, criticism, and insincerity."* An important requirement for the God chosen fast is to avoid judging and accusing others. Our words must be with grace and seasoned with salt as believers, *"Let your speech be always with Grace, seasoned with salt, that you may know how to answer" (Col. 4:6).*

Isaiah lists numerous blessings promised by God to those who practice the kind of fasting that is acceptable to God. Fasting is a requirement for victorious living.

# 21

# SPECIAL FASTING BLESSINGS

*"...Then shall thy light break forth as the morning, and thine health shall spring forth speedily: and thy righteousness shall go before thee; the glory of the LORD shall be thy rereward. Then shalt thou call, and the LORD shall answer; thou shalt cry, and he shall say, Here I am. If thou take away from the midst of thee the yoke, the putting forth of the finger, and speaking vanity; And if thou draw out thy soul to the hungry, and satisfy the afflicted soul: then shall thy light rise in obscurity, and thy darkness be as the noonday: And the LORD shall guide thee continually, and satisfy thy soul in drought, and make fat thy bones: and thou shalt be like a watered garden, and like a spring of water, whose waters fail not. And they that shall be of thee shall build the old waste places: thou shalt raise up the foundations of many generations; and thou shalt be called, The repairer of the breach, The restorer of paths to dwell in. If thou turn away thy foot from the sabbath, from doing thy pleasure on my*

*holy day; and call the sabbath a delight, the holy of the LORD, honourable; and shalt honour him, not doing thine own ways, nor finding thine own pleasure, nor speaking thine own words: Then shalt thou delight thyself in the LORD; and I will cause thee to ride upon the high places of the earth, and feed thee with the heritage of Jacob thy father: for the mouth of the LORD hath spoken it" (Isaiah 58: 8-14).*

There are a host of exceptional blessings that God has, and has specially reserved to honour His fasting saints with!

These blessings are listed in successive stages:

1. Isaiah described the blessing of health and righteousness:

*Then your light shall break forth like the morning, your healing shall spring forth speedily. And your righteousness shall go before you; The glory of the Lord shall be your rear guard" (verse 8).*

The NIV appears to paint the picture more vividly:

*Then your light will break forth like the dawn, and your healing will **quickly appear**; then your righteousness will go before you, and the glory of the Lord will be your rear guard(emphasis added).*

This is in consonance with Malachi 4:2, *"But to you who fear My name The Sun of Righteousness shall arise with healing in His wings; And you shall go out And grow fat like stall-fed calves"* There is a dealing (degree of relationship) with God that provokes divine healing. Fasting gives you opportunity to activate your faith for healing.

> **Fasting guarantees outstanding results where prayer is limited.**

Notice the phrase, "then your righteousness will go before you." What has righteousness got to do with it, you may ask? Jesus said, "But seek first the kingdom of God and His righteousness, and all these things shall be added to you." (Matt. 6:33).

*"...the glory of the Lord shall be thy rereward."* The word "rereward" literally means unique and exceptional reward, rare or uncommon protection.

The Lord Himself becomes your protector, such that if people try to ensnare you, God will fight on your behalf because you are one of His consecrated saints. This puts us on the offensive in the battle against the enemy of our souls.

2. In verse 9, Isaiah describes the blessing of answered prayer:

*"Then you shall call, and the Lord will answer; You shall cry, and He will say, 'Here I am.'"* Here, God commits Himself to answer your prayers and supply your needs. Are you tired

## THE TRANSFORMATIONAL POWER OF FASTING

> **Why will God answer your prayer when you fast? It is because when you fast, you are open to Him. Your spiritual capacity to hear and receive from Him is significantly increased.**

of praying without results? Fasting guarantees outstanding results where prayer is limited. God has committed Himself to answer your prayers when you fast. Why will God answer your prayer when you fast? It is because when you fast, you are open to Him. Your spiritual capacity to hear and receive from Him increases exponentially. Fasting puts you in readiness to be filed by God.

3. Further, Isaiah described the blessings of guidance and fruitfulness:

*"And if thou draw out thy soul to the hungry, and satisfy the afflicted soul; then shall thy light rise in obscurity, and thy darkness be as the noon day: And the Lord shall guide thee continually, and satisfy thy soul in drought, and make fat thy bones: and thou shalt be like a watered garden, and like a spring of water, whose waters fail not" (vv. 10-11).*

Notice, "then shall thy light rise in obscurity." What an amazing promise both of God's continual guidance and unceasing supply of His blessings. Promise of prosperity and abundance in the middle of recession! Or of a global pandemic! It must be noted, however, that these things have already been provided for in Christ, fasting merely positions us to receive them.

4. Next, Isaiah describes the blessings of restoration:

> "And they that shall be of thee shall build the old waste places: thou shalt raise up the foundations of many generations; and thou shalt be called, The repairer of the breach, The restorer of paths to dwell in" (verse 12).

> *It must be noted, however, that these things have already been provided in Christ, fasting merely puts us in a better position to receive them.*

The blessing of restoration is huge in the mind of God for His people. In Joel 2:25, God says, *"And I will restore to you the years that the locust hath eaten, the cankerworm, and the caterpiller, and the palmerworm, my great army which I sent among you."* In Amos 9:11,14, God declares,

> "In that day will I raise up the tabernacle of David that is fallen, and close up the breaches thereof; and I will raise up his ruins, and I will build it as in the days of old... And I will bring again the captivity of my people of Israel, and they shall build the waste cities, and inhabit them; and they shall plant vineyards, and drink the wine thereof; they shall also make gardens, and eat the fruit of them.

In fasting, God validates His promise of restoration to his saints. Nations have their destinies changed miraculously. Nineveh is a good example of this, *"When God saw what they did, how they turned from their evil way, God relented of the disaster that he had said he would do to them, and he did not do it" (Jonah 3:10).*

5. Finally, Isaiah describes the blessing of upliftment, promotion and exaltation:

> *"...Then shalt thou delight thyself in the Lord; and I will cause thee to ride upon the high places of the earth, and feed thee with the heritage of Jacob thy father: for the mouth of the Lord hath spoken it."*

What is the "heritage of Jacob" which we are to receive through fasting? Kenneth Copeland believes that Deuteronomy 32: 9-14 provides the answer to this pertinent question:

> *"For the Lord's portion is his people; Jacob is the lot of his inheritance. He found him in a desert land, and in the waste howling wilderness; he led him about, he instructed him, he kept him as the apple of his eye. As an eagle stirreth up her nest, fluttereth over her young, spreadeth abroad her wings, taketh them, beareth them on her wings: So the Lord alone did lead him, and there was no strange god with him. He made him ride on the high places of the earth, that he might eat the increase of the fields; and he made him to suck honey out of the rock, and oil out of*

the flinty rock; Butter of kine, and milk of sheep, with fat of lambs, and rams of the breed of Bashan, and goats, with the fat of kidneys of wheat; and thou didst drink the pure blood of the grape."

The heritage of Jacob, according to Kenneth Copeland, *"ensures that we hear the voice of the Good Shepard and that we are not led astray by the evil one…"*

Like Joel, Isaiah establishes a connection between fasting and the restoration of God's people. Isaiah ends his discussion on fasting with the theme:

> Thou shall build the old waste places: thou shalt raise up the foundations of many generations: and thou shalt be called, The repairer of the breach, The restorer of paths to dwell in (verse 12).

The work of restoration is, no doubt, an agenda that is uppermost in the heart of God in this hour. David's prophesy in this regard could not be more accurate. In Psalm 102:13, he says:

> "Thou shalt arise, and have mercy upon Zion: for the time to favour her, yea, the set time, is come".

A summary of the benefits of fasting is listed (below) in this form for ease of reference:

1. Then shall your light break forth like the dawn (Revelation).

2. Your healing shall spring up speedily (Divine healing and wholeness).

3. Your righteousness shall go before you (Righteousness).

4. The glory of the LORD shall be your rear guard (His Shekinah glory illuminating your paths).

5. Then you shall call, and the LORD will answer; you shall cry, and he will say, Here I am. Then your light shall dawn in the darkness (answered prayers).

6. And your darkness shall be as the noon-day (Divine wisdom).

7. The Lord will guide you continually (Continual guidance).

8. And satisfy your soul in drought (supernatural supply).

9. And strengthen your bones (Divine strength).

10. You shall be like a watered garden (Refreshment).

11. And like a spring of water, whose waters do not fail (Constant supply of life).

12. Those from among you shall build the old waste places (divine supply of labourers – the Aholiabs, and Bezaleels).

13. You shall raise up the foundations of many generations (Raising of future generations).

14. And you shall be called the Repairer of the Breach (A new name, restorer).

15. The Restorer of Streets to Dwell In (Restoration).

These verses reveal what Jesus meant when He spoke in Matthew 6 about fasting reward. No doubt, if done properly, and with the right attitude, fasting can be beneficial both physically, materially, spiritually and circumstantially. However, must heed the brilliant caution of Wiersbe: "… If we fast [just] in order to get something for ourselves from God, instead of to become better people for the sake of others, then we have missed the meaning of worship…"

## OTHER PROMISED BLESSINGS ASSOCIATED WITH FASTING

### Joy, Gladness And Cheerfulness

"Thus saith the Lord of hosts; The fast of the fourth month, and the fast of the fifth, and the fast of the seventh, and the fast of the tenth, shall be to the house of Judah joy and gladness, and cheerful feasts; therefore love the truth and peace" (Zech. 8:19)

## God's Open Reward

*"But thou, when thou fastest, anoint thine head, and wash thy face; That thou appear not unto men to fast, but unto thy Father which is in secret: and thy Father, which seeth in secret, shall reward thee openly" (Matt. 6:17, 18)*

## Spiritual Powers Over Demons

*"But this kind goes not out but by prayer and fasting" (Matt. 17:21)*

## Divine Empowerment And Supernatural Publicity

*"And Jesus returned in the power of the Spirit into Galilee: and there went out a fame of him through all the region round about" (Luke 4:14).*

# QUESTIONS AND ANSWERS ON BIBLICAL FASTING

# 22

# FASTING: QUESTIONS AND ANSWERS

This section provides answers to the most common questions people ask about the observance of biblical fast. Carefully selected, a great deal of grounds has been covered, with a bid to providing the believer with as much materials as are believed would help deal with areas of misinformation, misconceptions, sheer and blatant ignorance, people do have with regards to fasting, that has rendered the practice of it almost inconceivable for many. It is believed as earlier indicated, that most of the problems often associated with fasting stems from the legalistic and ritualistic view people hold about it.

We believe, therefore, that the answers that are provided to the questions dealt with in this section would go a long way to dispel much of these views.

## WHAT IS FASTING?

Fasting is the abstention from food for a period of time, for spiritual purposes.

Biblical fasting always centres on spiritual purposes. Fasting normally involves abstention from all food, solid or liquid, but not water, for a determined period of time, with specific spiritual goals in view. In exceptional circumstances, fasting could be total and absolute i.e., abstention from both food and water. As indicated, this should be the exception rather than the rule! A fast that goes beyond three days should include water intake!

It should be stressed however, that fasting is not only an abstention from food; it is also a concentration on God's glory, God's holiness and God's ways. It is man's total abandonment of all that matters to him in life in deep expression of his love and total devotion to God.

## WHY SHOULD A BELIEVER FAST?

You do not fast for the sake of fasting. You fast for specific purpose(s). You need to ask yourself the question: Why am I fasting? Is it for spiritual renewal, for guidance, for healing, for the resolution of problems, for special grace to handle a difficult situation? Ask the Holy Spirit to clarify His leading and objectives for your fast. This will enable you to pray more specifically and with great focus. There are several reasons why a believer should decide to fast. Usually you fast as a means of seeking God. God said, *"When you seek me with all your heart, I will be found by you" (Jer. 29:13, 14).* When a man or woman is willing to set aside the legitimate appetites of the body to concentrate on the work of fasting, they are demonstrating that they mean business; and that they are seeking God with all their heart.

Fasting is an expression of wholeheartedness. This is clear from Joel's call to the nation of Israel: *"Yet even now," says the Lord, "return to me with all your heart, with fasting. . ." (Joel 2:12).*

Also you fast when you are faced with situations that prayer alone cannot deal with. There are stubborn situations that have demonic undertone that prove too extreme to avert with prayer alone. Jesus said: "However, this kind does not go out except by prayer and fasting" (Matt. 17:21).

## HOW SHOULD I PREPARE FOR A FAST?

It is unwise to rush into any fast without adequate

spiritual and physical preparations. Jesus emphasised the importance of preparation in all our endeavours:

> *For which of you, desiring to build a tower, does not first sit down and count the cost, whether he has enough to complete it? Otherwise, when he has laid a foundation, and is not able to finish, all who see it begin to mock him, saying, 'This man began to build, and was not able to finish.' Or what king, going to encounter another king in war, will not sit down first and take counsel whether he is able with ten thousand to meet him who comes against him with twenty (Luke 14:28).*

The way you begin your fast will largely determine its success. Do not rush into a fast. Prepare your body for the fast. Eat smaller meals before starting a fast. Eat raw fruit and vegetables for, at least, two days before starting a fast. Withdraw from high-fat, high-sugar diets, and coffee and tea, days before you commence a lengthy fast. People generally experience a significant drop in their blood sugar, resulting in headaches, dizziness and nausea during a fast. These are withdrawal symptoms of forgoing these items you may have been used to before the fast.

Apart from these valuable physical preparations, devote quality time in fellowship with God; studying scriptures that deal with God's rewards for fasting. These would help to focus your mind on your fast.

Confess any known sin in your life, that the Holy Spirit calls to your remembrance and accept God's forgiveness (1 John 1:9).

## HOW DO I BEGIN MY FAST?

Evaluate why you are fasting and what you want the Lord to do as a result of your fast. People in the Bible fasted and prayed because they wanted something specific to happen; God's intervention, God's direction, a word from the Lord and, solution in critical situations. Prepare beforehand what you are going to do during the time you usually spend doing the thing you are fasting from.

Prepare yourself spiritually by spending time confessing and repenting from sin. Ask the Holy Spirit to reveal to you areas of sin in your life that you may be unaware of, and ask Him for His conviction.

Start with occasional short fasts to prepare your body for the fast. If your fast is for an extended period of time, it is important to prepare mentally, practically, and physically. Cut down on food intake a week before the actual fast and take on a vegetarian diet to help control cravings for food. You should reduce heavily caffeinated drinks and drink more water instead.

Begin your fast with an expectant heart!

# WILL FASTING FOR MORE THAN ONE PRAYER REQUEST DIMINISH MY REWARD?

I do not see how fasting for more than one issue is problematic if you are sincere and your motive is right before God. However, we must stress that, while God rewards fasting (Matt. 6:17-18), fasting is not a magical rite that invokes a quantity of blessings on the object of the fast, with the consequence that those blessings might diminish if spread too thin. We are not trying to bribe God or secure His divine favour through His appreciation of our performance of a fast. God knows all your needs even before you ask Him, in the first place, but whether He chooses to help or not, more than likely, has to do with whether your requests are aligned with His will and purposes for your life in the situation.

As Mahesh Chavda puts it, *"We don't fast to earn something; we fast to make a connection with our supernatural God..."* A fact alluded to by Shane Idleman when he said, *"Fasting doesn't twist God's arm; it realigns our heart with His and gets us back on track; it gives us wisdom and discernment for crucial issues..."* Further, Edith Schaeffer agrees that *"fasting is never a bribe to get God to pay more attention to the petitions? No, a thousand times no. It is simply a way to make clear that we sufficiently reverence the amazing opportunity to ask help from the everlasting God, the Creator of the universe, to choose to put everything else aside and concentrate on worshiping, asking forgiveness, and making our requests known-considering His help more important than anything we could do ourselves in our own strength and with our own ideas."*

God will reward the sacrifice of fasting, as we have seen throughout this book, no doubt. However, we must get our perspectives right, as discussed.

The fast (and the prayer that should always accompany it) is a blessing that God has given to us. It is completely for our own benefit. The fast is designed to increase and deepen our own spiritual sensitivity, allowing us more intimate communication with God. In that state, we can more easily determine God's will and understand how our own actions might affect the course of events. We become more sensitive to impressions and ideas that can help us and those we love.

That said, a study of the original meaning of the word "fast" from the verb *tsom*, indicates that fasting is often associated with emergency or distress; which gives the impression that we usually fast for one compelling issue, but still pray for the other items on our prayer lists. Consequently, a person who is fasting and praying usually does not attach all his prayer requests to the fast.

In the true sense of fasting, we pray for one deep burden. The fasting individual usually puts himself in a state of emergency concerning a particular burden. This is why the Bible associates afflicting one's soul with fasting, *"But as for me, when they were sick, my clothing was sackcloth.* ***I afflicted my soul with fasting****. My prayer returned into my own bosom"* (Psalm 35:13 World English Bible, emphasis added).

# SHOULD I ALWAYS WITHDRAW TO A SOLITARY PLACE DURING MY FAST?

*"So I lay prostrate before the Lord for these forty days and forty nights, because the Lord had said he would destroy you. And I prayed to the Lord, 'O Lord God, do not destroy your people and your heritage, whom you have redeemed through your greatness, whom you have brought out of Egypt with a mighty hand. Remember your servants, Abraham, Isaac, and Jacob. Do not regard the stubbornness of this people, or their wickedness or their sin, lest the land from which you brought us say, Because the Lord was not able to bring them into the land that he promised them, and because he hated them, he has brought them out to put them to death in the wilderness. For they are your people and your heritage, whom you brought out by your great power and by your outstretched arm" (Deut. 9:25-29 ESV).*

In Breth Mckay's masterpiece, we learn, "In the hush of silent solitude, you find the space needed for undistracted and thus fruitful reflection; you can finally focus on picking up on sacred signals and listening to their urgent broadcasts. The more time you spend alone with God, the better you can hear the "still, small voice" and discern his will. The more you can quiet the cacophony of the crowd, the better able you'll be to attend to your inner nudging, and become self-reliant."

Henry David Thoreau concurs *"I never found the companion that was so companionable as solitude."*

The question, undoubtedly, will arise in the hearts of many fasting people of God as to whether or not they are to withdraw to a lonely or solitary place during their times of fasting.

The huge need and profound place of fasting retreat cannot be over-emphasised. If silence and solitude are so compelling and vitalising, why do so few people seek them, and why are they so difficult to seek? When was the last time you found yourself in a space of simple solitude and silence, much less intentionally carve out time to cultivate these practices as disciplines?

Given the fact that solitude and silence seem to scratch a basic human itch, and, when pursued as spiritual disciplines, can provide such an edifying effect on the soul, why is it that the majority of people so seldom experience these states?

The answer to these probing questions is in the huge demand our modern way of living has placed on us.

If you are like most people, your life is probably filled with noise (audible and otherwise) from morning until night. As soon as you wake up, you check your phone and turn on music or the radio. Your time in the car is no less different with your car stereo. At the office, you are never fully disengaged from the people around you, or from your phone — which continues to provide a constant stream of input throughout the day. After work it is another music or podcast-filled commute to a noise-filled gym, and then home to converse with your family, scroll through your phone. Even when you are not actively attending to it, you may put the radio and television on in the background, to sort of keep you company. Even the shortest stretches of quiet feel empty, uncomfortable. You have observed "a minute silence" before… You know the feeling!

While one does not advocate that every observance of fast should be conducted in isolation, there is, no doubt, a strong case for it, if it is possible, given the huge spiritual dividends it offers. Bob Sorge opines that, "… retreats can be highly significant in our spiritual journey to augment and complement our daily disciplines." Jesus was accustomed to spending personal time in isolation; a time of deep reflection and fellowship with the Father:

*"And in the morning, rising up a great while before day, he went out, and departed into a solitary place, and there prayed" (Mark 1:35).* This was not just a practice, this was His life; a strong, unbroken and unweaning attachment to the Father. This, no doubt, accounted for the tremendous power with the breath-taking miracles that followed His earthly ministry. The Bible sums it up this way, "How God anointed Jesus of Nazareth with the Holy Ghost and with power: who went about doing good, and healing all that were oppressed of the devil; for God was with him" (Acts 10:38).

## SHOULD I CARRY ON WITH MY USUAL BUSINESS OF LIFE WHILE I AM FASTING?

Just as in prayer, a believer leading a fasted life, will periodically engage in fasting of varying duration, for example, a -twenty-four hour long fasting - two to three times a week. It is expected that a person fasting at such frequency would carry on with his usual business of life while fasting. The same applies to a person on a partial fast for a longer duration, say 30 – 40 days. It is perfectly in order for him to carry on with his business of life, while he reserves his evenings for special session with God. However, in his contacts and dealings with men, he must avoid religious ostentation or public display of his fast. He must heed the lord's warning:

> "Moreover when ye fast, be not, as the hypocrites, of a sad countenance: for they disfigure their faces, that they may appear unto men to fast. Verily I say unto you, They have their reward. But thou, when thou fastest, anoint thine head, and wash thy face: That thou appear not unto men to fast, but unto thy Father which is in secret: and thy Father, which seeth in secret, shall reward thee openly" (Matt. 6:16-18).

Apart from special periods of prayer or other spiritual activities, your life and general conduct while fasting should be as normal and unpretentious as possible.

I have undertaken fasts of varying length, ranging from 3 days, 7 days, 14 days, 21 days, even up to 40 days. Whilst undergoing these different periods of fasts, including the longest – 40 days, with the help of God, I carried on with my usual responsibilities of life, including family and ministerial duties albeit, with lesser degree of intensity, as the fasting progressed.

As stated, answering the preceding question however, a time of fasting necessitates no doubt, a time of solitude, isolation and seclusion. Our earlier stance notwithstanding, we take the view that a far better option or approach will be that the fasting believer withdraws to a place of seclusion and devote that time in seeking the Lord, as exemplified in the scripture below:

Said Moses:

> "So I lay prostrate before the Lord for these forty days and forty nights, because the Lord had said he would destroy you. And I prayed to the Lord, 'O Lord God, do not destroy your people and your heritage, whom you have redeemed through your greatness, whom you have brought out of Egypt with a mighty hand. Remember your servants, Abraham, Isaac, and Jacob. Do not regard the stubbornness of this people, or their wickedness or their sin, lest the land from which you brought us say, Because the Lord was not able to bring them into the land that he promised them, and because he hated them, he has brought them out to put them to death in the wilderness. For they are your people and your heritage, whom you brought out by your great power and by your outstretched arm" (Deut. 9:25-29 ESV).

If at all possible, all fasting should be done with retreat. There are undoubtedly, ample reasons that lend weight to this notion.

First, the fact that this was the practice exemplified by Jesus. Jesus often withdrew to spend time with His father, yet, He is the perfect Son of God. How much more do we need to withdrew to a solitary place to spend time talking with God? As you pursue your creator, you will discover a divine love exchange that will fuel your supernatural path through the rugged roads of this earthly life.

Second, fasting is ministering to the Lord, as demonstrated by the elders of the Early Church:

> *"Now there were in the church that was at Antioch certain prophets and teachers; as Barnabas, and Simeon that was called Niger, and Lucius of Cyrene, and Manaen, which had been brought up with Herod the tetrarch, and Saul. As they ministered to the Lord, and fasted, the Holy Ghost said, Separate me Barnabas and Saul for the work whereunto I have called them. And when they had fasted and prayed, and laid their hands on them, they sent them away" (Acts 13:1-3).*

The fasting believer should be able to spend quality time in the presence of the Lord in isolation.

Furthermore, given that fasting is a time of serious business with God, the ideal position should be to seek Him with absolute focus and concentration, thereby avoiding the distractions that could result from interacting with people and the general affairs of life.

Everything should be done to withdraw from people, and anything that has a potential to cause distraction from the task at hand. It is not possible to be caught up with God and be caught up with man at the same time. It is not possible to be hearing the voice of God and the voice of man at the same time. There is a choice to be made, and the fasting saint ought to determine which voice must be pre-eminent.

Lastly, fasting, being warfare in the unseen realm, the personality to be encountered most is the devil. The need to be single-minded on the task of overcoming the adversary cannot therefore, be overemphasised. It is, accordingly, unwise to take on too much in the course of the fast, thereby loosing grips on the essence of the assignment. Notice the enemy rejoices at your too many exploits (busyness); what he hates is the believer on his knees. Learn the lesson!

## WHAT ARE THE USUAL INDICATORS THAT YOU NEED TO FAST?

The leading of the Spirit of God is very vital in knowing when to fast. The occasion for fasting is a totally voluntary decision. Some of the specific times when people in the Bible fasted are listed in the appendix section of this book. But basically we can say a Christian may decide to fast whenever there is a spiritual concern or struggle in his or her life. Of course, there may be times when those in authority over us proclaim fasts, as was done by King Saul (1 Sam. 14:24) or Jehoshaphat (2 Chr. 20:3). But normally and ultimately, that decision is solely between us and the Lord.

Here is a principle: In God's Word, we always find fasting connected with a very troubled spirit or a very anxious heart before the Lord. So, a reason for fasting is not something you choose on the spur of the moment. There are times when simply pressing into God through more time in His Word and in prayer, will reopen the flow of the supernatural in your life. But, at other times, you need something more—a time dedicated wholly to Him. As argued by R.A Torrey, "*… there are times of emergency or special crisis in work or in our individual lives, when men of downright earnestness will withdraw themselves even from the gratification of natural appetites that would be perfectly proper under other circumstances, that they may give themselves wholly to prayer. There is a peculiar power in such prayer. Every great crisis in life and work should be met that way. There is nothing pleasing to God in our giving up in a purely Pharisaic and legal way things which are pleasant, but there is power in that downright earnestness and determination to obtain in prayer the things of which we sorely feel our need, that leads us to put away everything, even things in themselves most right and necessary, that we set our faces to find God, and obtain blessings from Him.*" These should be among the things that should prompt us to fast.

# CAN THE PRACTICE OF FASTING BE ABUSED?

The practice of fasting has, for a very long time, been a subject of much controversies and misconceptions. This has led to several aspects of it, such as its meaning, what it entails, the motive and the general conduct of it, being misunderstood and abused. This is tantamount to a very potent and dangerous weapon in wrong hands.

Let us now examine the groups of people most culpable of this heinous act.

## Hypocrites

> "Why have we fasted,' they say, 'and you have not seen it? Why have we humbled ourselves, and you have not noticed?' "Yet on the day of your fasting, you do as you please and exploit all your workers. Your fasting ends in quarrelling and strife, and in striking each other with wicked fists. You cannot fast as you do today and expect your voice to be heard on high" (Isa. 58:3-4, NIV).

> "Then the Lord said to me, "Do not pray for the well-being of this people. Although they fast, I will not listen to their cry; though they offer burnt offerings and grain offerings, I will not accept them. Instead, I will destroy them with the sword, famine and plague" (Jer. 14:11,12 NIV).

*"Moreover when ye fast, be not, as the hypocrites, of a sad countenance: for they disfigure their faces, that they may appear unto men to fast. Verily I say unto you, They have their reward" (Matt. 6:16).*

## The Pharisees

*"The Pharisee stood and prayed thus with himself, God, I thank thee, that I am not as other men are, extortioners, unjust, adulterers, or even as this publican. I fast twice in the week, I give tithes of all that I possess" (Luke 18:11,12).*

## Queen Jezebel

*And she wrote in the letters, saying, Proclaim a fast, and set Naboth on high among the people: And set two men, sons of Belial, before him, to bear witness against him, saying, Thou didst blaspheme God and the king. And then carry him out, and stone him, that he may die (I Kings 21:9,10).*

## The Leaders of Jezreel

*And the men of his city, even the elders and the nobles who were the inhabitants in his city, did as Jezebel had sent unto them, and as it was written in the letters which she had sent unto them. They proclaimed a fast, and set Naboth on high among the people. And there came in two men, children of Belial, and sat before him: and the men of Belial witnessed against him, even against Naboth, in the presence of the people, saying, Naboth did blaspheme God and the king. Then they carried him forth out of the city, and stoned him with stones, that he died (1 Kings 21:11-13).*

### False Teachers

*"Now the Spirit speaketh expressly, that in the latter times some shall depart from the faith, giving heed to seducing spirits, and doctrines of devils; Speaking lies in hypocrisy; having their conscience seared with a hot iron; Forbidding to marry, and commanding to abstain from meats, which God hath created to be received with thanksgiving of them which believe and know the truth" (1 Tim. 4:1-3).*

During a fast, toxins will be flushed out of the body, primarily through the kidneys, lungs and skin. Bowel movements will be few or will stop completely as the body rests and rejuvenates itself.

# I WANT TO FAST BUT CANNOT BECAUSE OF AN ILLNESS

If your illness requires constant taking of medication, it is wise to abstain from fasting, until you have your physician's permission to do so.

If you cannot fast as a result of an illness, you should not feel ashamed.

Let these words of a veteran address your situation:

*"If you cannot go without eating all day because of an ailment of the body, beloved one, no logical man will be able to criticize you for that. Besides, we have a Lord who is meek, loving and generous, who does not ask for anything beyond our power. Because He neither requires the abstinence from foods, neither that the fast take place for the simple sake of fasting, neither is its aim that we remain with empty stomachs, but that we fast to offer our entire selves to the dedication of spiritual things, having distanced ourselves from secular things... because human nature is indifferent and gives itself over mostly to comforts and gratifications, for this reason the philanthropic Lord, like a loving and caring father, devised the therapy of the fast for us, so that our gratifications would be completely stopped and that our worldly cares be transferred to spiritual works..."* - St John Chrysostom.

## SHOULD I TAKE MULTI-VITAMINS DURING A FAST?

The simple answer is you cannot; and in fact, if you do, you are not actually fasting and are putting yourself in potential danger, as well as exacerbating existing issues. Much of the benefits of fasting accrue as a result of the physiological changes that result in the complete absence of nutrients and calories coming in. When we consume nutrients or calories of any kind, we are not fasting, and we do not get nearly the same benefits. Without moving into the specific adaptations to the fasting state, you could put your body in serious

danger of starving, by consuming nutrients with few, or no calories.

## WILL MY FASTING BE REWARDED?

Without any iota of doubt, God has committed Himself to reward the fasting of the saint. However, note the cautious tone of Jesus on the subject:

> *"Moreover when ye fast, be not, as the hypocrites, of a sad countenance: for they disfigure their faces, that they may appear unto men to fast. Verily I say unto you, They have their reward. But thou, when thou fastest, anoint thine head, and wash thy face; That thou appear not unto men to fast, but unto thy Father which is in secret: and thy Father, which seeth in secret, shall reward thee openly" (Matt.6:16-18).*

When fasting for the right reasons, no fast will go in vain, and will always benefit you or those around you. Please read the chapter on the benefits of fasting, under section seven of this book for a more comprehensive answer to this question.

# WHY IS FASTING IMPORTANT?

Perhaps the most important reason for us to practice fasting is because Jesus fasted (Matt 4.1-4), and He assumes that we will fast also. In Matthew 6.16, Jesus says: *"When, or, as often as [hotan, in the Greek] you fast, do not put on a gloomy face as the hypocrites do, for they feign their appearance so that they will be noticed by men when they are fasting."* The idea is not if you fast, but as often as you fast. Jesus assumes that Christians will fast, just as He assumes that Christians will give to the poor (Matt 6.2) and pray (Matt.6.5-6).

However, it is important to note that fasting does not make an individual a Christian, and neither does not fasting disqualify us from being one. The Pharisees were rigorously concerned with fasting, but they treated it as a legalistic exercise instead of one that was both heart-felt and faith-induced (Luke 18.12). The thief on the cross never fasted, and yet was assured by Jesus that he would be with Him in paradise that very day.

# DOES JESUS EXPECT THE CHRISTIANS TO FAST?

As earlier discussed, Jesus, in His teaching on the subject, said: "When ye fast..." (Matt. 6:18), and not if you fast, which presupposes that Jesus expects fasting to be part of our regular services to God. Jesus did not only teach fasting, He validated the practice by actually doing it at the highest level – forty days.

And in Matthew 9:15, He did not say His followers "might" fast; but "they will fast."

It is something that He expects us to incorporate into our service, as part of deeper our relationship with Him. Although it is not specifically commanded by Scripture, fasting should be a regular part of the Christian life. There is no reason for a Christian not to fast, especially when Jesus clearly expects His followers to fast regularly.

# HOW OFTEN CAN I FAST?

The Bible nowhere explicitly answers this question. We are told that we ought to fast as part of our spiritual expression of our Christian life and faith in Christ Jesus (Matt 6.16-17), but we are not told how often fasting should be done. Luke 18.12 refers to a practice among certain Pharisees of fasting twice a week. In mentioning this, however, Luke's point is to say that their fasting was a legalistic and rote practice; it was not induced by a pure heart, a good conscience, and a sincere faith (1 Tim 1.5).

An important point worth noting, however, is: If the Pharisees, who concentrated on the outward religion only, with no internal, forgiving, and renewing grace, fasted twice a week, what does this mean for us, who have been saved by divine grace and freed from the necessity of outward obedience, and forgiven of all our sins through the atonement of Jesus Christ?

Fasting should be a regular part of a Christian's life, not just on God's Holy Day known as the Day of Atonement (Levi. 23:32), but several times in a year. Periodic fasting is of immense benefit. The Bible says that Paul did this often (2Cor. 11:27). The Apostle Paul knew that fasting would be a way of life for Christians (1Cor. 7:5).

As to the question of how often you should fast, you need to be guided and led by the Holy Spirit. Apart from its valuable spiritual benefits, periodic fasting helps to eliminate some of the unpleasant body reactions such as headaches, and toxins.

## HOW SHOULD I GO ABOUT FASTING?

Once again, the Bible nowhere explicitly answers this question. Some fasts in Scripture are complete abstentions, where both food and water are not partaken (Est. 4.16). Others appear to be only partial abstentions (Daniel

1.15; 10.3), in which certain aspects of a "normal" and permissible diet are refrained from for a given period of time. Examples of partial fasts might be abstaining from something that is particularly relished (i.e., sweets, ice cream, meat,) or, perhaps, abstaining from one or more meals that would normally be eaten. The idea is to deny yourself and, correspondingly, to devote yourself to prayer, focusing the time and energy that you would have used in eating to prayerfully seeking God.

## HOW DO I KNOW WHAT TYPE OF FAST TO OBSERVE?

This question takes into account the fact that there are different types of fasting, such as proclaimed or public fast, personal fast, the normal fast, the absolute fast and the partial fast. This knowledge can help deal with much of the misconceptions and, at times, frustrations that are very often associated with fasting. Further, this gives the believer a wide variety of fasting to choose from.

*(Please see part three of this book for a full discussion on this topic).*

# WHY SHOULD I CONSIDER FASTING?

There are many reasons in the Bible to fast. The following list provides the most common:

## To seek the Lord:

Fasting helps us to express earnestness in our seeking the Lord's help (2 Chr. 20.3; Est 4.16; Acts 14.23). In denying ourselves food, we are telling the Lord that we mean business. Andrew Murray states: "Fasting helps to express, to deepen, and to confirm the resolution that we are ready to sacrifice anything, to sacrifice ourselves, to attain what we seek for the kingdom of God."

## To express a wholehearted faith:

Oftentimes in the Bible, fasting is an expression of wholehearted response to God. It shows that He is more important to us than mere physical pleasures. (Joel 2.12-13).

## To prepare for ministry:

Jesus spent 40 days and nights in the wilderness fasting and praying before He began God's work on earth. He needed time alone to prepare for what His Father had called Him to do (Matt. 4:1-17; Mark 1:12-13; Luke 4:1-

14). Also the elders of the church in Antioch prayed and fasted before Barnabas and Saul were released to the work of the ministry (Acts 13:2-3).

### To seek God's wisdom:

Paul and Barnabas prayed and fasted for the elders of the churches before committing them to the Lord for His service (Acts 14:23).

### To gain victory:

After losing 40,000 men in battle in two days, the Israelites cried out to God for help. Judges 20:26 says all the people went up to Bethel and "sat weeping before the Lord." They also "fasted that day until evening." The next day the Lord gave them victory over the Benjamites.

### To repent:

After Jonah pronounced judgment against the city of Nineveh, the king covered himself with sackcloth and sat in the dust. He then ordered the people to fast and pray. Jonah 3:10 says, "When God saw what they did and how they turned from their evil ways, He relented and did not bring on them the destruction He had threatened."

### To show grief:

Nehemiah mourned, fasted, and prayed when he learned Jerusalem's walls had been broken down, leaving the

Israelites vulnerable and disgraced (Neh. 1:1-4). At other times, fasting is practiced as an expression of mourning, either over death (2 Sam. 12.16) or over sin (Jonah 3.5), and a medium of pleading with the Lord that He might hear the accompanying prayer and answer it from on high. A good example of this is in Jonah 3.5, where Nineveh repents before God with prayer and fasting, and pleads with Him to show mercy upon them. See also (Est. 9.31 and Joel 1.14).

## To seek deliverance or protection

Ezra declared a corporate fast for a safe journey for the Israelites returning to Jerusalem from exile in Babylon. A situation very extreme and desperate – a case of imminent danger - warranted this fast. It shows an absolute reliance and trust in God.

Now, let us see what drove Ezra into fasting:

"Then I proclaimed a fast there, at the river of Ahava, that we might afflict ourselves before our God, to seek of him a right way for us, and for our little ones, and for all our substance. For I was ashamed to require of the king a band of soldiers and horsemen to help us against the enemy in the way: because we had spoken unto the king, saying, The hand of our God is upon all them for good that seek him; but his power and his wrath is against all them that forsake him. So we fasted and besought our God for this: and he was intreated of us" (Ezra 8:21-23, emphasis added).

To seek wisdom and guidance and intervention:

In 2 Chronicles 20.1-30, Jehoshaphat proclaimed a national fast in order that all the people might seek the Lord's wisdom and guidance in the face of an encroaching military invasion that was coming upon him from Edom. This suggests that fasting and praying in the face of overwhelming circumstances is entirely appropriate for us.

*(Please also see chapter 6 of this book for our full discussion on the purposes of fasting).*

## IS FASTING ALWAYS VOLUNTARY?

Fasting is a voluntary abstention from food for a pre-determined period of time, in other to seek God with focus and intensity, for a definite purpose.

Fasting is meant to be a private act between the believer and God. In other words, the decision to fast, when to fast, the purpose of the fast, the length of the fast, where to fast, how to prepare for and break the fast, are made solely by the person to undertake the fast.

However, there are times where such decisions are taken by others for the fasting believer. For example, people in a local church's leadership, on behalf of members of the church or Christian Fellowship, can declare a fast. Thus, it is a common practice for a decision to undertake a fast to be made by the leadership of a church for the congregation.

Accordingly, spiritual leaders and people in governmental leadership positions may invite others to join in corporate fasting, with a specific goal in mind and for a specific period of time.

For instance, Queen Esther said to her uncle Mordecai, *"...fast for me, and do not eat nor drink three days, night or day. My maidservants and I will also fast in the same way" (Est. 4:16)*. Also in 2 Chr. 20:3, the Bible says, *"And Jehoshaphat feared, and set himself to seek the Lord,* **and proclaimed a fast throughout all Judah** *(emphasis added)."*

However, fasting should never be forced or made compulsory or supper- imposed on anyone or group of people; but can be promoted and encouraged as a biblically and historically proven means of positioning our hearts to receiving more of God's grace, in the context of commitment to prayer and to the word of God (Joel 2:15).

Jesus attested to this fact when He was interrogated by the disciples of John on the apparent neglect of His disciples to the discipline of fasting:

> "Then the disciples of John came to Him, saying, 'Why do we and the Pharisees fast often, but Your disciples do not fast?' And Jesus said to them, 'Are the children of

*the bridechamber able to mourn while the bridegroom is with them?* **But the days will come when the bridegroom shall be taken away from them, and then they shall fast**" *(Matt. 9:14-15, emphasis added).*

Jesus taught fasting and lived a fasted life, yet He did not impose the practice on His disciples.

In all, Jesus had an undisguised dislike to any ostentatious display of religious sentiments, especially in relation to fasting. He warned against public display of fasting as practiced by the Pharisees (Matt. 6:16-18). It is also important to remember that fasting is not an end to itself. It should, of course, draw us closer to God and focus our minds to think like Him. But it should ultimately lead us to help those who are oppressed, feeding those who are hungry, providing shelter for those who have none, and giving clothes to those who are in grave need (Isaiah 58:6-7).

However, the level at which a person engages in fasting should be determined according to physical limitations (health), age and experience. Those with known or suspected physical disability or illness, or those with any history of eating disorder should never fast, except in consultation with, and under the supervision of a qualified doctor. Pregnant or nursing mothers should not fast food or drink, as it could negatively affect the health and development of their baby and their own personal health.

# SHOULD I ALWAYS FAST IN SECRET?

As much as possible, you should fast in secret especially, where you are undertaking a personal fast. Apart from very few exceptional circumstances, your fast must be conducted in secret, as a matter entirely between you and God. Remember Jesus' warning: *"That thou appear not unto men to fast, but unto thy Father which is in secret: and thy Father, which seeth in secret, shall reward thee openly"* (Matt. 6:18).

When we examined the account of Jesus' fast (Matt. 4:1-11), we saw that He went into the wilderness. He did not go into the city and advertised His fasting.

Matthew 6:17-18 earlier examined, is abundantly clear in context:

"But when you fast, put oil on your head and wash your face, so that it will not be obvious to others that you are fasting, but only to your Father, who is unseen; and your Father, who sees what is done in secret, will reward you".

The Scripture is clear here, when it says that your fasting should not be obvious to others. It is wise to tell a spouse or a close and trusted friend to help hold you up in prayer, but it is both unwise and unbiblical to go around telling others of your fast. Remember, your reward is not from people, but from God.

# CAN I FAST AND NOT LET MY WIFE OR HUSBAND KNOW?

Very clearly Jesus taught that we are to observe our fasts in secret:

> *Moreover when you fast, be not, as the hypocrites, of a sad countenance: for they disfigure their faces, that they may appear to men to fast. Truly I say to you, They have their reward. But you, when you fast, anoint your head, and wash your face: That you appear not to men to fast, but to your Father which is in secret: and your Father, which sees in secret, shall reward you (Matt. 6:16-18).*

However, when it comes to fasting within the premise of a husband and wife relationship, there seems to be an apparent exception. Paul's warning is noteworthy. Paul cautioned Christian couples not to "Deprive ...one the other, except it be with consent for a time, that you may give yourselves to fasting and prayer; and come together again, that Satan tempt you not for your lack of self-control" (1 Cor. 7:5). Within the context of Paul's reasoning, it is absolutely impossible for a party to a marriage to engage in a fast without the other party having knowledge of it.

As a matter of fact, due consent of the 'non-fasting' partner is to be obtained well ahead of time.

Explaining this point beyond the boundary of sexual relationship in marriage, it could be argued that in a proper family setting, it is expected that crucial matters such as fasting would be thoroughly discussed, at least, between the husband and wife, for adequate adjustments – perhaps in area of food – and other vital aspects to be made ahead of time.

Further, I strongly believe that who we choose to reveal our fasting to is entirely our decision. Motive is no doubt, an issue of critical importance, and must be carefully considered in all cases.

## ARE THERE CIRCUMSTANCES THAT MAKE GIVING KNOWLEDGE OF OUR FASTING TO OTHERS LEGITIMATE OR UNAVOIDABLE?

There are situations that may justify your decision to disclose your fasting to others. In his thought-provoking work, Zachariah Fomum identifies some of such factors, including where the person fasting:-

## FASTING: QUESTIONS AND ANSWERS

1. Feels that he is weak and cannot complete the fast without the prayers of the brethren. He therefore, announces his fast to them so as to solicit their prayers.

2. Is a leader who is setting example in fasting for those he is leading so that they may do likewise. He therefore, tells them, not because he wants them to "see" him, but because he desires their growth in this area.

3. Has a major battle before him and wants people to fast with him for the overthrow of the enemy. He must therefore, tell them about his fast and solicit their co-operation.

4. May want to demonstrate to young believers that God does honour fasting, that fasting is not something that has outlived its usefulness, and that they should commit themselves to a life of fasting. In doing this he might have to share how it has worked in his own life. He can therefore, talk about his experience in fasting without seeking to draw attention to himself or to his record in fasting.

The golden rule, I believe, should be *'guard your heart and motive.'* You can do any of the above without drawing attention to yourself. We know about the forty-days fast of the Lord Jesus because He told the disciples about it. His motive was clear and legitimate.

Paul couldn't be more precise when he said:

*"But with me it is a very small thing that I should be judged of you, or of man's judgment: yea, I judge not mine own self. For I know nothing by myself; yet am I not hereby justified: but he that judgeth me is the Lord. Therefore judge nothing before the time, until the Lord come, who both will bring to light the hidden things of darkness, and will make manifest the counsels of the hearts: and then shall every man have praise of God (I Cor. 4:3-5)."*

In the same vein, Moses made his forty-day fasts public, the same goes for Paul who spoke quite openly about his fasted life; otherwise, they would not have been sources of inspiration to us, yet none of these people suddenly became hypocrites because of that.

# DOES FASTING REQUIRE ABSTENTION FROM WATER?

The key issue raised by this question hinges on whether water can be categorised as food. You guessed right; absolutely not, I hear you say! Let us remind ourselves of the definition of fasting, to clear the air. Both the Webster and Bible Dictionaries define fasting as, "abstinence from food." Webster Dictionary goes further to define food as "…nutriment; nourishment in solid form." Food and water-drinking are two different things. As Franklin Hall puts it, "*…to do without water results in thirsting, and thirsting means a great desire to drink. Fasting will be* *understood better if we recognise these facts. One should not associate abstinence from water with the subject of fasting."*

Now let us consider the same matter from a pure scriptural stand-point:

*"And when he had fasted forty days and forty nights, he was afterward an hungred" (Matt. 4:2).*

It is quite evident from the above Scripture that Jesus fasted from, not water but food. We are told very clearly, *"... when he had fasted ... he was afterward an hungred (emphasis added),* not "He was afterward thirsty." This consideration opens up a vast field for reflection. We shall only indicate few of the many directions in which it applies.

1. As said, "…he was afterward an hungred" gives a clear indication of the type of fast that the Lord had; which only involved abstinence from food and not from water. It is a known fact that when a person goes without food and water for a considerable period of time, his crave for water is far more intense than that for food. It seems evident that Jesus did drink water. This is to be the believer's example in fasting.

2. The temptation of Jesus centred on food and not water. The Bible says, "And when the tempter came to him, he said, If thou be the Son of God, command that these stones be made bread" (Matt. 4:3, emphasis added). Water was not at all the centre of the temptation of Jesus.

Only one feasible explanation is credible; the fact that Jesus consumed water in His fast. He couldn't have been tempted with what He already had at His disposal.

3. The above line of reasoning is further strengthened in the response that Jesus gave to the temper (satan): "But he answered and said, It is written, Man shall not live by bread alone, but by every word that proceedeth out of the mouth of God" (Matt. 4:4, emphasis added). It is evidence that Jesus did not say, 'Man shall not live by bread and water alone', which further suggests that Jesus had not partaken in water fast.

Undoubtedly, the confusion that exists in the minds of many who believe that they must abstain from water in the course of a fast must be overcome. *"Our fasts should include plenty of water or they can be life threatening;"* warned Bill Bright.

The Bible, no doubt, also describes some extreme times that people fasted from everything, including water. For instance, Exodus 34:28, Deuteronomy 9:9, Ezra 10:6, Esther 4:16 and Acts 9:9. This type of fast is usually reserved for extreme circumstances. Believers should never attempt such fasts, beyond three days, and under the supervision of a health practitioner.

It is absurd for people to think about fasting and prayer without drinking water. Those who do this, do it in ignorance, and should be corrected by some constructive teachings. Your body is the temple of the Holy Spirit (1 Cor.6:19). To attempt a major fast without water can destroy vital organs in the body. According to experts, water is the human principal chemical component and makes up about sixty per cent of your body weight. Every system in the body depends on water. For example, water flushes toxins out of vital organs, carries nutrients to your cells, and provides a moist environment for ear, nose and throat tissues. Lack of water can lead to dehydration, a condition that occurs when you do not have enough water in your body to carry out normal functions. Even mild dehydration can drain your energy and make you tired.

## ARE THERE PEOPLE THAT SHOULD NOT FAST?

No doubt, spiritual leaders may invite others to join in corporate fasting with specific goals in mind and for a specific time; people should never be compelled to fast. The level at which a person engages in fasting should be determined by several factors including age, health, and God's leading.

• To start with, fasting is not within the realm of those who have never received Jesus as their Lord and personal saviour and have made up their minds to live in enmity with their creator. The Bible clearly states that "The sacrifice of the wicked is an abomination to the LORD:

but the prayer of the upright is his delight." The position is further substantiated in Proverbs 21:27, "The sacrifice of the wicked is abomination: how much more, when he bringeth it with a wicked mind?" Fasting is a unique privilege of the Sons of the Kingdom (Matt. 15:26).

• Further, you should not fast if you have liver or kidney weakness or disease, or are extremely frail, malnourished, anaemic, or exhausted. You should consult a doctor and be under his or her care during fasting if you have a weakened immune system, severe high blood pressure, medication-dependent diabetes, or weak circulation causing frequent fainting. Those with a physical disability or illness, or those with any history of an eating disorder, should never fast, except in consultation with, and under the supervision of, a qualified doctor.

• In addition, surgery or a major illness. Time should be taken to recuperate before attempting a fast. Also, don't fast directly prior to major surgery.

• Also, pregnant or nursing mothers should not fast food or liquids as it could negatively affect the health and development of their baby and their own personal health.

• Minors are discouraged from fasting food and should never engage in fasting without express parental consent and oversight.

- Finally, if older teenagers fast food under their parents' supervision, we encourage them to use juice and protein drinks to sustain their health and metabolism.

# IS THE DISCIPLINE OF FASTING TAUGHT THROUGH OUT SCRIPTURE?

The Bible mentions fasting over 70 times. The practice of fasting is not taught in the Pentateuch (the first 5 books of Moses), but in the historical books (2 Sam. 12:16; 1 Kings 21:9-12; Ezra 8:21), and the prophet's writings (Isa. 58:3-5; Joel 11:14; 2:15; Zech. 8:19). There was no fasting when Israel was led out of Egypt into the Promised Land. The first time fasting was mentioned in Scripture; it was in connection with Moses. We have the record in Chapter 34 of Exodus. We are told, Moses did not eat for forty days and nights, while He was on the mount with God receiving the Ten Commandments. In Verse 30 we read:

> "And when Aaron and all the children of Israel saw Moses, behold, the skin of his face shone: and they were afraid to come nigh him."

The Day of Atonement—also called "the Fast" (Acts 27:9)—is the only fast day commanded by God (Lev. 23:27), though other national fast days are mentioned in the Bible. Also, personal fasts are clearly expected of Christ's disciples (Matt. 9:14-15).

## WHAT SCRIPTURES DO YOU RECOMMEND FOR STUDY DURING FAST?

There are several Scriptures a believer in fasting can draw inspirations and directions from; notably: Isaiah 58, Esther 4:16, Zechariah 7 and 8, Matthew 6:16-18, Luke 4 and a host of others referenced throughout this book. They serve as good foundations to build your fasting life on.

## HOW OFTEN SHOULD A CHRISTIAN FAST?

Fasting is as important a Christian discipline as prayer and Bible study. Just as it could not be said that Christian should resort to prayer only in times of great crisis, reserving fasting observance for challenging times only, is wrong and misleading. Fasting should be a natural part of the life of a believer.

Prayer and fasting are equal and integral part of the same ministry. In Matthew 6:5-6, Jesus said, "When ye pray…"

(emphasis added). He did not say, "If you pray", In the same passage, He said, "When ye Fast..." (verses 16-17, emphasis added), which gives an apparent assumption that Christians should regard the observance of biblical fasting as a normal and natural part of the Christian life. This further indicates that the discipline of fasting has not been left at the discretion of the believer, perhaps, because of its incredible benefits. Just as prayer is not an option for the believer, fasting is not either. It is undoubtedly, a natural expectation of God from His Saints.

There are times when the believer or a group of believers will be prompted by the Holy Spirit to embark on a fast, perhaps to avert an imminent danger. Yet majority of the time, fasting is an act of our faith and will. It is a decision we make based on our love and obedience to Christ. It is part of our service and worship to Him, as seen in the life of Prophetess Anna:

> *"And there was one Anna, a prophetess, the daughter of Phanuel, of the tribe of Aser: she was of a great age, and had lived with an husband seven years from her virginity; And she was a widow of about fourscore and four years, which departed not from the temple, but served God with fastings and prayers night and day" (Luke 2:36-37).*

Prophetess Anna exemplified a life that is wholly devoted to sacrificial service to the Lord through conscious and deliberate denial of life necessities. She striped herself of the pleasures of life in other to give her all to God.

Further, in His response to the seeming accusation levied by the Pharisees against His disciples' refusal to fast - an apparent violation of the Jewish custom - Jesus referred to a time when, after the departure of the Bridegroom (referring to the post - ascension era), the disciples would see fasting as a divine obligation placed on them. Said Jesus:

And Jesus said to them, Can the children of the bridal chamber fast, while the bridegroom is with them? as long as they have the bridegroom with them, they cannot fast. But the days will come, when the bridegroom shall be taken away from them, and then shall they fast in those days (Mark 2: 19, 20).

Accordingly, after the Lord's death, His disciples frequently fasted as of necessity, and went through much deprivation and trial. In essence, this prophetic word, as it were, has found fulfilment in the lives of His 'immediate disciples'; and should be also for the His present day 'disciples', until He returns to take to Himself His Bride, when there will be a glad and everlasting feasting.

Fasting is to be a natural outcome of discipleship. We are meant to fast for the same reason we pray. This does not, by any means, indicate that we are to fast every time we pray.

As said, Jesus addressed fasting in association with both prayer and almsgiving. Jesus declared "when you give alms" (Matt. 6:2), "when you pray" (Matt. 6:6), and "when you fast" (Matt. 6:16). The logical conclusions from these texts are: though, the Bible is silent as to how often we should fast, Jesus intends fasting to be undertaken by the believer as a discipline. Just as Jesus expects us to pray and give alms, He expects us to fast.

Finally, in the Sermon on the Mount, when Jesus spoke about prayer and fasting, He used similar expressions in addressing both subjects. The main difference, however, is that in relation to prayer; he included a structure of prayer we often refer to as 'the Lord's Prayer.'

# HOW DO I KNOW WHEN TO QUIT FASTING?

Fasting that is pleasing to God also requires wisdom. Watch your body signs!

Some have erroneously advised for these signs to be ignored, and attribute them to part of the pranks of the enemy to get you to give up your fast. Undesired outcomes have, sadly resulted by ignoring these vital signs altogether. Be warned! This caution is particularly for those that undertake very lengthy fasts. While it is normal as we have already examined, to experience some unpleasant reactions within the first few days of a fast, such as headaches, nausea, sleeplessness, weakness, and tight neck, it is common experience that these all withdraw with hunger pangs as the fast progresses.

However, hunger pangs do return after your body has burnt off all excess fat, and detoxified. When it comes to the point of beginning to burn off tissue from vital organs, it will give signal of severe hunger pangs, at which time you should break your fast; in fact, immediately! Some have ignored these signs to their detriment. As said, this is usually the case with lengthy fasts.

While it is often the case that at the beginning of a fast, its duration is pre-determined, as advised in this book; it is, however, emphasised that in fasting that go beyond fourteen days, for the vital signs to be looked out for. Once hunger pangs return, please break the fast; it does not matter whether you have covered the period you have set to fast or not.

## HOW DO I OVERCOME SATAN'S TEMPTATION TO VIOLATE MY FAST?

If you have ever been tempted to violate your fast, you are not alone! Everyone that has ever fasted or lives a fasted life faces this temptation. Instead of giving-in to the temptation, be encouraged in the fact that your fast is causing the enemy some irritations and fierce disturbances, hence the attacks, and temptation to violate the fast! The enemy does not border himself with matters that do not hold significance before him.

Once again, use the word of God to overcome such temptations. Focus on the promised rewards to fasters. At such times make Isaiah 58 one of your favourite scriptures. Claim the promises in the face of satan's cheap tricks.

# WAS FASTING PRACTISED BY THE EARLY CHURCH?

## Fasting Associated with Saul's Dramatic Conversion:

*"And he was three days without sight, and neither did eat nor drink" Acts 9:9.*

The first reference to fasting in the Book of Acts was in connection with the dramatic conversion of Saul on the road to Damascus. After his unusual experience Saul was left blinded. He was led into the city of Damascus, where for three days he was "without sight, and neither ate nor drank" (Acts 9:9). It has been argued by some that this experience lacks the essential elements of a true fast. In the first place, they contend, the experience appears to have been imposed on Saul (Paul); he did not of his free will abstain from food and drink, which fasting entails. Second, the experience, they argue, was more of Paul falling into a trance than it being a voluntary abstinence from food and water. Be that as it may, it cannot be denied that Paul later became one of the greatest advocates of the discipline of fasting (2 Cor. 6: 3-10, 11: 23-27), as would be seen in the next question.

## Fasting Associated with the First Missionaries

The early New Testament Christians not only practiced fasting individually, they took fasting as a corporate discipline also. Significantly, in the early church, prayer and fasting were the means by which the first missionaries were commissioned. This was attested to by Luke in Acts 13:1-3:

Now there were in the church that was at Antioch certain prophets and teachers; as Barnabas, and Simeon that was called Niger, and Lucius of Cyrene, and Manaen, which had been brought up with Herod the tetrarch, and Saul. As they ministered to the Lord, and fasted, the Holy Ghost said, Separate me Barnabas and Saul for the work whereunto I have called them. And when they had fasted and prayed, and laid their hands on them, they sent them away.

As these leading ministers – prophets and teachers - were ministering to the Lord with fasting, the Holy Ghost gave a clear leading concerning God's mandate for two of the leading ministers in their midst.

> *"Separate me Barnabas and Saul for the work whereunto I have called them" (emphasis added).*

The phrase "…the work unto which I have called them" is significant.

God had called Barnabas and Saul to the work of the ministry; they did not know it for a fact, until it was revealed to them through the corporate fasting of the leaders of the church.

Thank God, these leaders obeyed the leading of the Spirit and fasted, otherwise Barnabas and Saul (Paul), could have been out of the perfect will of God for their lives. Thank God for leaders that led the right way; paving a way for upcoming leaders to be impacted and released into God's assignment.

This meeting –the corporate fast –of the leadership of the church could be said to be the birth-place of all the exploits the Bible attributes to Paul.

Having experienced the formidable power of prayer and fasting first-hand, Paul and Barnabas later employed the same tool in the establishment of churches, and appointment of their leaders thereafter. After Paul and Barnabas completed the first officially church-sponsored foreign missionary effort, they visited each church they had established to be sure proper leadership was in place.

> *"And when they had preached the gospel to that city, and had taught many, they returned again to Lystra, and to Iconium, and Antioch, Confirming the souls of the disciples, and exhorting them to continue in the faith, and that we must through much tribulation enter into the kingdom of God. And when they had ordained them elders in every church, and had prayed with fasting, they commended them to the Lord, on whom they believed" (Acts 14:21-23).*

It should be noted that everything we have read about the practice of fasting in the early church had a beginning or foundation to it. First, was the outpouring of the Holy Spirit which was ushered in through the prayer and fasting of the disciples. In Acts 1:13 we read:

> *"And when they were come in, they went up into an upper room, where abode both Peter, and James, and John, and Andrew, Philip, and Thomas, Bartholomew, and Matthew, James the son of Alphaeus, and Simon Zelotes, and Judas the brother of James".*

This became the tradition of the disciples after the ascension of Jesus; giving themselves "continually to prayer and the ministry of the word" (Acts 6:4). They put prayer first! Prayer gives an edge and weight to the word.

And the dispensation of the Holy Ghost was born. This marked the beginning of an outstanding ministry for the disciples – a ministry characterised with notable miracles and amazing wonders. Indeed, God's church has always waited more on prayer than on anything else for its success. This was clearly demonstrated by the early church. From this humble beginning grew the practice of fasting. With fasting, the Church entered into a new phase that shaped the spiritual landscape of Jerusalem and its environs, and indeed, the whole world. Everyone acknowledged that a force to reckon with had been born – the church.

# FASTING AS PRACTICED AND TAUGHT IN THE EPISTLES

Fasting played a vital role in the life and ministry of Paul. Immediately after his dramatic encounter with Christ on his way Damascus, Paul spent the next three days without food and water (Acts 9:9). Later, he referred to fasting as one of the great pillars of his missionary ministry; also presenting it as one of the ways we can demonstrate, authenticate and manifest ourselves as true ministers of God.

"... *in all things,*" Paul admonishes, "*approving ourselves as the ministers of God, in much patience, in afflictions, in necessities, in distresses, In stripes, in imprisonments, in* *tumults, in labours, in watchings, **in fastings**; By pureness, by knowledge, by long suffering, by kindness, by the Holy Ghost, by love unfeigned, By the word of truth, by the power of God, by the armour of righteousness on the right hand and on the left, By honour and dishonour, by evil report and good report: as deceivers, and yet true; As unknown, and yet well known; as dying, and, behold, we live; as chastened, and not killed; As sorrowful, yet alway rejoicing; as poor, yet making many rich; as having nothing, and yet possessing all things (2 Cor. 6:3-10, emphasis added).*

Further, in 2 Corinthians 11: 23-27, Paul contends:

*Are they ministers of Christ? (I speak as a fool) I am more: in labours more abundant, in stripes above measure, in prisons more frequent, in deaths oft. Of the Jews five times received I forty stripes save one. Thrice was I beaten with rods, once was I stoned, thrice I suffered shipwreck, a night and a day I have been in the deep: In journeyings often, in perils of waters, in perils of robbers, in perils by mine own countrymen, in perils by the heathen, in perils in the city, in perils in the wilderness, in perils in the sea, in perils among false brethren; In weariness and painfulness, in watchings often, in hunger and thirst, **in fastings often**, in cold and nakedness" (emphasis added).*

Furthermore, the phrase, "fastings often" (plural), as used in verse 27, proves that Paul devoted himself to a life of fasting, and saw it as a prerequisite for success in ministry. As a matter of fact, for the early church and Apostle Paul, fasting was a normative practice. It was the rule rather than the exception; the life – wire of the church.

# HOW SHOULD I BREAK A FAST SUCCESSFULLY?

Another significant aspect of a fast is bringing it to a successful end. It could be very difficult to break a fast, especially those that have gone on for a lengthy period of time. The importance of breaking a fast with due caution cannot be overemphasised. Care needs to be taken in this regard, so as not to overburden your digestive system. Introducing foods carefully and gradually is the key.

Your digestive system has rested and needs time to become accustomed to food again. It is imperative to gradually reintroduce food so as not to overburden the body after its period of rest and healing. Metabolism slows during a fast and requires time to re-adjust. This is achieved by carefully adding small amounts of easily-digested foods on the days following a fast.

Much of the body's toxins are stored in fat tissue. During a fast, toxic fats are released and eliminated; however, if too much food is reintroduced too quickly, the body will easily regain more than the lost fat. A good practice is to consume raw fruits and a good amount of filtered water on the first day following a fast.

Break your fast gradually. Begin eating gradually. Do not eat solid foods immediately after your fast. Suddenly reintroducing solid food to your stomach and digestive tract will likely have negative, even dangerous consequences. Try several smaller meals or snacks each day. If you end your fast gradually, the beneficial physical and spiritual effects will result in continued good health.

Gradually return to regular eating with several small snacks during the first few days. Start with a little soup and fresh fruit such as watermelon and cantaloupe. Advance to a few tablespoons of solid foods such as raw fruits and vegetables or a raw salad and baked potato.

Fruits and vegetables, raw or lightly steamed may be eaten on the second day. By the third day, some the pre-fast diet may be resumed. Generally, the longer the fast, the longer it should take to return to the normal diet. It is also important to chew thoroughly and avoid overeating.

Your ability to resume toilet successfully (without some delivery pangs), depends largely on the way you started the fast. To achieve easy passing of stool at the end of the fast, you have to see to it that few days before you commence the fast, you consume a great deal of fruits and vegetables, preferably, broccoli.

# FASTING FROM THE LEGENDS' PERSPECTIVES

These golden nuggets are included to encourage, inspire, supercharge and build up your faith. Please make use of them.

## ANDREW MURRAY

*"The faith that can overcome stubborn resistance such as you have just seen in this evil spirit [in Matthew 17:14-21], Jesus tells them, is not possible except for men living in very close fellowship with God and in very special separation from the world—in prayer and fasting. And so [Jesus] teaches us two lessons of deep importance in regard to prayer. The one so that faith needs a life of prayer in which to grow and keep strong. The other is that prayer needs fasting for its full and perfect development. Faith needs a life of prayer for its full growth."*

*"Prayer is reaching out after the unseen; fasting is letting go of all that is seen and temporal. Fasting helps express, deepen, confirm the resolution that we are ready to sacrifice anything, even ourselves to attain what we seek for the kingdom of God."*

## ALBERT HAASE

*"Fasting can be a painful admission that I am not free, that my life is enslaved, obsessed or addicted to external things such as food, drink, co-dependent relationships, sex, television, privacy and the like."*

## BILL BRIGHT

*"Fasting with a pure heart and motives, I have discovered, brings personal revival and adds power to our prayers. Personal revival occurs because fasting is an act of humility. Fasting gives opportunity for deeper humility as we recognize our sins, repent, receive God's forgiveness, and experience His cleansing of our soul and spirit. Fasting also demonstrates our love for God and our full confidence in His faithfulness."*

## C.S. LEWIS

*"It is impossible to accept Christianity for the sake of finding comfort: but the Christian tries to lay himself open to the will of God, to do what God wants him to do. You don't know in advance whether God is going to set you to do something difficult or painful, or something that you will quite like; and some people of heroic mould are disappointed when the job doled out to them turns out to be something quite nice. But you must be prepared for the unpleasant things and the discomforts. I don't mean fasting, and things like that. They are a different matter. When you are training soldiers in manoeuvres, you practice in blank ammunition because you would like them to have practices before meeting the real enemy. So we must practice in abstaining from pleasures which are not in themselves wicked. If you don't abstain from pleasure, you won't be good when the time comes along. It is purely a matter of practice."*

## DAVID R. SMITH

*"Fasting with a pure heart and motives, I have discovered, brings personal revival and adds power to our prayers. Personal revival occurs because fasting is an act of humility. Fasting gives opportunity for deeper humility as we recognize our sins, repent, receive God's forgiveness, and experience His*

*cleansing of our soul and spirit. Fasting also demonstrates our love for God and our full confidence in His faithfulness."*

## DIETRICH BONHEOFFER

*"Jesus takes it for granted that his disciples will observe the pious custom of fasting. Strict exercise of self-control is an essential feature of the Christian's life. Such customs have only one purpose—to make the disciples more ready and cheerful to accomplish those things which God would have done."*

## DALLAS WILLARD

*"Fasting confirms our utter dependence upon God by finding in Him a source of sustenance beyond food."*

## ELMER TOWNS

*"It's important to note that religious practices such as fasting are less important than doing God's will. As Micah 6:8 points out, what the Lord truly requires of us is devotion to Himself: "To do justly, to love mercy, and to walk humbly with your*

God." Fasting is not an end in itself; it is a means by which we can worship the Lord and submit ourselves in humility to Him. We don't make God love us any more than He already does if we fast, or if we fast longer. As Galatians states, "Stand fast therefore in the liberty by which Christ has made us free, and do not be entangled again with a yoke of bondage" (5:1). The goal of any discipline is freedom. If the result is not greater freedom, something is wrong."

"Even if we wanted to, we could not manipulate God. We fast and pray for results, but the results are in God's hands. One of the greatest spiritual benefits of fasting is becoming more attentive to God—becoming more aware of our own inadequacies and His adequacy, our own contingencies and His self-sufficiency—and listening to what He wants us to be and do."

"Christian fasting, therefore, is totally antithetical to, say, Hindu fasting. Both seek results; however, Hindu fasting focuses on the self and tries to get something for a perceived sacrifice. Christian fasting focuses on God. The results are spiritual results that glorify God—both in the person who fasts and others for whom we fast and pray."

## EDITH SCHAEFFER

*"Is fasting ever a bribe to get God to pay more attention to the petitions? No, a thousand times no. It is simply a way to make clear that we sufficiently reverence the amazing opportunity to ask help from the everlasting God, the Creator of the universe, to choose to put everything else aside and concentrate on worshiping, asking for forgiveness, and making our requests known—considering His help more important than anything we could do ourselves in our own strength and with our own ideas."*

## FRANCIS OF ASSISI

*Everyone must study his own nature. Some of you can sustain life with less food than others can, and therefore I desire that he who needs more nourishment shall not be obliged to equal others, but that everyone shall give his body what it needs for being an efficient servant of the soul. For as we are obliged to be on our guard against superfluous food which injures body and soul alike, thus we must be on the watch against immoderate fasting, and this the more, because the Lord wants conversion and not victims.*

## GLEN ARGON

*A spiritually awake person would see everything as a gift, even suffering. We deserve nothing and yet we so often act as though we deserve everything. Nothing should be taken for granted. We should say thank you every day to God and to each other for all that is provided for us. This is one reason why fasting is such an important spiritual discipline. Not just fasting from food, but also fasting from cars, shopping centres, the news – whatever we have an inordinate attachment to. Fasting can help re-kindle our gratitude for all that we have been given.*

## HUDSON TAYLOR

*"In Shansi I found Chinese Christians who were accustomed to spend time in fasting and prayer. They recognized that this fasting, which so many dislike, which requires faith in God, since it makes one feel weak and poorly, is really a Divinely appointed means of grace. Perhaps the greatest hindrance to our work is our own imagined strength; and in fasting we learn what poor, weak creatures we are–dependent on a meal of meat for the little strength which we are so apt to lean upon."*

# JOHN WESLEY

*"The man who never fasts is no more in the way to Heaven than the man who never prays."*

*"[Fasting] is a help to prayer; particularly when we set apart larger portions of time for private prayer. Then especially it is that God is often pleased to lift up the souls of his servants above all the things of earth, and sometimes to rap them up, as it were, into the third Heaven. And it is chiefly, as it is a help to prayer, that it has so frequently been found a means, in the hand of God, of confirming and increasing, not one virtue, not chastity only, (as some have idly imagined, without any ground either from Scripture, reason, or experience,) but also seriousness of spirit, earnestness, sensibility and tenderness of conscience, deadness to the world, and consequently the love of God, and every holy and Heavenly affection."*

*"But, if we desire this reward, let us beware . . . of fancying we merit anything of God by our fasting. We cannot be too often warned of this; inasmuch as a desire to 'establish our own righteousness,' to procure salvation of debt and not of grace, is so deeply rooted in all our hearts. Fasting is only a way which God hath ordained, wherein we wait for his unmerited mercy; and wherein, without any desert of ours, he hath promised freely to give us his blessing."*

*"Bear up the hands that hang down, by faith and prayer; support the tottering knees. Have you any days of fasting and prayer? Storm the throne of grace and persevere therein, and mercy will come down."*

## WESLEY DUEWEL

*"You and I have no more right to omit fasting because we feel no special emotional prompting than we have a right to omit prayer, Bible reading, or assembling with God's children for lack of some special emotional prompting. Fasting is just as biblical and normal a part of a spiritual walk of obedience with God as are these others....*

*"How do you take up your cross? To take up a cross is not to have someone place the cross upon you. Sickness, persecution, and the antagonism of other people are not your real cross. To take up a cross is a deliberate choice. We must purposely humble ourself [sic], stoop down, and pick up the cross for Jesus. Fasting is one of the most biblical ways to do so....*

*"Fasting can deepen hunger for God to work. Spiritual hunger and fasting have a reciprocal power. Each deepens and strengthens the other. Each makes the other more effective. When your spiritual hunger becomes very deep, you may even lose the desire for food. All of the most intense forms of*

*prevailing prayer . . . can be deepened, clarified, and greatly empowered by fasting...."*

*"Fasting is natural when you are burdened sufficiently, wrestling with mighty prevailings, and warring in hand-to-hand conflict with satan and his powers of darkness. Fasting becomes sweet and blessed as your hunger reaches out to God. Your hunger gains tremendous power as you fast and pray— particularly if you set apart time from all else to give yourself to fasting and prayer. It can become a spiritual joy to fast...."*

*"Fasting feeds your faith. . . . Your confidence begins to deepen. Your hope begins to rise, for you know you are doing what pleases the Lord. Your willingness to deny self and voluntarily to take up this added cross kindles an inner joy. Your faith begins to lay hold of God's promise more simply and more firmly."*

*"Fasting is still God's chosen way to deepen and strengthen prayer. You will be the poorer spiritually and your prayer life will never be what God wants it to be until you practice the privilege of fasting."*

# THOMAS A KEMPIS

*"Jesus has many lovers of His kingdom of Heaven, but he has few bearers of His Cross. Many desire His consolation, but few desire His tribulation. He finds many comrades in eating and drinking, but He finds few hands who will be with Him in*

*His abstinence and fasting...But those who love Jesus purely for Himself, and not for their own profit or convenience, bless Him as heartily in temptation and tribulation and in all other adversities as they do in time of consolation. And if He never sent them consolation, they would still bless and praise Him."*

# EPILOGUE

*I was so taken aback with my discovery that I trawled through scores of church history and revival books (electronically!) looking for references to fasting. What I found was astounding! There is clear, documented evidence that all the great leaders and revival movements of church history used this amazing key to add power to their prayers! In one collection of church history documents the software I used, refused to reveal its findings, stating 'the search exceeds the 5,000 limit of this software!' Could it be that fasting is a vital, but missing ingredient in the 21st century church?...Men and women that God has used mightily throughout history, have similarly believed this. They saw God's glory manifest in their day. The possibility of joining their ranks is offered to every believer today. Right around the world thousands of believers are practicing prayer with fasting. The Lord is preparing his great army for a glorious and final outpouring of his Spirit to restore the glory to the church and in the world, before his return. Let's put fasting back on our menu* - Tony Cauchi.

With surgical precision, careful exegesis, and engaging breath-taking illustrations, this book has expressed the deepest cry of our generation. As Cauchi has cleverly analysed, there is no better time to bring biblical fasting back on the scene, as the irrefutable key to successful living, proven weapon of breakthrough that cuts through all satanic barriers.

There is therefore, no better time for the church to awake to the huge significance of this highly potent weapon the Lord has blessed her with and engage it in its full ramifications, in every facet of life. We need no reminding that the church is at the cusp of a very significant phase in the calendar of God for the earth. Like the biblical nation of Israel, the church is in a transition, just as Joshua led the nation of Israel into the promise land as a transitional leader, leading a transitional nation at God's pre-ordained transitional time. So the church is entering into a glorious phase in her eternal destiny. The challenges the world faces today – climate change, global economic meltdown, a global pandemic with enormous capability are all, in my view, part of the events that will cause a resurgence or escalation of the life of fasting in the church. Lack of fasting will rub the church of her glorious status, a requirement of her rapture experience. Only the saints of God that heed the Masters call to fast will be fine –tuned to her the-end-of- the -age trumpet sound. Said Jesus, *"But the days will come, when the bridegroom shall be taken*

# EPILOGUE

*away from them, and then shall they fast in those days (Luke 5:35)*.

This is nothing short of a glorious invitation to the highly privileged life of fasting ordained for the saints of God. Our time, indeed, our generation fulfils the requirements of the Master's prediction. The bridegroom absence is a pre-condition to fulfilling the Master's command. We know it won't be much longer before He returns to take those who love Him home. May He find us obeying His clarion call to fasting, when He comes. Jesus' instruction to us before He went to be with the Father was, *"...Occupy till I come" (Luke 19:13)*.

On a personal level, Jesus teaches the believer the power of fasting on many fronts. First, He told His disciples that prayer could be limited in its effect; a lesson that transcends the generation of His immediate audience. In His temptation in the wilderness by the devil, the Lord demonstrated mastering over the enemy through the power of fasting. The combined effect of both experiences, as demonstrated by the Lord, leaves us with one incontestable conclusion: fasting is a powerful tool to living a victorious life. The plethora of material and individual cases contained in this book bears witness to this significant and time – tested fact.

The transformative power of fasting should never be underestimated! We have seen that the mystery God has packaged for us in fasting defiles every situation when applied in the right way, with the right motive.

Is there a stronghold that has been gripping your life? What is dead in your life that you know God wants to resurrect? What dream, goal, or godly ambition is waiting to be realised? Do you desire a deeper walk with God and increased spiritual hunger? Do you need help in the area of self-discipline and temperance? Are you struggling with a sin that has become a stronghold in your life? I mean a sin that you just cannot seem to get rid of; you have spent time in prayer but you just cannot seem to break its hold. Do you need a breakthrough, direction, or peace? Is all hell breaking loose in your life? Are there great obstacles ahead? Then it is time to prepare for battle through prayer and fasting.

Fasting is the key to breakthrough in life! For everyone that desires a significant and enviable leap in life, for everyone that passionately and desperately needs a 'turn around' in life, for those believers that are fed up of the status quo and urgently and intently hunger for a change, for the individuals who have come to the end of themselves and are badly desirous of Heaven's intervention, for the many of God's wonderful children who had once tasted of the goodness of the Lord and are now singing the Lord's song in a 'strange land', and desperately desire restoration! For those who have prayed on end without any remarkable results, fasting is the answer. Jesus said, *"this kind goeth out not except by prayer and fasting" (Matt. 7:21).*

# VARIOUS FASTINGS IN THE BIBLE AND THEIR DURATIONS

As seen in the word of God, fasting is of different durations, ranging from just missing a meal, to one full day, to days, even weeks. In this section, we will examine the various fasting revealed in the word of God and their durations.

# PART OF THE DAY FAST

*Then the king went to his palace, and passed the night fasting: neither were instruments of music brought before him: and his sleep went from him (Daniel 6:18).*

# ONE DAY FAST

*Also on the tenth day of the seventh month there shall be a day of atonement: it shall be an holy convocation unto you; and ye shall afflict your souls, and offer an offering made by fire unto the Lord. And ye shall do no work in that same day: for it is a day of atonement, to make atonement for you before the Lord your God (Lev. 23:27 KJV).*

*The tenth day of this seventh month is the Day of Atonement. Hold a sacred assembly and deny yourselves, and present a food offering to the Lord. 28 Do not do any work on that day, because it is the Day of Atonement, when atonement is made for you before the Lord your God (Lev 23:27 NIV).*

*And they gathered together to Mizpeh, and drew water, and poured it out before the Lord, and fasted on that day, and said there, We have sinned against the Lord. And Samuel judged the children of Israel in Mizpeh (1 Sam. 7:6).*

*And the men of Israel were distressed that day: for Saul had adjured the people, saying, Cursed be the man that eateth any food until evening, that I may be avenged on mine enemies. So none of the people tasted any food (1 Sam. 14:24).*

*Therefore go thou, and read in the roll, which thou hast written from my mouth, the words of the Lord in the ears of the people in the Lord's house upon the fasting day: and also thou shalt read them in the ears of all Judah that come out of their cities (Jer. 36:6).*

*Now in the twenty and fourth day of this month the children of Israel were assembled with fasting, and with sackclothes, and earth upon them (Neh. 9:1)*

EPILOGUE

# THREE DAYS

*And they gave him a piece of a cake of figs, and two clusters of raisins: and when he had eaten, his spirit came again to him: for he had eaten no bread, nor drunk any water, three days and three nights I Sam. 30:12).*

Many people may have difficulty regarding this as a fast, given our definition of fasting as a deliberate abstention from food for a spiritual purpose. In the first place, the subject of the supposed fast could not be said to have abstained from food deliberately (voluntarily). Had he had access to food he could have eaten and drank. Secondly, his abstention from food could not have been said to be for a spiritual purpose, given that he was not even an Israelite (or to be more specific from Judah) he was an Egyptian who was among the enemy's allies that evaded Ziglag, the habitant of the people of God at the time.

> *"And David said unto him, To whom belongest thou? and whence art thou? And he said, I am a young man of Egypt, servant to an Amalekite; and my master left me, because three days ago I fell sick. We made an invasion upon the south of the Cherethites, and upon the coast which belongeth to Judah, and upon the south of Caleb; and we burned Ziklag with fire" (I Sam. 30: 13-14).*

However, the discussion leads us to the question I'm so often asked: *"Can one observe a fast involuntarily?"*

Recently I found an interesting material on the topic by Arthur Wallis I would like to share with you.

These are his thoughts:

*"...we should observe that fasting may also refer to abstaining from food involuntarily." "The two kinds of involuntary fasting"*, he adds *"are:*

1. Where there is no desire for food because of anxiety, sorrow or mental distress (Dan 6:18), and

2. Where persons find themselves in a situation where no food is available [as in the case of the Egyptian], also in Matt 15:32.

Paul evidently knew a good deal of this second sort. No doubt his mention of "fastings" in 2 Corinthians 6:5 and 11:27 refers to this kind of involuntary hardship. Evidently Paul had no difficulty in reconciling such want with the promise, *"My God will supply every need of yours." (Phil. 4:19).* He knew that the experience of finding himself temporary without food, and without the means to obtain it, was a necessary trial of faith permitted by God for his ultimate blessing. "I have learned, in whatsoever state I am, to be content. I know both how to be abased, and I know how to abound: in any and all circumstances I have learned the secret of facing plenty and hunger, abundance and want" (Phil 4:11, 12). And he concludes, *"If God should call us to walk 'the path of necessity', and we find ourselves on a fast that is not our choosing, let us not fear. He will yet "... turn our captivity... and bless our latter end more than our beginning (Job 42:10).*

# FURTHER RECORDS OF THREE DAY FASTS

*Go, gather together all the Jews that are present in Shushan, and fast for me, and neither eat nor drink three days, night or day: I also and my maidens will fast likewise; and so will I go in unto the king, which is not according to the law: and if I perish, I perish (Est. 4: 16).*

*Then Jesus called his disciples unto him, and said, I have compassion on the multitude, because they continue with me now three days, and have nothing to eat: and I will not send them away without food, lest they faint in the way (Matt. 15:32, Mark 8: 2, 3).*

*And he was three days without sight, and neither did eat nor drink (Acts 9:9).*

# SEVEN DAYS

*And when the inhabitants of Jabeshgilead heard of that which the Philistines had done to Saul; All the valiant men arose, and went all night, and took the body of Saul and the bodies of his sons from the wall of Bethshan, and came to Jabesh, and burnt them there. And they took their bones, and buried them under a tree at Jabesh, and fasted seven days (1 Sam. 31:11-13, 1 Chron. 10:11, 12).*

*And Nathan departed unto his house. And the Lord struck the child that Uriah's wife bare unto David, and it was very sick. David therefore besought God for the child; and David fasted, and went in, and lay all night upon the earth. And the elders of his house arose, and went to him, to raise him up from the earth: but he would not, neither did he eat bread with them. And it came to pass on the seventh day, that the child died. And the servants of David feared to tell him that the child was dead: for they said, Behold, while the child was yet alive, we spake unto him, and he would not hearken unto our voice: how will he then vex himself, if we tell him that the child is dead? Then said his servants unto him, What thing is this that thou hast done? thou didst fast and weep for the child, while it was alive; but when the child was dead, thou didst rise and eat bread. And he said, While the child was yet alive, I fasted and wept: for I said, Who can tell whether God will be gracious to me, that the child may live? But now he is dead, wherefore should I fast? Can I bring him back again? I shall go to him, but he shall not return to me (2 Sam. 12: 15-18, 21-23)*

## FOURTEEN DAYS

*And while the day was coming on, Paul besought them all to take meat, saying, This day is the fourteenth day that ye have tarried and continued fasting, having taken nothing. Wherefore I pray you to take some meat: for this is for your health: for there shall not an hair fall from the head of any of you. And when he had thus spoken, he took bread, and gave thanks to God in presence of them all: and when he had broken it, he began to eat (Acts 27:33-35)*

## TWENTY ONE DAYS

*I ate no pleasant food, neither came meat nor wine in my mouth, neither did I anoint myself at all, till three whole weeks were fulfilled (Dan. 10:2, 3).*

# FORTY DAYS

*And he was there with the Lord forty days and forty nights; he did neither eat bread, nor drink water. And he wrote upon the tables the words of the covenant, the Ten Commandments (Exod. 34:28)*

*When I was gone up into the mount to receive the tables of stone, even the tables of the covenant which the LORD made with you, then I abode in the mount forty days and forty nights, I neither did eat bread nor drink water (Deut. 9:9)*

*And I fell down before the LORD, as at the first, forty days and forty nights: I did neither eat bread, nor drink water, because of all your sins which ye sinned, in doing wickedly in the sight of the LORD, to provoke him to anger (Deut. 9:18)*

*And he arose, and did eat and drink, and went in the strength of that food forty days and forty nights unto Horeb the mount of God (1 Kings 19:8)*

*Then was Jesus led up of the Spirit into the wilderness to be tempted of the devil. And when he had fasted forty days and forty nights, he was afterward an hungred (Matt. 4:1-2)*

# JESUS IS LORD: A CALL FOR SALVATION

You need to know Jesus personally.
Do not gamble with your eternal destination!
Religion, good works, good intentions are not good enough to get you into Heaven.

Jesus said:

*"Behold I stand at the door and knock: if any man hear my voice and open the door, I will come into him, and will sup with him he with me" (Rev.3:20).*

If you have not yet given your life to the Lord Jesus please do so by praying the following Prayer of Salvation:

*Lord Jesus I come to you just as I am*

*Thank you for dying on the cross for my sins*

*Thank you for being the substitute for all my wrong doings*

*Today I open my heart to you*

*Lord come in and be my Master, Be my Lord*

*I surrender the rest of my life to you*

*satan, I refuse you today*

*I refuse all your operations my in life*

*I reject all the works of the flesh I have been used to*

*Jesus, I Surrender all to you*

*I am born again by your grace.*

*Amen*

I rejoice with you and the angels in Heaven rejoicing over your salvation. Please find a living Bible believing Church where you can grow and fellowship with other Christians.

If you have prayed this prayer, please we will very much like to hear from you. Kindly contact us through the following address:

**Email:** hopeofglory@btinterent.com
**Website:** www.hopeofgloryinternational.com

# BIBLIOGRAPHY

B. Sorge, Secret of the Secret Place (Oasis House, USA, 2001).

B. Sorge, Unrelenting Prayer (Oasis House, USA, 2005).

D. Prince, Experiencing God's Power (Whitaker House, New Kensington, 1998).

D. Prince, Fasting (Whitaker House, USA, 1986).

D. Prince, How To Fast Successfully (Whitaker House, USA, 1976).

D. Colbert, Toxic Relief, Restore health and energy through fasting and detoxification (Siloam, USA, 2001).

E. Towns, Fasting For A Miracle, (Regal, USA, 2012).

E. Towns, Fasting For Spiritual Breakthrough, A Guide To Nine Biblical Fasts (Regal, USA, 1996).

F. Hall, The Fasting Prayer (Martino Publishing, USA).

R. W. Floyd, The Power of Prayer and Fasting (B&H Publishing Group, Tennessee, USA, 2010).

R. Smith, Fasting (Garden City Press Ltd, UK, 1968).

R. Smith, Some Light on Fasting (Rushworth Literature Enterprise Ltd, UK, 1966).

Z. Fomum, The Ministry of Fasting (Vantage Press, New York, 1996, 1968).

Z. Fomum, Waiting On The Lord In Prayer (Books4revival.com, 1996).

www.ingramcontent.com/pod-product-compliance
Lightning Source LLC
Chambersburg PA
CBHW021951160426
43209CB00030B/1910/J